IMAGES
of America

HEARNE

On the Cover: Black and white, immigrant and native-born, white collar and blue collar stand shoulder to shoulder on a Hearne downtown street. (Courtesy of Hearne Chamber of Commerce.)

IMAGES
of America

HEARNE

Melissa Freeman

ARCADIA
PUBLISHING

ISBN 978-0-7385-8540-6

Published by Arcadia Publishing
Charleston, South Carolina

Printed in the United States of America

Library of Congress Control Number: 2011945487

For all general information, please contact Arcadia Publishing:
Telephone 843-853-2070
Fax 843-853-0044
E-mail sales@arcadiapublishing.com
For customer service and orders:
Toll-Free 1-888-313-2665

Visit us on the Internet at www.arcadiapublishing.com

To Cathy Lazarus, whose commitment to Hearne and help with this book cannot be over estimated

Contents

Acknowledgments

My sincere thanks to all who provided pictures and information for this book, including Kent Brunette and Polly Morgan with the Hearne Chamber of Commerce; Carolyn Palmos Lampo, Larry Blackmon, and the First Baptist Church of Hearne; Dorothy Starkey, Laura Chesner, Susan Freeman, Kathy Brimhall, and the Robertson County Clerk's Office; the Carnegie Library in Bryan; the Cushing Library at Texas A&M University (TAMU); Dr. Mike Waters with TAMU; Ed Luster; Dr. Dale Baum; the Texas State Library and Archives; the Texas Preservation Board; Anna Florida and Robert Nelson with the City of Hearne; Kendra Maness and the *Robertson County News*; Frank Adams; Cindy Wallace; Sue Gandy; Uncommon Productions; Quaker Oats; and the NFL Hall of Fame.

INTRODUCTION

Hearne, Texas, began as Brown's Station, a watering hole on the Houston–Port Sullivan stagecoach line in the 1840s. There, tired travelers and horses found a spring with tasty water and a tavern serving medicinal (or that was the claim) whiskey needed for passage across the malaria-infested Brazos River Bottoms. The Bottoms were "no place for a white man," said some.

After Code Brown built his cabin, tavern, store, and post office (actually, a box for dropping off and picking up), sure enough, settlers came. In 1851–1852, the Hearnes, a pioneering cotton-growing family that had traveled from Alabama through Mississippi and Louisiana—farming along the way—began staking out tracts of land in the Bottoms. Undeterred by threat of disease, the family—brothers, sisters, cousins, and in-laws led by Christopher Columbus (C.C.) Hearne—contracted for about 10,000 acres of prime bottomland in what had originally been within the Ruiz, Manchaca, Martinez, and Nixon Spanish land grants. In some parts, these grants overlapped giving rise to years of conflicting claims.

The Bottoms and Hearne slaves produced so much cotton that C.C. Hearne brought in the railroad to carry it away. When the Houston & Texas Central Railroad neared Brown Station in 1868, the area became known as Hearne Station, and the modest whiskey-supplying tavern was swallowed by about 20 saloons in tents serving 30 Irish railroad crews. Understandably, Hearne earned its "rough town" reputation early on.

But the wells—at least three by 1870—still rendered tasty water. Good water, roads and rails, and people with vision—white, black, and Hispanic—went on to create a town that has weathered repeated storms: natural, cultural, and economic. With a will to survive, Hearne continues to make its mark on the Lone Star State as the Crossroads of Texas.

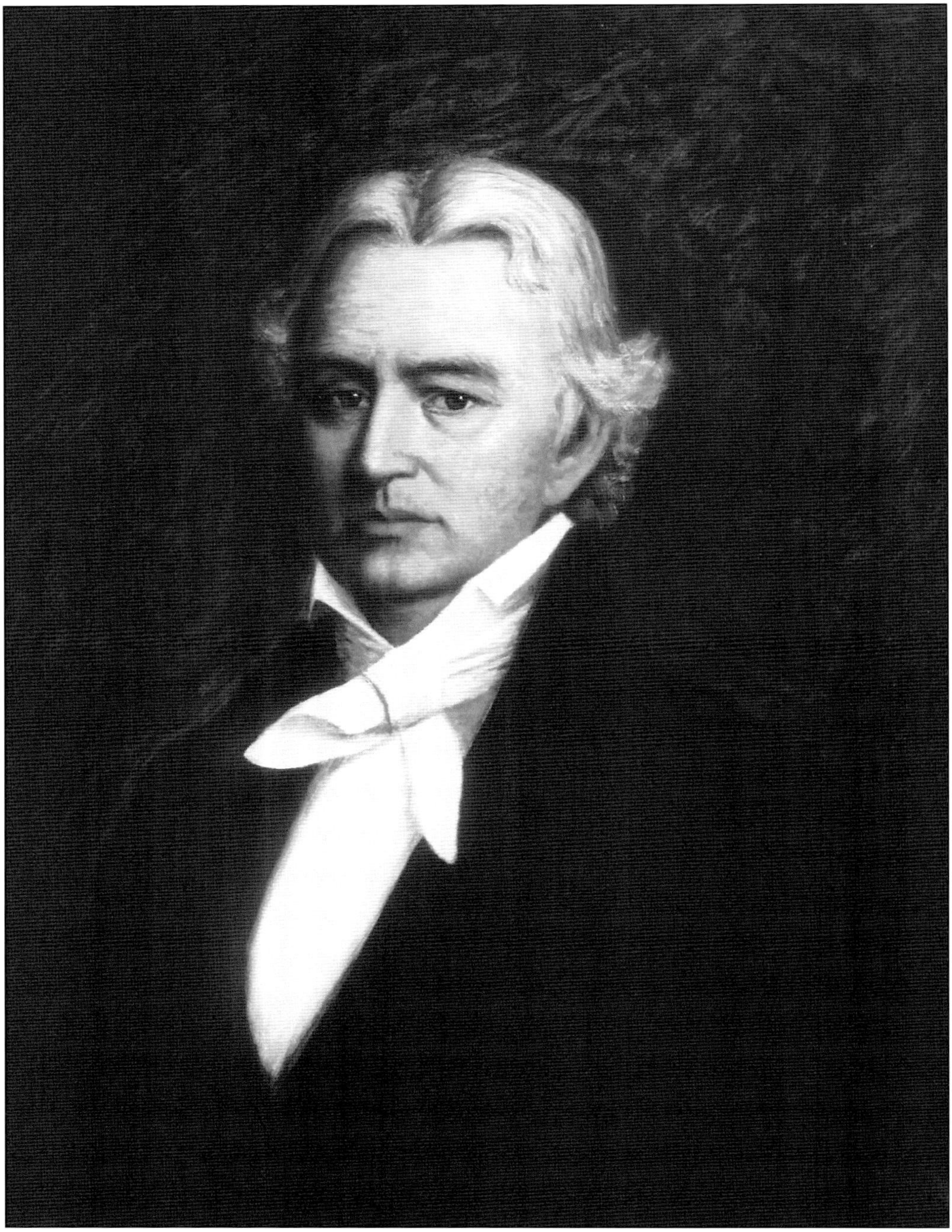

By 1830, a total of 148 families had left the green hills of Tennessee, traveled long, rough, dusty roads, and crossed swollen streams and turbulent rivers to claim land in hostile, Indian-held territory on this man's say-so. Tennessee-born Texas impresario Sterling Clack Robertson had gravitas. The tall, handsome, well-spoken Robertson probably had little trouble convincing his fellow Tennesseans to come to Texas and claim large tracts of land for a song—$30 a league (4,428 acres). (Courtesy of Texas State Preservation Board.)

One

Hearne Beginnings

When Sterling Clack Robertson established his colony a few years before Texas independence, he opened up for American pioneers a vast stretch of Texas land on either side of the Brazos River. The first towns in what would become Robertson County (a relatively small section of the original claim) were Owensville, Sterling, and Wheelock. All three would be passed up, the first two fading into history, when cotton became king and the railroads came to haul it. A new town born of cotton and the iron horse was established in their wake: Hearne, Texas.

The Hearnes, a family of cotton farmers who had already tested the soils of Georgia, Alabama, Mississippi, and Louisiana, established their first residence in Wheelock and had an eye on the Brazos Bottoms over 20 miles to the west. They knew good cotton-growing land when they saw it. The previous year, cousins Samuel "Sam" Hearne and Horatio "Rasche" Ransome Hearne and Sam's brother-in-law Charles Lewis had explored thousands of acres along the river, and Sam had purchased about 2,000 acres of bottomland in 1851. From their Wheelock headquarters, the rest of the family followed suit.

In a county with a population of fewer than 1,000 people, land was plentiful and cheap—except perhaps for the attorney fees and legal-settlement costs. Since Brazos bottomlands (generally located between the Brazos and Little Brazos Rivers) fell within overlapping Spanish land grants, land purchasers could expect to spend time in court arguing their claims with heirs of the original grantees: Francisco Ruiz, Antonio Manchaca, Marcelino Martinez, and George Antonio Nixon. The Hearnes were repeatedly successful, having secured their purchases with contracts rather than deeds, but they did have to pay a few settlements to convince claimants to leave court.

By 1860, the county's population would swell to almost 5,000 with nearly half being enslaved African Americans, many of whom worked in or near the Brazos River Bottoms. Hearne's future demographics were shaping up before the town did.

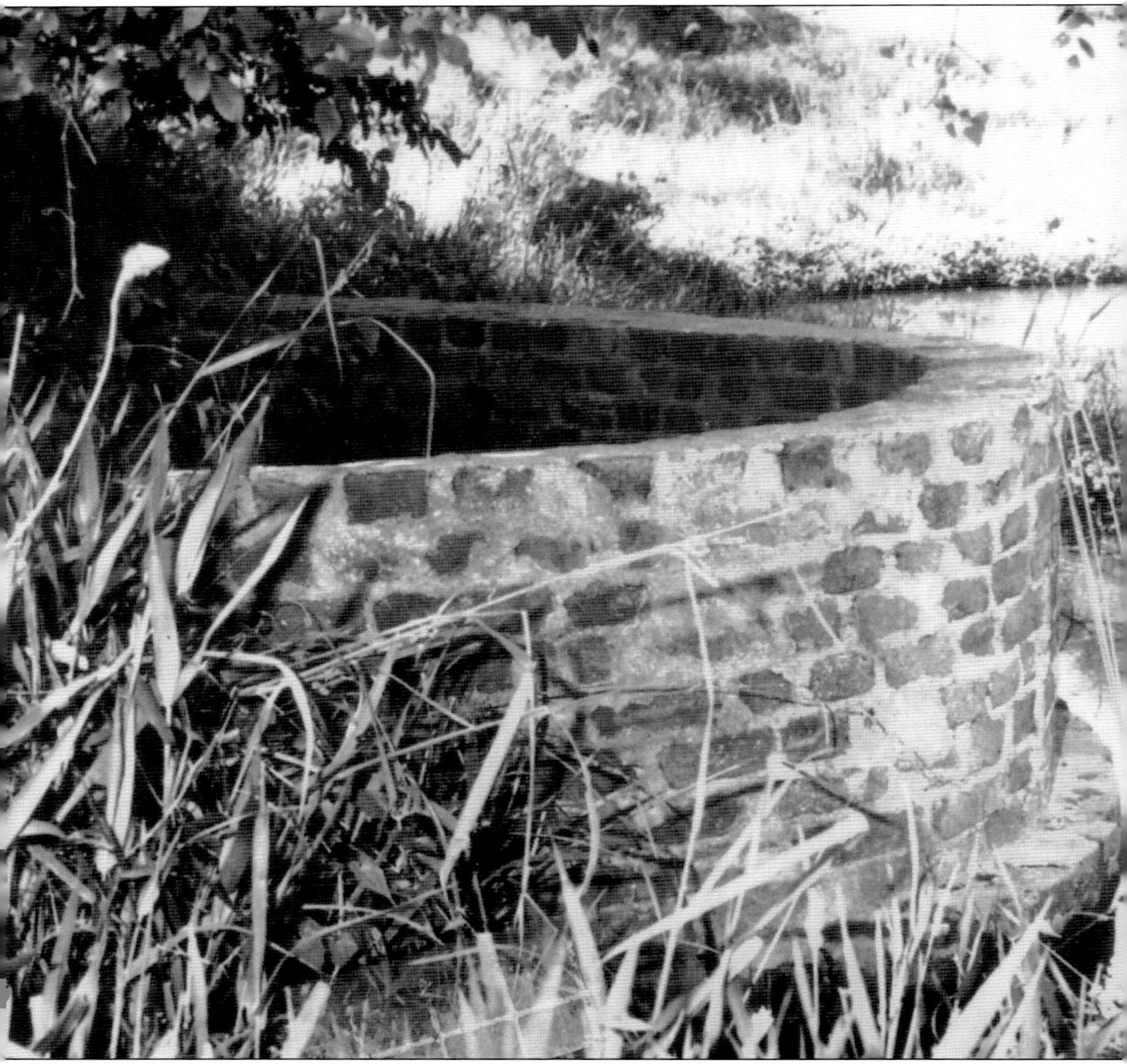

Around 1836, Code Brown found good spring water near the Houston–Port Sullivan (a colonial town on the Brazos River) stagecoach road. He built a cabin, which by the early 1840s had developed into a tavern, store, and post office to take care of travelers' needs—particularly the need of whiskey to fortify them for the journey through the malarial Brazos River Bottoms. His, according to McCarver and McCarver's *Hearne on the Brazos*, was the first settlement in what would become Hearne. (Courtesy of Robertson County Clerk's Office.)

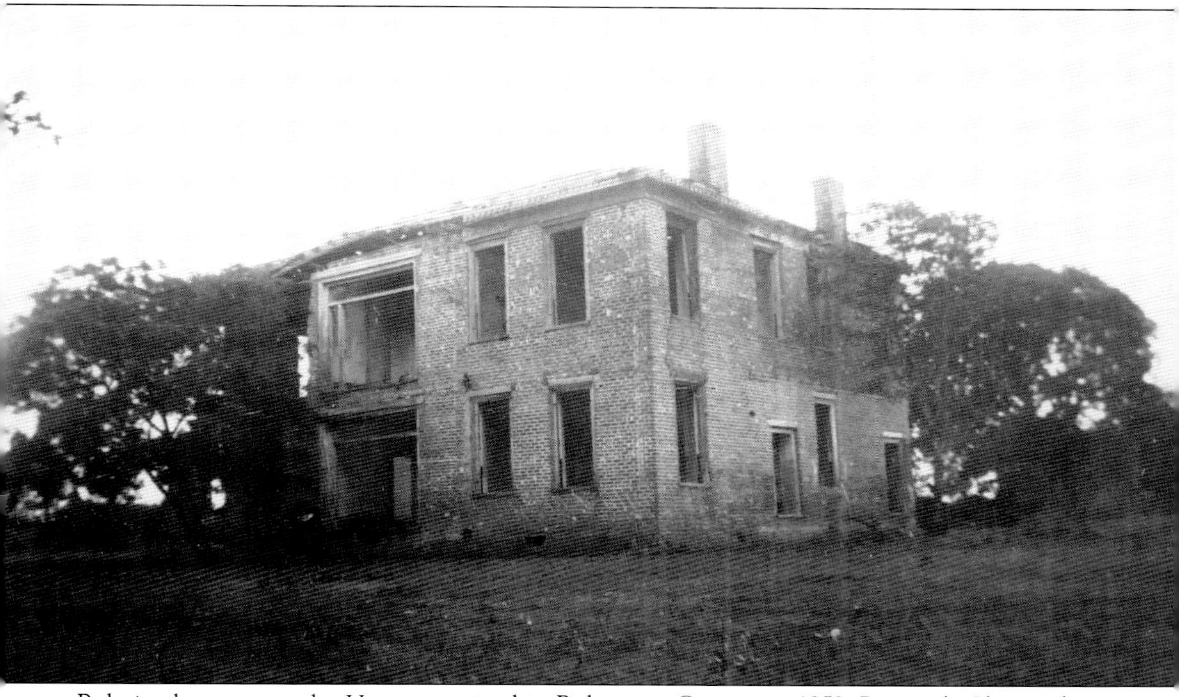

Relative latecomers, the Hearnes arrived in Robertson County in 1852. Patriarch Christopher Columbus Hearne settled near Wheelock, building this large two-story house while the family, beginning with brother Samuel and cousin Ebenezer ("Ebb"), claimed thousands of acres of rich Brazos River bottomland southwest of Code Brown's tavern. (Courtesy of Texas State Library and Archives.)

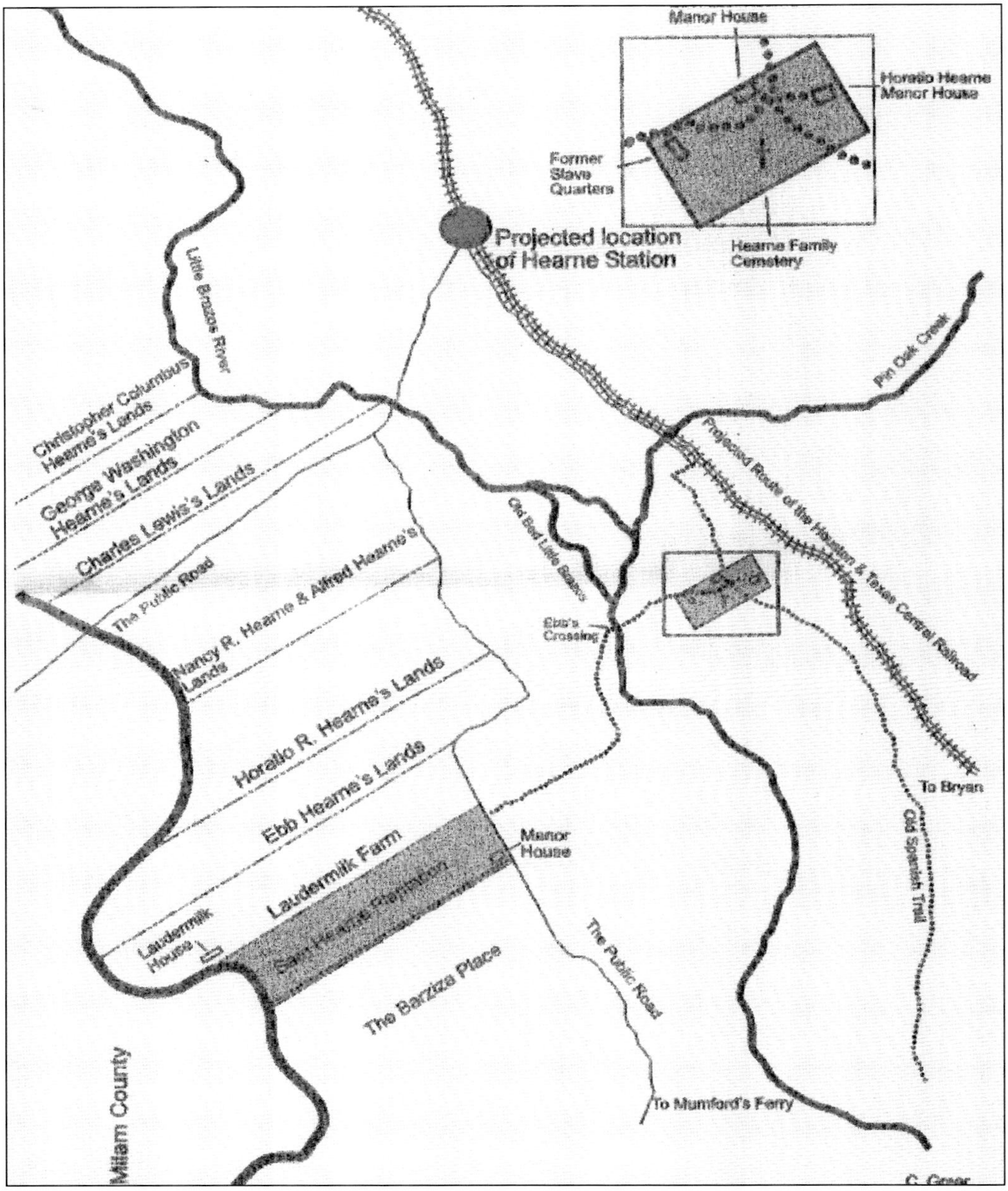

By the end of the Civil War, several of the Hearnes held large tracts of Brazos River bottomland south and west of present-day Hearne. Tracts in bands from south to north included brother Sam's, cousin Ebb's, cousin Rasche's, brother Albert's (with his mother-in-law Nancy), brother-in-law Charles Lewis's, brother Washington's, and patriarch C.C. Hearne's own extensive acreage. (Courtesy Baum, *Counterfeit Justice*.)

C.C. Hearne was a millionaire by today's reckoning. According to the 1860 US census, Christopher Columbus, or "Lum" as the family called him, had wealth totaling $141,000. In today's dollars, that translates to between $2.5 and $5 million, depending on the inflation calendar one uses. (Courtesy of Hearne Chamber of Commerce.)

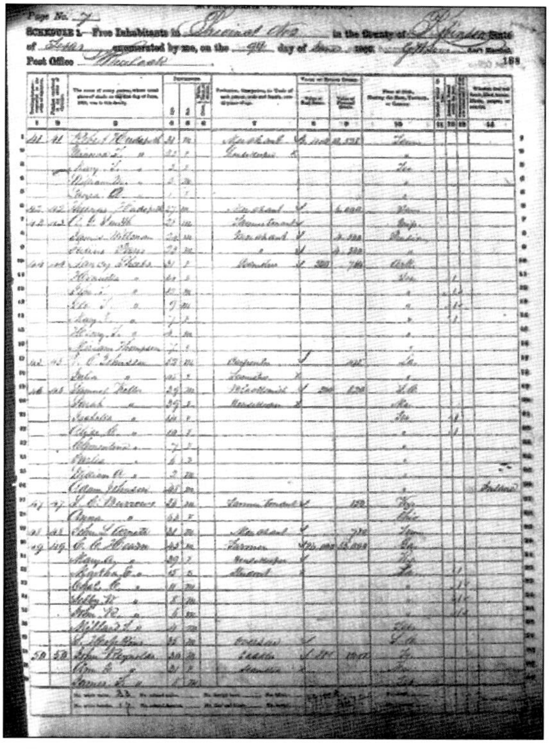

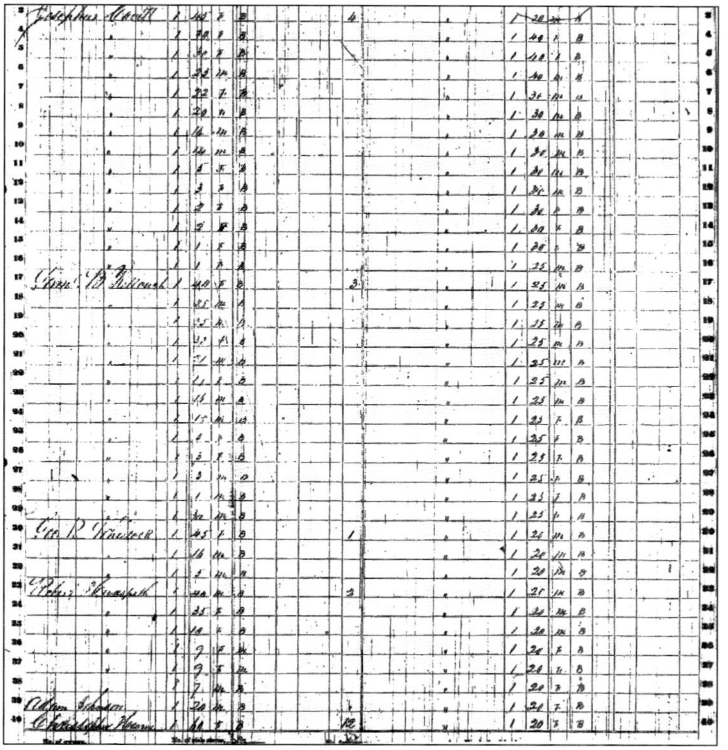

The 1860 slave rolls (C.C. Hearne's pictured) indicated each Hearne had his own. Were Hearne slaves treated well? In 1854, the *San Antonio Ledger* reported the capture of two of eight escapees from the "Columbus Herron" plantation. One had been beaten and his arm broken. Hattie Cole, a slave on Ebenezer's plantation, recalled Ebb saying "taint fo' parties he have de plantation, but 'tis fo' wo'k." Ebb's slaves were fed well, doctored well, and worked hard. (Courtesy of Federal Archives and Records Administrator.)

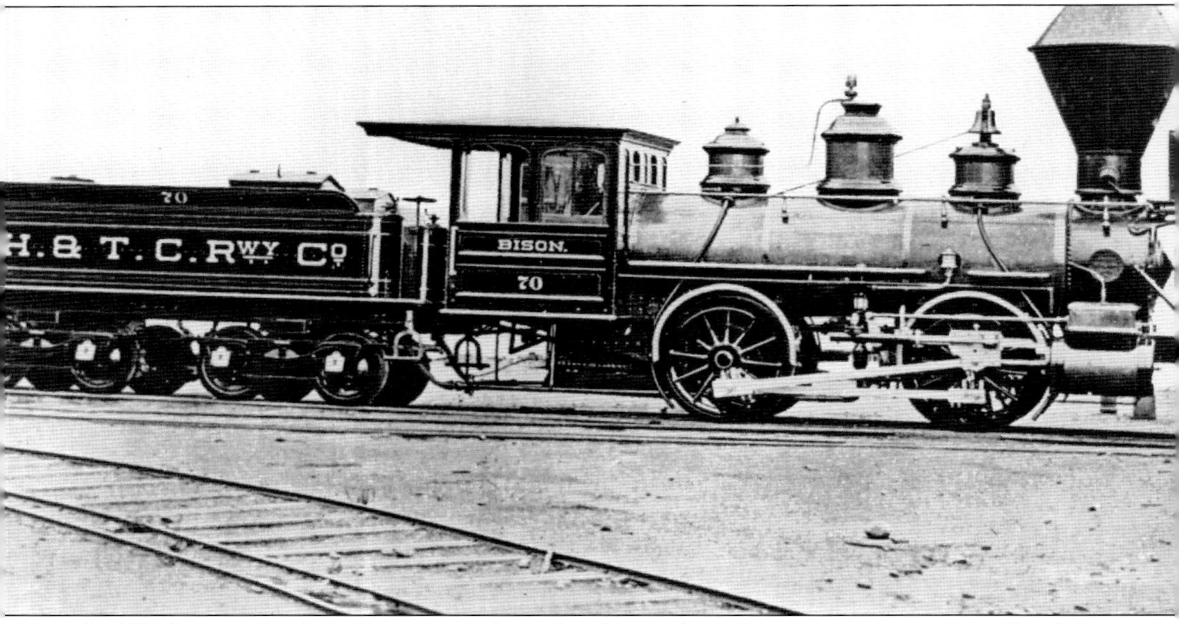

In 1858 forward-thinking Lum, seeing the railroad as the best way to transport cotton, offered the Houston & Texas Central (H&TC) land in exchange for a station. The Civil War halted track laying, but Hearne Station became the line's terminus in 1868; the Bison (pictured) was one of H&TC's workhorses. Saloons accommodating thirsty train men sprang up like bluebonnets in April. Ironically, Lum, who had moved to Houston, died in 1867. His wife, Mary Ellen, honored his 700-acre land commitment. (Courtesy of Hearne Chamber of Commerce.)

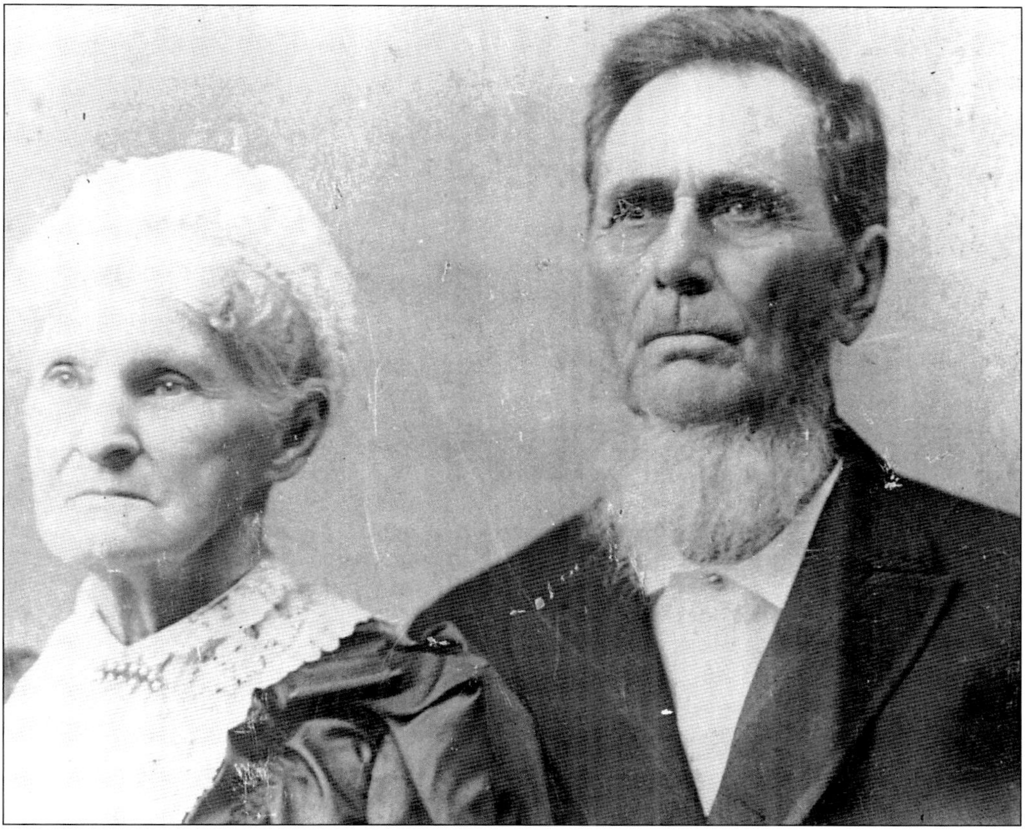

In Robertson County, little is left of the family that brought the cotton business and the railroad. In time, most moved to the larger cities of Houston and Austin to make larger fortunes. Though Rasche Hearne and wife, Priscilla (pictured), and Wash Hearne and wife, Francis, continued to shape the future of the Brazos River Bottoms and the city of Hearne for decades after Lum's death, all the Hearnes eventually died or moved away. Some family members lie in the Ebenezer Hearne Cemetery (pictured) south of the city and some in Hearne's Norwood Cemetery, but their legacy lives on in humming rails and sometimes challenging race relations. (Above, courtesy of Hearne Chamber of Commerce; below, courtesy of Cathy Lazarus.)

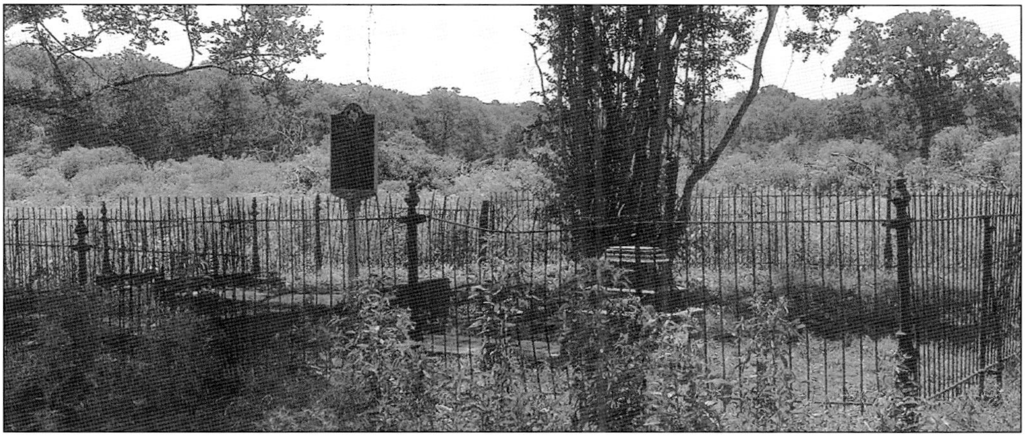

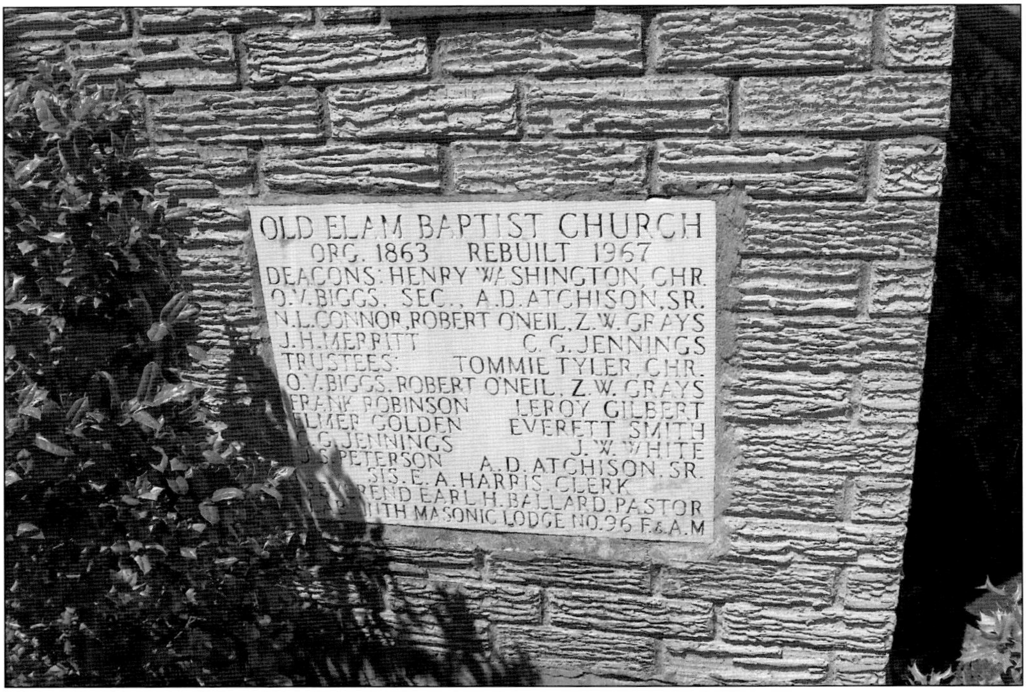

Initially, Hearne churches were rare. For whites, the Union Church serving members of all denominations was first. Old Elam (shown), a slave congregation established in 1863, was the first African American house of worship—originally constructed of wooden planks in the Brazos River Bottoms and later moved into Hearne where the St. Emmanuel Church already had a building. (Courtesy of the author.)

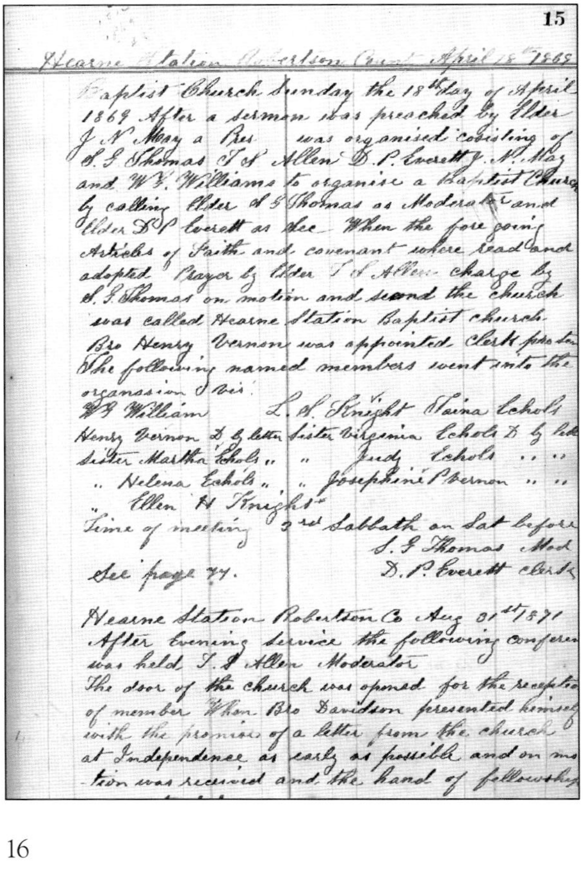

15

Hearne Station Robertson Count April 18th 1869

Baptist Church Sunday the 18th day of April 1869 After a sermon was preached by Elder J N May a Pres was organised consisting of S S Thomas T S Allen D P Everett J N May and W S Williams to organise a Baptist Church by calling Elder S S Thomas as Moderator and Elder D P Everett as Sec When the fore going Articles of Faith and covenant where read and adopted Prayer by Elder T S Allen charge by S S Thomas on motion and second the church was called Hearne Station Baptist church Bro Henry Vernon was appointed Clerk pro tem The following named members went into the organsion to wit

W S William — L S Knight — Saina Echols
Henry Vernon by letter — sister Virginia Echols by let
sister Martha Echols " — " Judy Echols " "
" Helena Echols " — " Josephine P Vernon " "
" Ellen H Knight "

Time of meeting 3rd Sabbath on Sat before
S S Thomas Mod
D P Everett clerk
See page 77.

Hearne Station Robertson Co Aug 31st 1871 After evening service the following conference was held T S Allen Moderator The door of the church was opened for the reception of member When Bro Davidson presented himself with the promise of a letter from the church at Independence as early as possible and on motion was received and the hand of fellowship

In 1869, Hearne Station Baptist Church was established—the first Anglo church to pull out of the union congregation. Until members could afford to build a worship center, Hearne Station Baptist met in the Masonic lodge building. The church kept meticulous records, indicating that it grew from 11 members in 1869 to over 100 in 1888. The congregation built its first of three sanctuaries in 1877. (Courtesy of First Baptist Church of Hearne.)

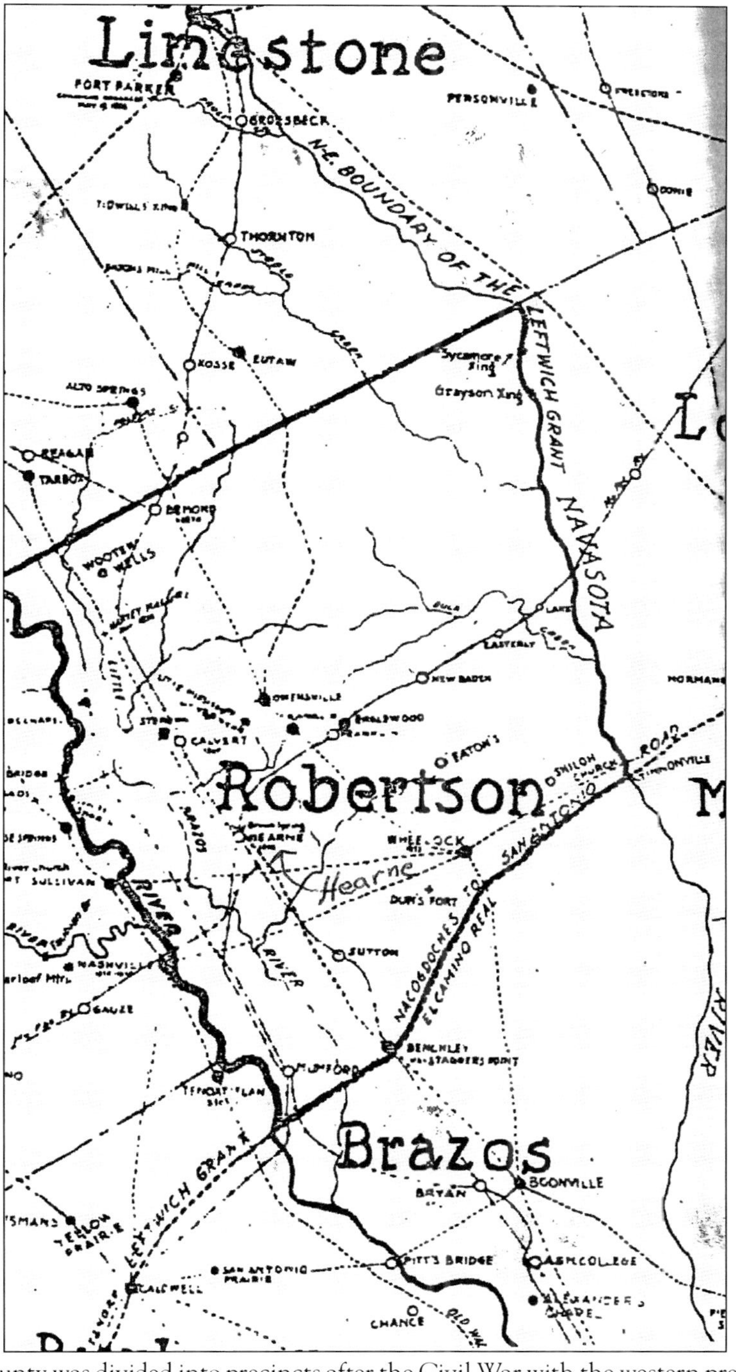

Robertson County was divided into precincts after the Civil War with the western precincts nearer the Brazos River referred to as the "Black Precincts" because of their large African American population. Within those precincts, the new towns of Hearne and Calvert were rapidly growing, despite the presence of a large military garrison in Calvert that was called "Yankee Hole" by the white locals. (Courtesy of Baker, *The History of Robertson County*.)

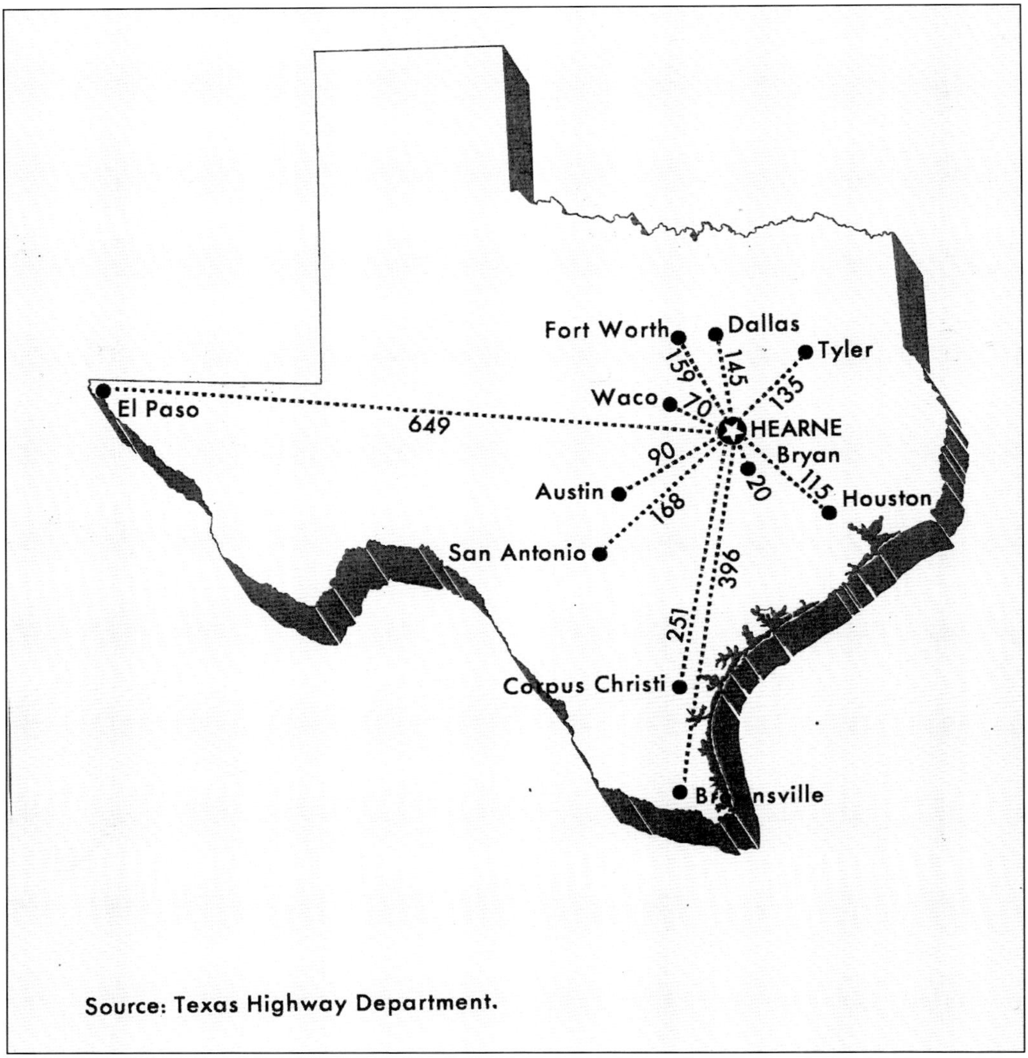

Hearne was quickly becoming one of the hubs of a large county in the Union's largest state. Its expanding rail yards, roundhouse, and connections with Houston, Dallas, San Antonio, and Austin made it a "name" in post–Civil War Texas. (Courtesy of Texas Department of Public Safety.)

Two

Seeds of Prosperity and Bitterness

The years from 1867 to 1896 were marked by both unprecedented growth and violence. Railroads and thousands of acres under cotton cultivation provided the "boom" and spared Hearne the economic depression that gripped the post–Civil War South. However, the Hearne area did not escape the violence engendered by Reconstruction, the attempt to give newly freed slaves an equal place in society. In a county with almost as many black as white residents, most residing near the Brazos River, living could be a hazardous business.

Immediately after the Civil War, white supremacy groups rode roughshod over Robertson County, attempting to reestablish an antebellum social order. According to historian Dale Baum, in 1867 alone, 20 African Americans residents were "deliberately shot," but not one of the assailants stood trial. By year's end, the Freedman's Bureau, a federal agency created to help former slaves assume roles as citizens, and federal troops had stepped in to quell the violence.

One Hearne tale dating back to 1871 illustrates the racial tension. According to local legend, an African American state policeman sent by Texas's "carpetbag government" to curb the city's racial violence was lured into a Hearne saloon and shot dead before he could begin his job. Actually, says Baum, the state policeman was white, showing that Hearne gunslinger Calvin Brown was an equal-opportunity killer. However, the presumed motive for the murder, to oppose state efforts to stop violence against former slaves, is probably true.

In 1868, African American influence in western Robertson County blossomed, and for almost three decades, a Robertson County black voice was consistently heard in the state capital in Austin. But that political influence abruptly ended in 1896 when Hearne attorney O.D. Cannon, then county judge, stationed white men with guns around the courthouse in Franklin, and with a six-shooter in hand, personally guarded the ballot box to bar black voters. In 1886, Cannon shot and killed former Hearne congressman and self-taught attorney Harold "Hal" Geiger (who was black) for making a "disrespectful" comment in court. Cannon shot and wounded Calvert congressman Alexander Asberry when he challenged the 1896 election (though a black man, Asberry almost regained his seat in the Texas Legislature despite Cannon's firepower). For almost a century, African Americans stayed away from the polls.

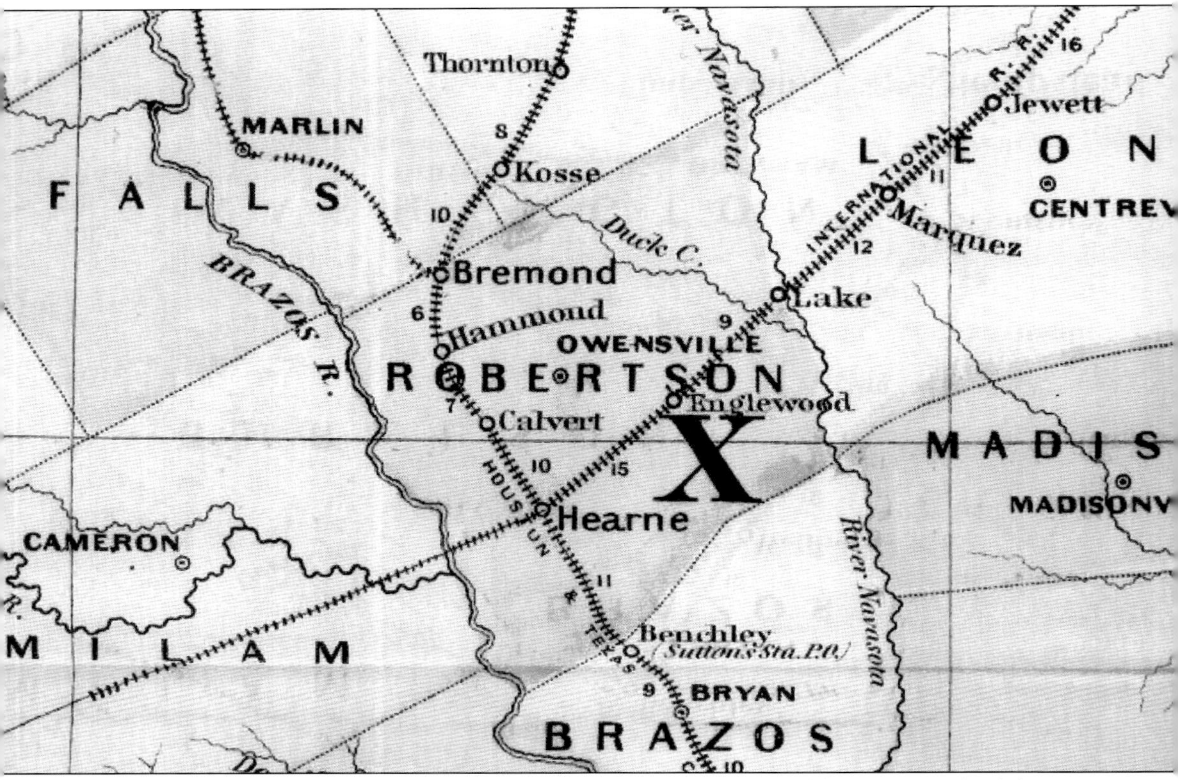

In 1870, the International & Great Northern Railroad (I&GN), enabled by a 700-acre land donation from Charles Lewis, Lum's brother-in-law, agreed to come through Hearne on its east-west route. Disputed land claims held up progress for months, according to McCarver and McCarver, but later that year, a compromise was worked out, and tracks were laid by 1872 as promised. Meanwhile, new rail crews filled the saloons, and Hearne earned its "crossroads" title with tracks running north-south and east-west. (Courtesy of Hearne Chamber of Commerce.)

The Methodist church was also established in 1870 with Methodist preacher Horace Bishop arriving on his horse Ku Klux. Joe Lambert, owner of the town's largest saloon, befriended Bishop and allowed him to "set up church" on the saloon's second floor. Local rowdies' efforts to run off Bishop failed, and worship services began. That same year, Bishop and congregants Nathan Kilgore and Jonathan Wilkerson built one of Hearne's first schools. (Courtesy of author.)

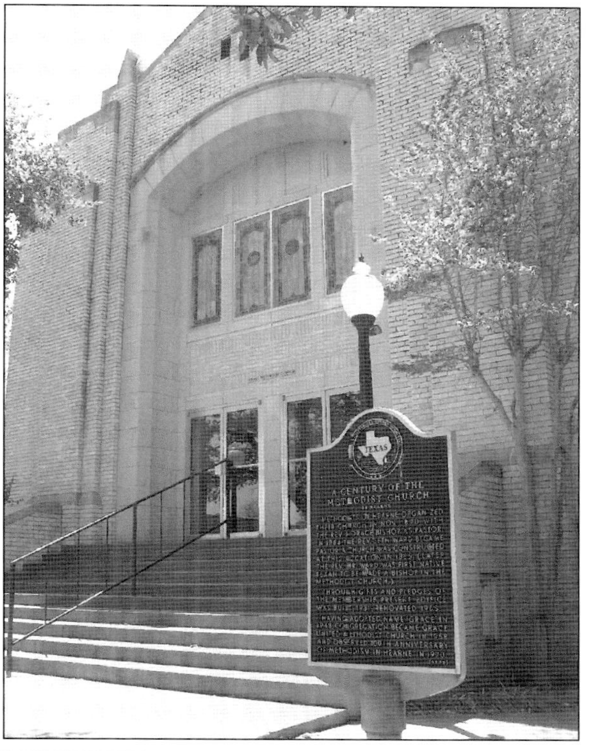

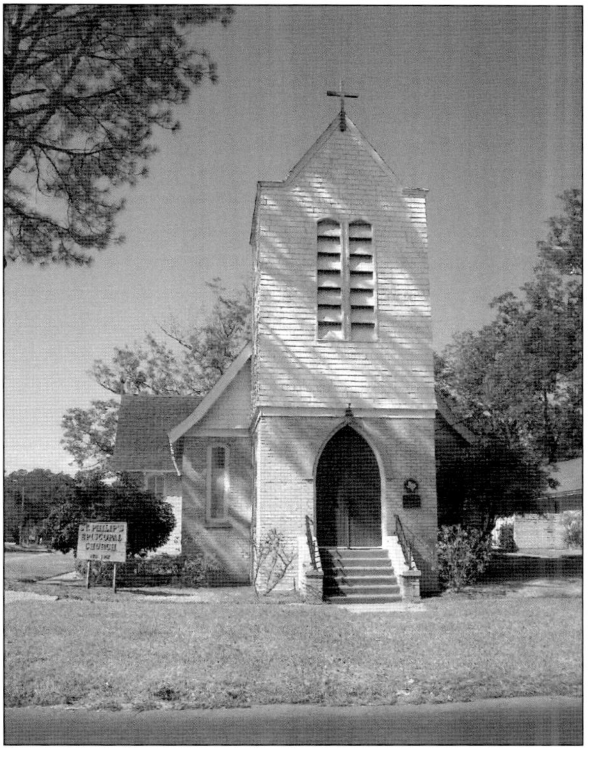

Soon after the Methodist church arrived, St. Philip's Episcopal Church (pictured) and the First Presbyterian Church withdrew from Union Church, and the Catholic archdiocese established a hospital/church for a growing Catholic population. (Courtesy of author.)

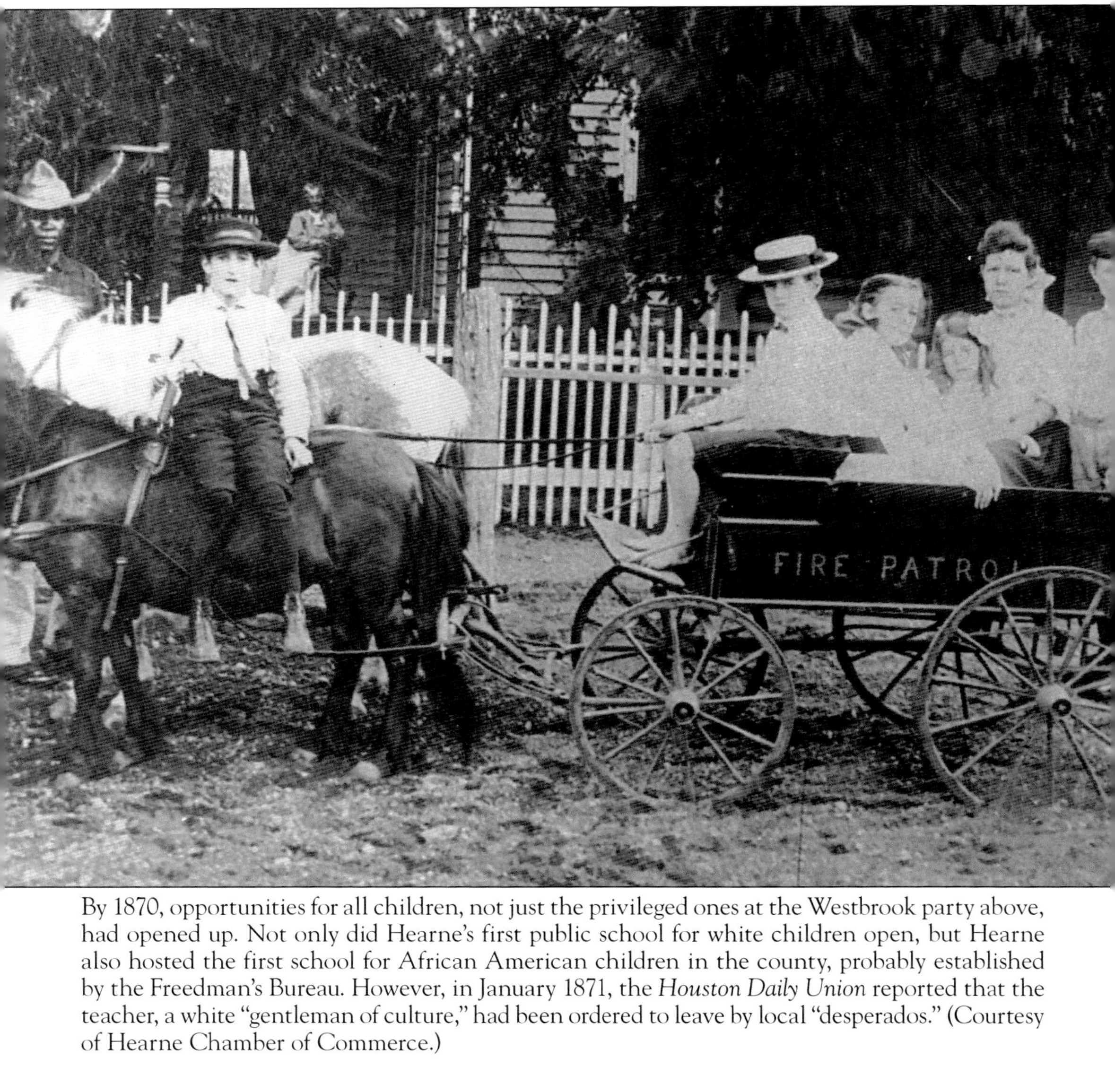

By 1870, opportunities for all children, not just the privileged ones at the Westbrook party above, had opened up. Not only did Hearne's first public school for white children open, but Hearne also hosted the first school for African American children in the county, probably established by the Freedman's Bureau. However, in January 1871, the *Houston Daily Union* reported that the teacher, a white "gentleman of culture," had been ordered to leave by local "desperados." (Courtesy of Hearne Chamber of Commerce.)

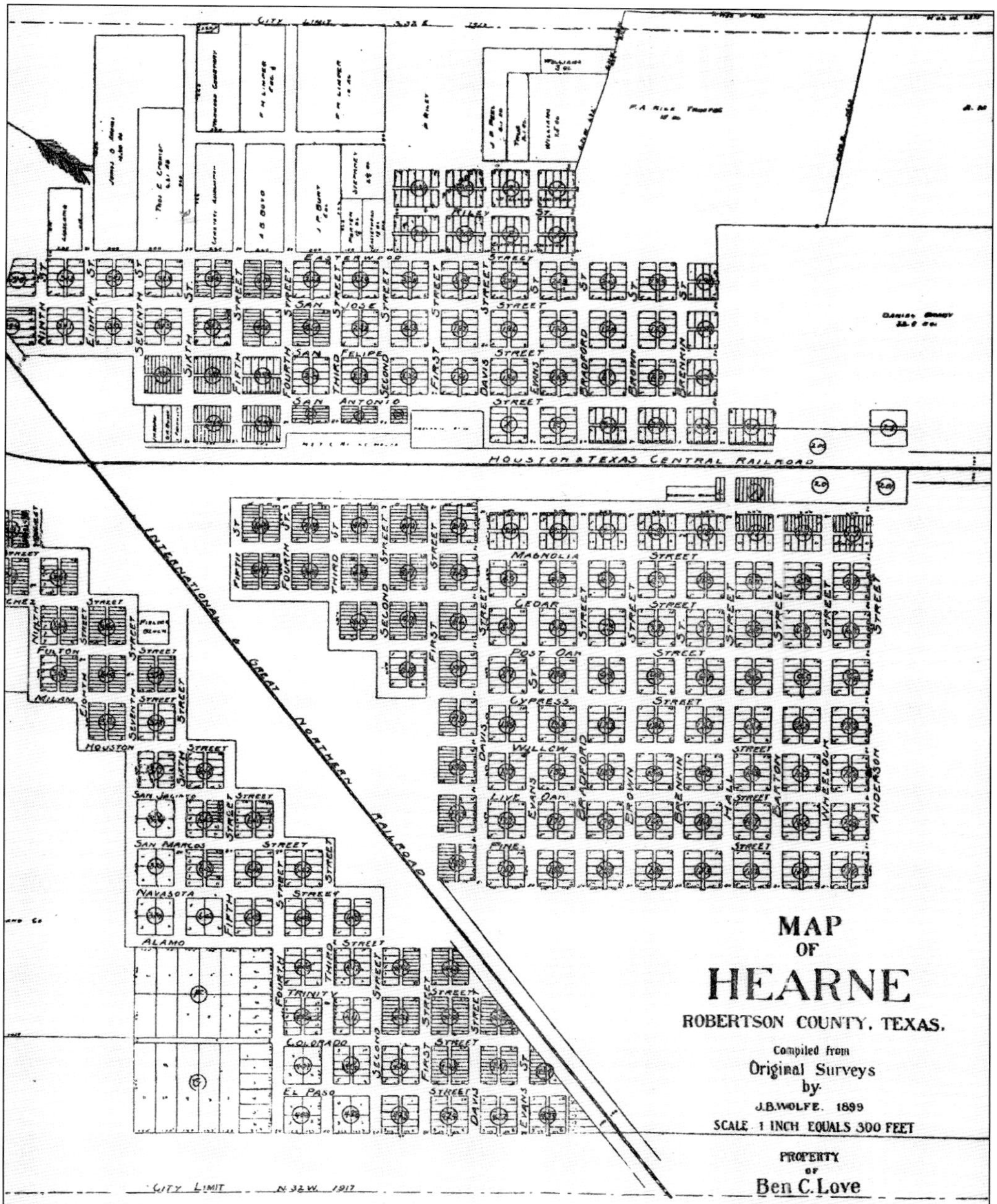

In 1871, Hearne incorporated; the New York and Texas Land Company surveyed and sold Hearne city lots. Hearne's three artesian wells provided ample water for businesses, including Hale & Evans Dry Goods, S.C. Brown's meat market, Adams and Leonard's bank, Brown and Wilkerson's general store, Wash Hearne's hotel, and saloons owned by Lambert and John Teeling. Drs. D.M. Morrison and E.M. Matkin hung shingles with Matkin opening the first pharmacy. (Courtesy of Hearne Chamber of Commerce.)

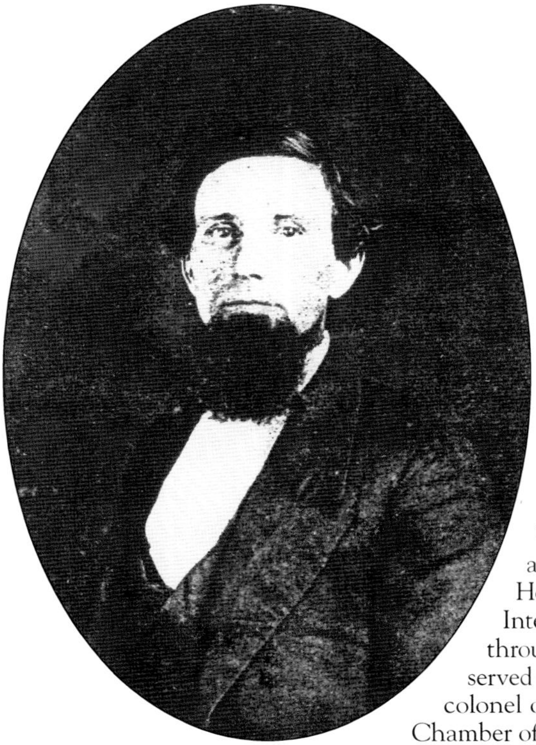

Col. Charles Lewis and his wife, Adeline (Lum's sister), who are both buried in Hearne's Norwood Cemetery, contributed as much to Hearne Station as any other couple. In addition to his own home, Lewis constructed the first house of worship for Caucasian Christians—Union Church—and the first business structure, a general store. Most of the land divided into Hearne's first lots had been Lewis property, and the International & Great Northern Railroad barreled through on land he donated. Widely respected, Lewis served two terms in the state legislature and was named colonel of the local militia. (Left, courtesy of Hearne Chamber of Commerce; below, courtesy of author.)

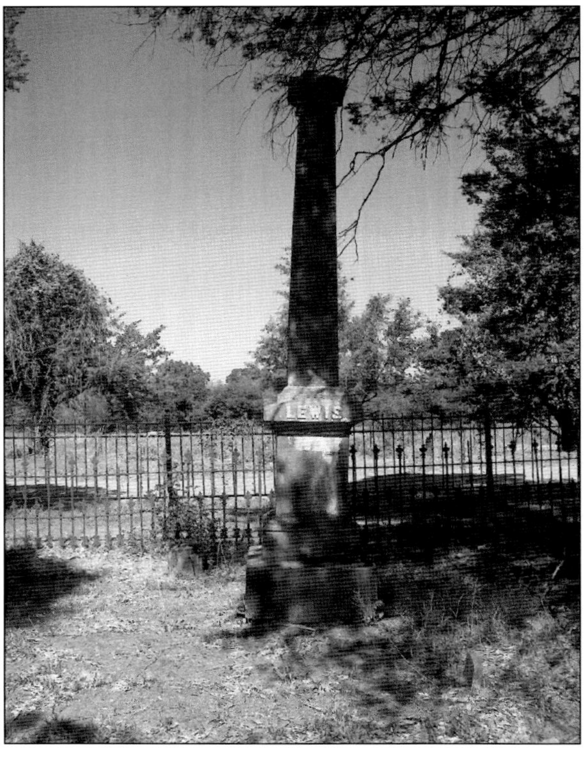

As business boomed in Hearne and Calvert, African American political influence was exploding. Of the 52 black representatives to the state legislature and the constitutional convention from 1868 to 1896, six were either representing Robertson County and/or had matriculated there. Matthew Gaines, arguably the most influential of the 52, represented Washington County but served his "time on the cross" as a slave on Lum's plantation, making him a product of the Hearne plantation system, according to Dr. Dale Baum. (Courtesy of Texas Preservation Board.)

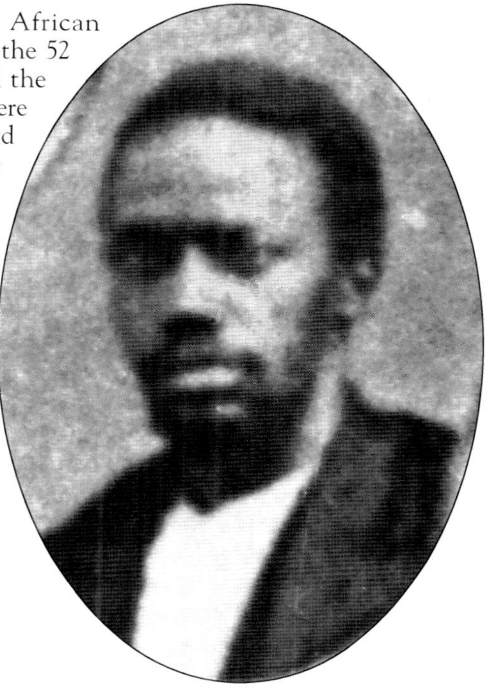

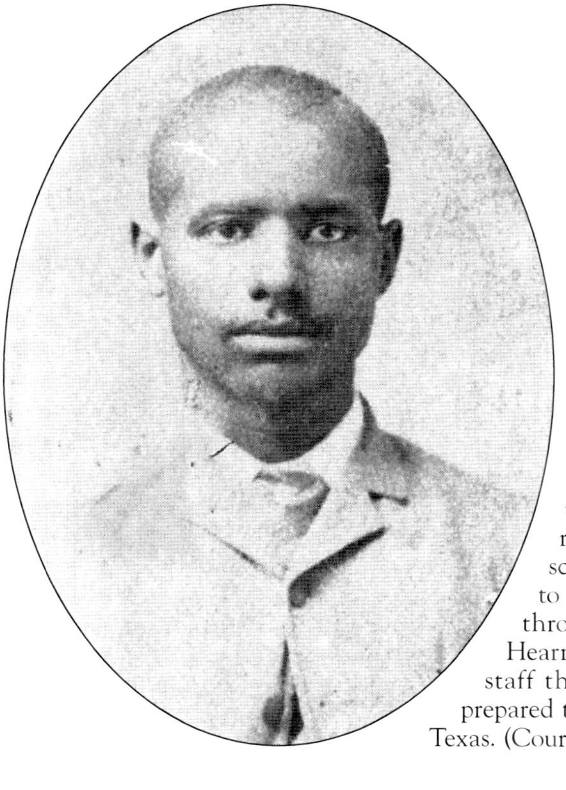

Alexander Asberry, a soft-spoken, modest man, served in the legislature form 1889 until 1896. Though from Calvert, he was a product of the Hearne Academy, a remarkable trade and college-preparatory school operating north of Hearne from 1881 to 1909. Supported by blacks throughout Texas through the Baptist Lincoln Association, the Hearne Academy had an all–African American staff that either trained students for trades or prepared them to enter Bishop College in Marshall, Texas. (Courtesy of Texas Preservation Board.)

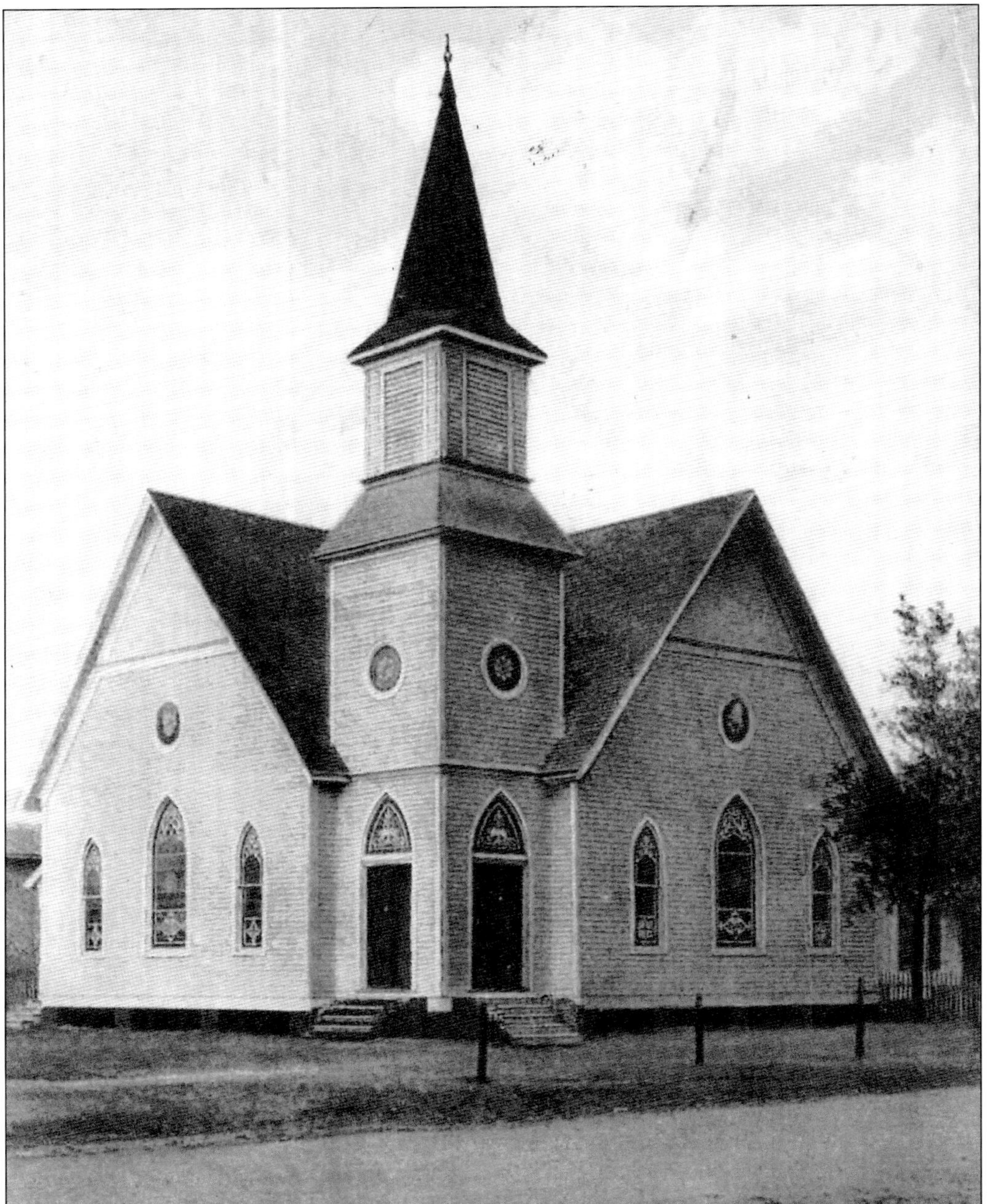

Little Flock Missionary Baptist, Hearne's second-oldest African American church, was established in 1881. St. Emmanuel Baptist joined several families traveling from Red Top (now Shiro), Texas, to Kansas, who had stopped in Hearne. The new congregation built a church on the east side—Little Flock. St. Mark Baptist and the African Methodist Episcopal (AME), pictured, soon followed. Hearne's black Methodists attempted to erect a building three times before J.S. Whitaker—a remarkable church-builder, writer, and preacher—came to Hearne and completed the job. (Courtesy of Cathy Lazarus, "Church Histories.")

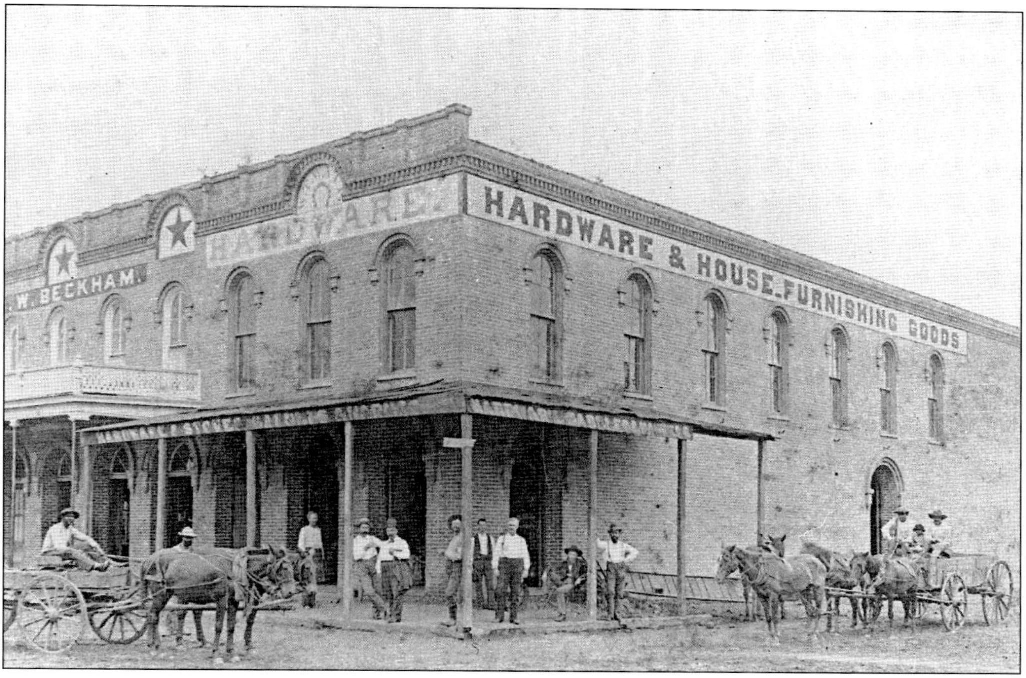

Fire tore through Hearne's wooden downtown structures in December 1883, making room for the brick buildings standing today. Robert A. Allen had come to Hearne in 1872, buying out Watt's hardware, only to lose it to fire in 1891. Relocating to the Beckham building, Allen and son R.C. made Allen Hardware Company one of the most significant in Texas. Another co-occupant of the Beckham building was Col. Robert Martin's opera house, but as Allen expanded, the opera house moved out. (Both, courtesy of Hearne Chamber of Commerce.)

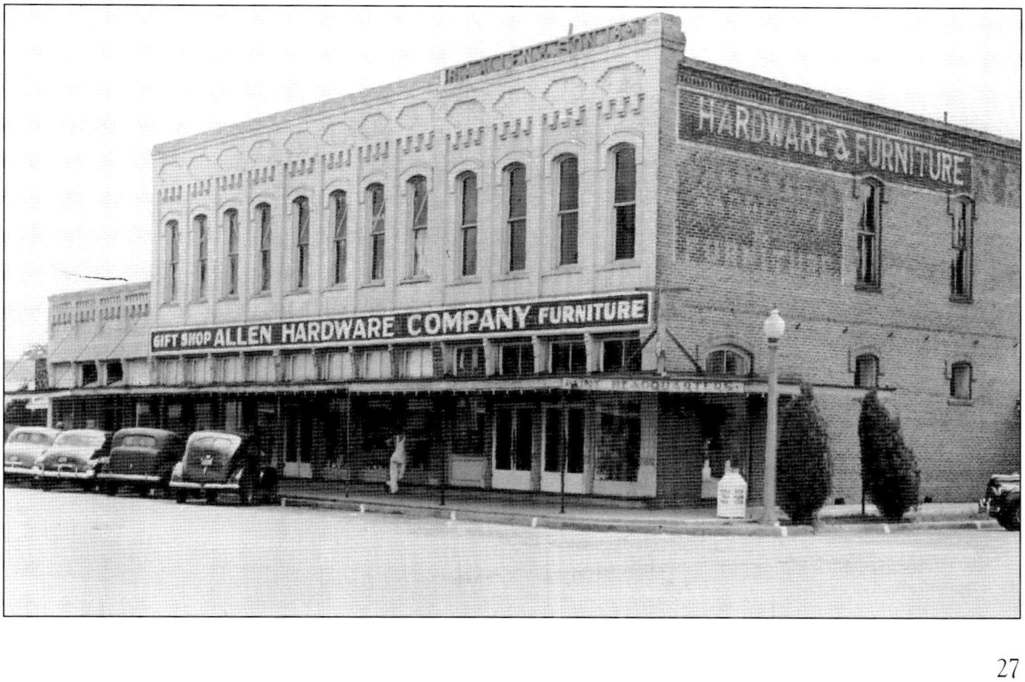

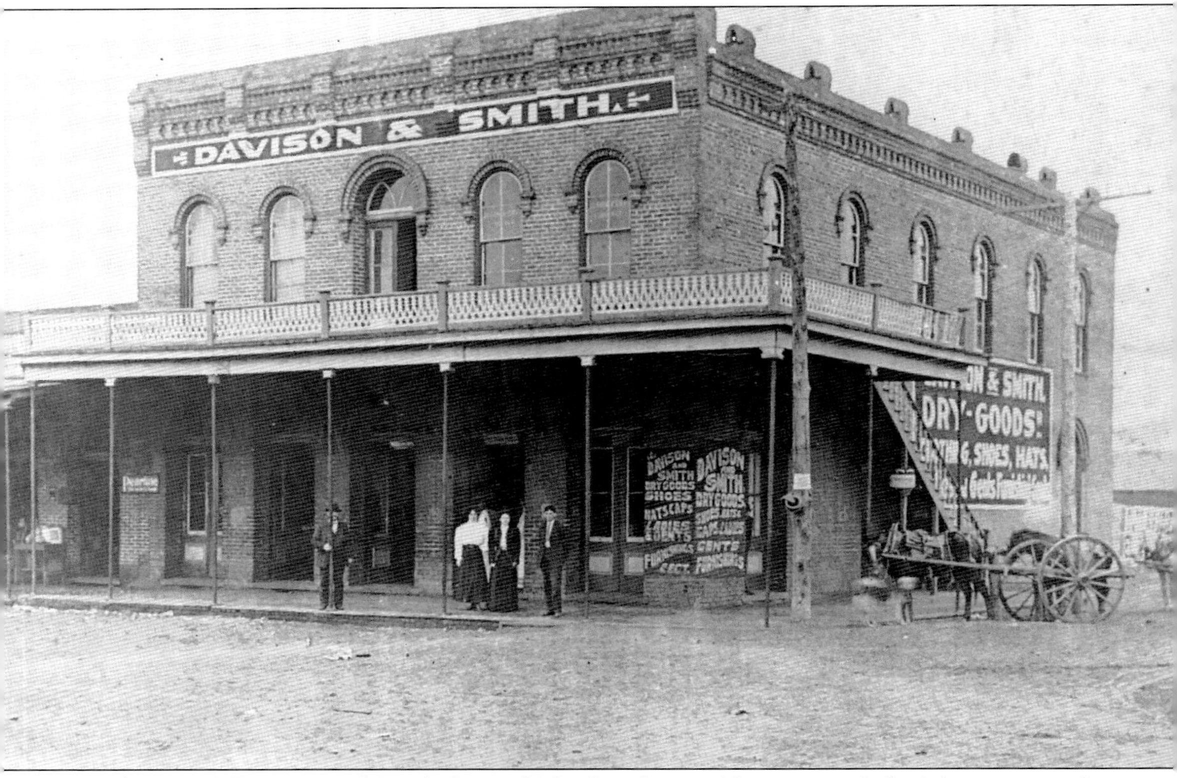

Built in 1896, Davison and Smith General Merchandise could meet most ladies' shopping needs. Constructed on the corner of Magnolia and Fourth Streets, it—along with three other dry goods stores, eight grocery stores, Allen Hardware, two furniture stores, three drugstores, a dozen or more saloons, four hotels, four restaurants, two millinery shops, three lumberyards, and three livery stables—provided goods and services to Hearne. (Courtesy of Hearne Chamber of Commerce.)

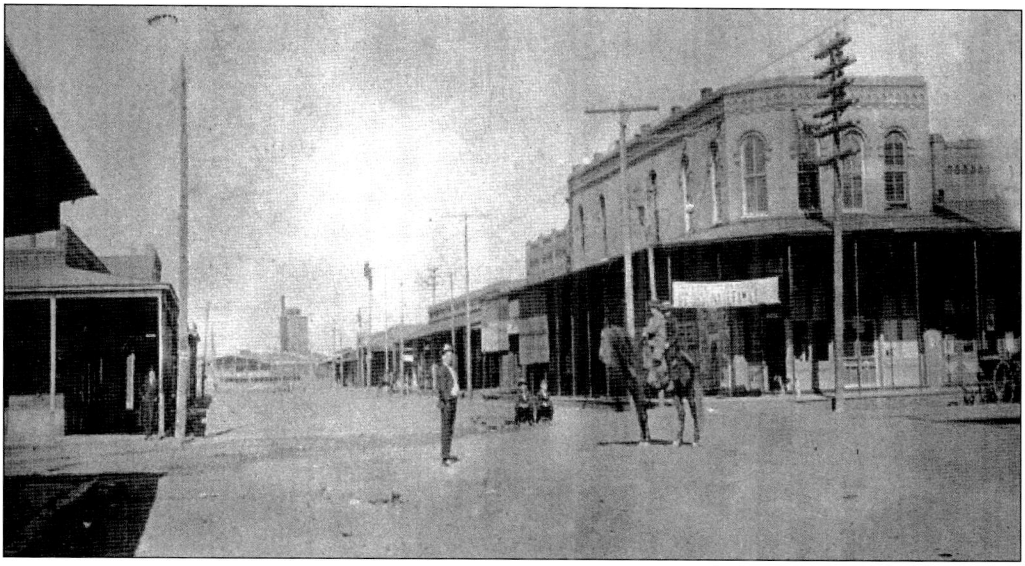

Hearne's downtown structures were mostly complete by 1900. Though the facades and the names have changed (many times in some cases), the 1900 buildings still, for the most part, house Hearne's downtown enterprises. Hearne officials at the turn of the century include Thornton Peyton Griffin (standing), the city marshal for 43 years and reputed to be the "man who tamed Hearne," and Peter L. Brady (seated in center), its mayor for 23 years and the man most responsible for the Hearne Municipal Power Company. Brady, successful owner of Brady's cotton gin and the son of Irish Catholic immigrants, first electrified Hearne by erecting a private generating plant. True to his Irish roots, Brady was a pillar of St. Mary's Church. (Above, courtesy of Hearne Chamber of Commerce; below, courtesy of the City of Hearne.)

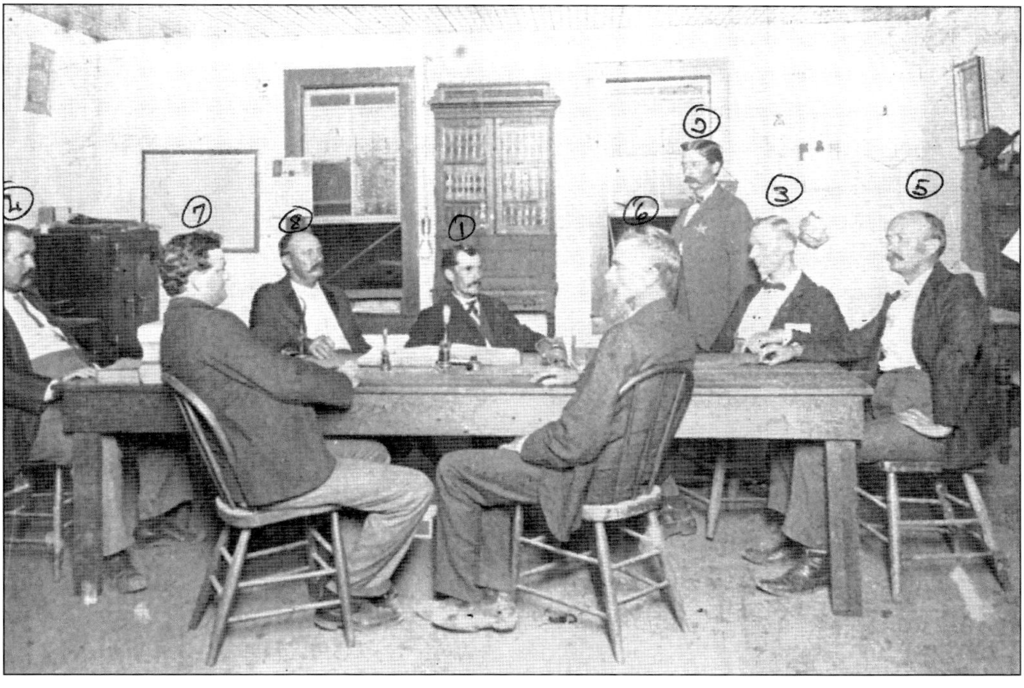

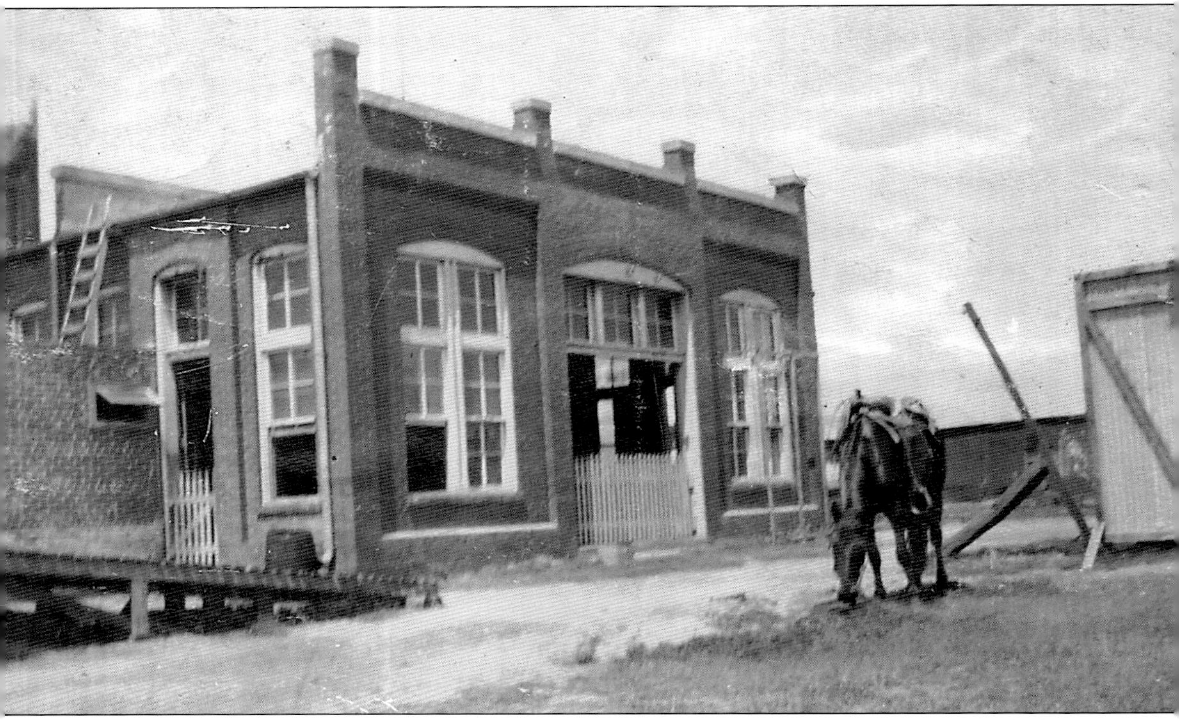

Though Peter Brady built Hearne's first power plant as a private enterprise, he probably believed that it would go public and become one of Hearne's primary assets. Soon after, the city purchased the plant, replacing the original building with a larger, better equipped one. It did, indeed, become the city's primary source of income. (Courtesy of Hearne Chamber of Commerce.)

Three

Big Railroads and Big Cotton

By the 1890s, Hearne and the Brazos River Bottoms plantations to its west and southwest were growing, ginning, baling, and loading on to railcars tens of thousands of bales of cotton a year. Production had been hampered by labor problems in the 1870s and 1880s, first remedied by the particularly cruel practice of using (and abusing) convict labor from the prisons (a practice both Hal Geiger and Alexander Asberry fought against in the Texas Legislature) then solved when Rasche Hearne made repeated trips to North Carolina to lure cotton field hands to the Bottoms. Many generations of Hearne residents trace their roots to North Carolina. With hands in the fields, cotton became the driving force of Hearne's economy. In 1895, according to McCarver and McCarver's *Hearne on the Brazos*, "The Hearne [cotton] compress handled 78,000 bales of cotton."

Even with all of the Bottoms cleared and cultivated, it took the railroads to make cotton the undisputed king. Throughout the 1890s, Hearne was served not only by the H&TC and I&GN but also its own Hearne & Brazos Valley Railway (H&BV), running from Hearne to Stone City in Brazos County. Created by Hearne businessmen, the H&BV hauled not only cotton but also plantation owners from homes in town to the Bottoms and field hands from the Bottoms to Hearne's stores.

But a cotton-based economy lives at the mercy of the weather. A good crop meant booming business downtown, and a bad crop meant "one step closer to the poorhouse," according to one Hearne businessman (McCarver and McCarver). When cotton farmers harvested a bumper crop, the wealth passed down to field hands, cotton gin and compress owners and workers, and oil plant workers. In a bad year, the flow of money constricted to a trickle.

The other side of the economic equation (the railroads) also was not without occasional tragedy. Several monumental train wrecks make up part of Hearne's lore, including the wreck of the Owl at the Hammond siding a few miles north of Hearne in January 1918. A switch connecting the siding with the main line had been damaged, and when the Owl barreled through, the first of several passenger coach cars split the switch, sending the back end of the train onto the siding and smack into a freight engine with caboose parked there. As a result of the accident, 16 passengers were killed and 17 injured, including many burned by scalding water gushing from broken steam pipes (McCarver and McCarver).

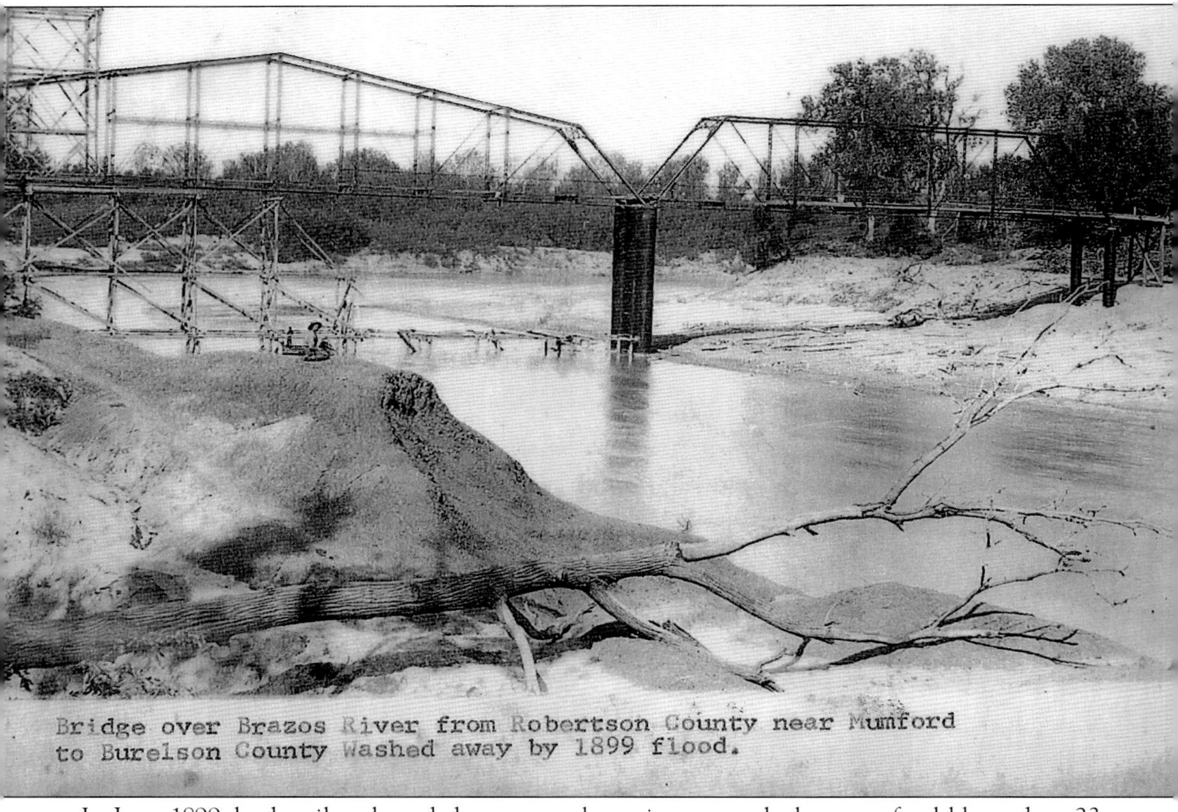

In June 1899, both railroads and the cotton plantations were dealt a near-fatal blow when 23 inches of rain fell in three days. Floodwaters rampaged over Bottoms plantations, washing away crops and damaging bridges and rails. The H&BV never recovered and sold out to the H&TC. In 1913, floods rose again. According to McCarver and McCarver, only 40 percent of the cotton crop made it to harvest, and what was salvaged was dark, stained by Williamson County black dirt from two counties away. (Courtesy of Hearne Chamber of Commerce.)

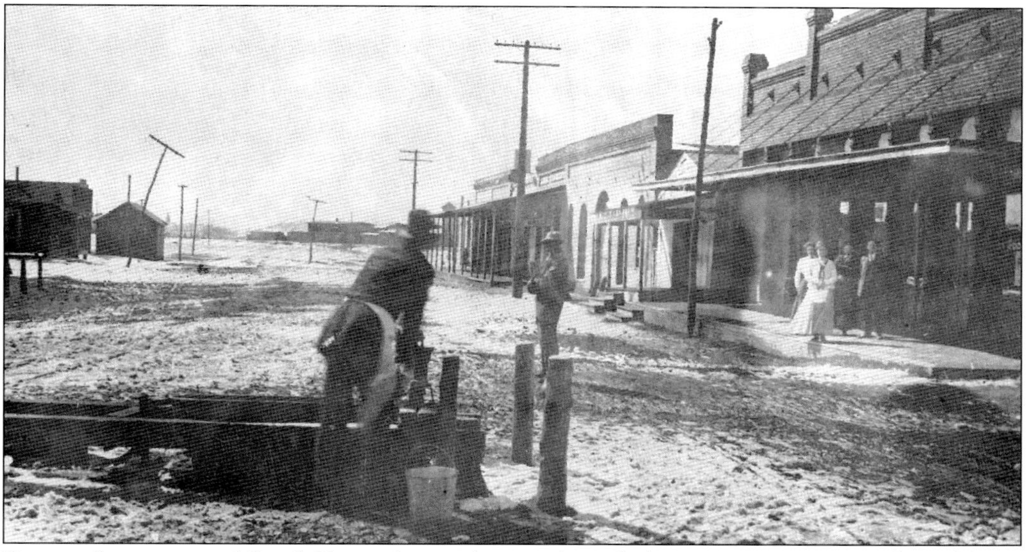

Despite the occasional flood, Hearne's growth proved steady from 1890 to 1920, as reflected by its growing downtown and customers in the stores (Hazlett Drugstore is pictured below). Following the 1890 census, Hearne could claim a population of 1,873, up 462 from the previous count in 1880. By 1920, Hearne was a town of 2,741, with its population increasing by almost 400 between 1910 and 1920 despite losses in World War I and the influenza pandemic of 1918–1919, according to McCarver and McCarver. Though it had good times punctuated by bad times, overall, Hearne prospered. (Both, courtesy of Hearne Chamber of Commerce.)

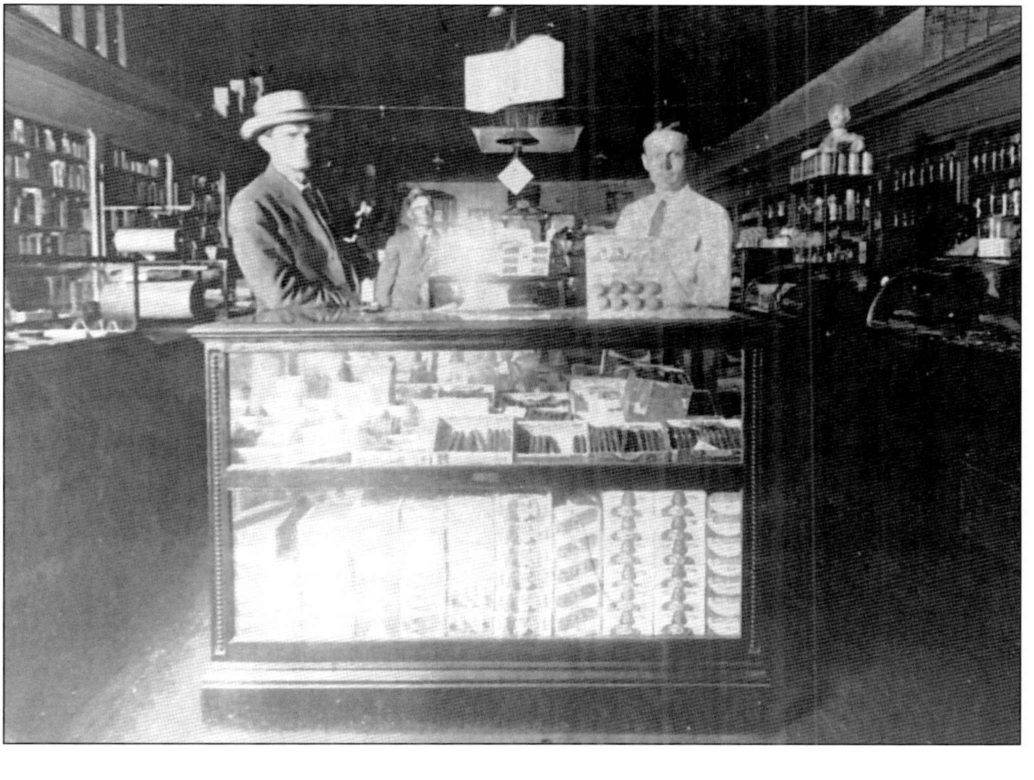

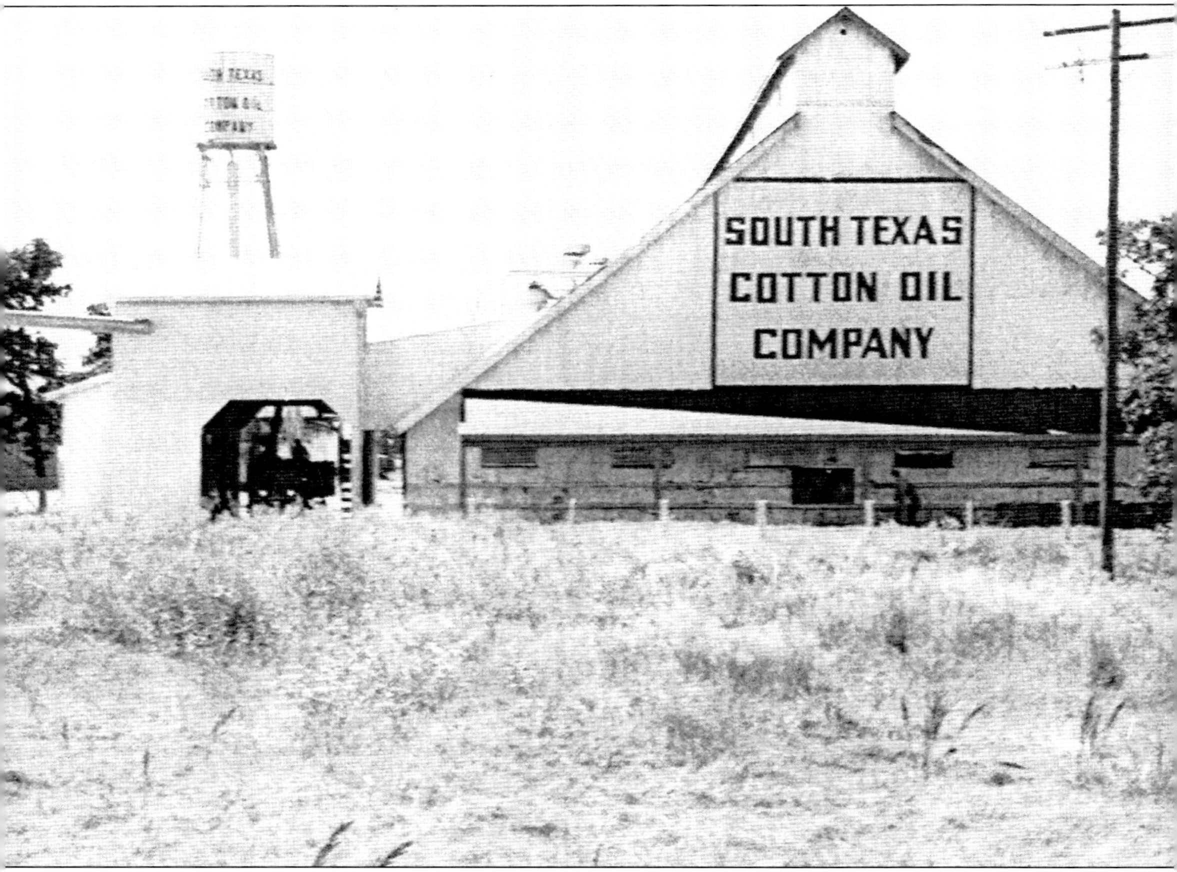

Once cotton was ginned, cottonseed was pressed for its oil or crushed for animal feed. Hearne's first cottonseed mill was built in 1874 from Hearne's original depot; a larger mill followed in 1892. According to McCarver and McCarver, the mill crushed 10,000–13,000 tons of seeds annually and produced feed for 900–13,000 head of cattle. The oil plant (pictured) was built by Brazos Bottom Cotton Planters in 1899 and operated until 1969. (Courtesy of Dorothy Starkey.)

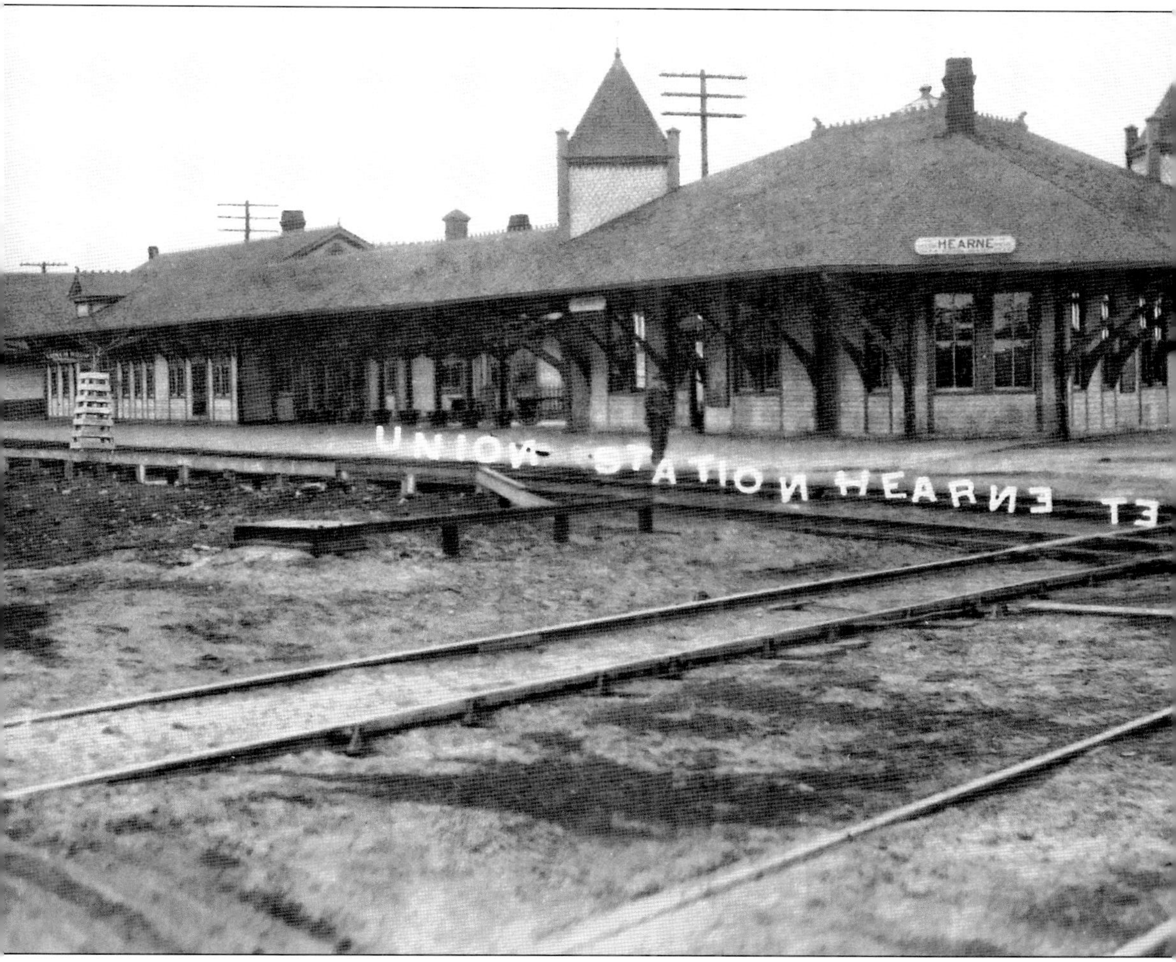

In 1901, Hearne's final train depot was completed. A second commercial station south of the depot featured large loading docks to handle hundreds of 500-pound cotton bales. Later, stockyards were added to accommodate hundreds of head of cattle to be loaded into northbound railcars. (Courtesy of Hearne Chamber of Commerce.)

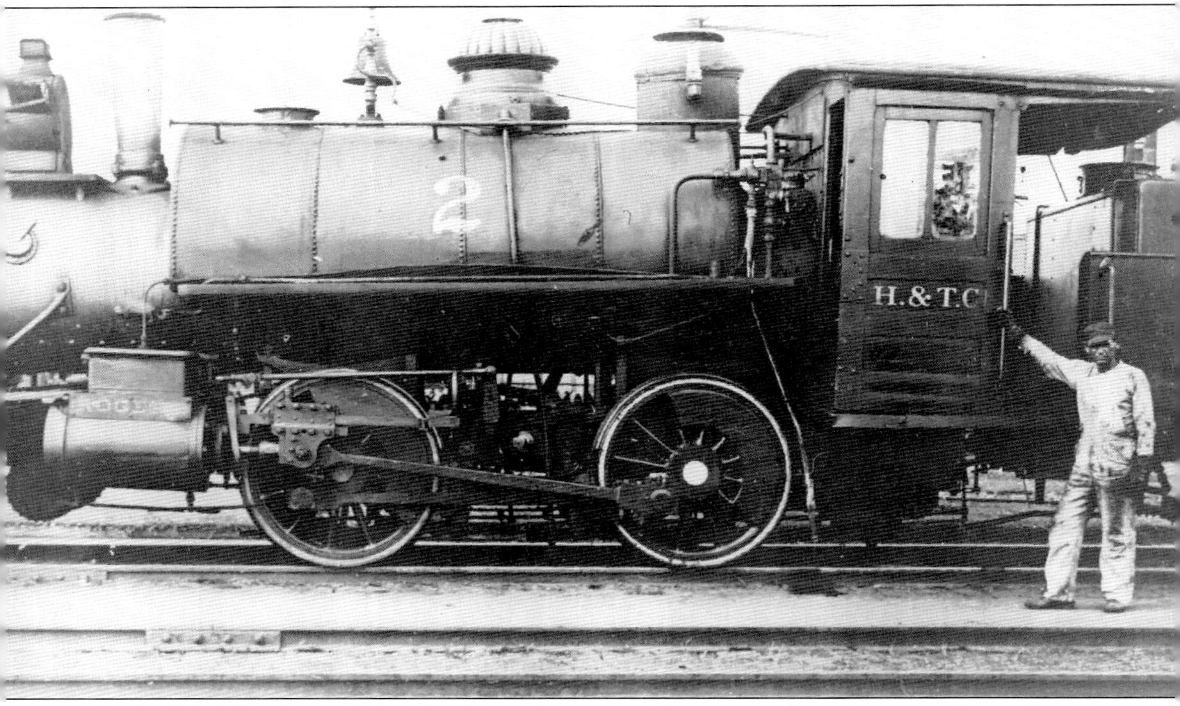

In 1874, H&TC had installed a 10-stall roundhouse and division machine shops, employing from 30 to 40 men. The Buffalo, Hearne's never-fail rail yard engine, soon began its many years of service. With Hearne serving as H&TC division headquarters, rail crews swarmed over the yards at all hours of the day and night. In time, even youngsters could find employment as runners—boys who tracked down and often woke up train crews before their shift began. (Courtesy of Hearne Chamber of Commerce.)

Until washed out, the H&BV owned by a Hearne group headed by Titus C. Westbrook (pictured), H.B. Easterwood, and R.A. Allen, was an unqualified success, taking cotton transport to the plantations themselves. The H&TC had purchased the H&BV by 1901, but people still had fond memories of "waitin' on the Jack" at Brown and Magnolia Streets and riding the Jack, like the four happy customers pictured. (Both, courtesy of Hearne Chamber of Commerce.)

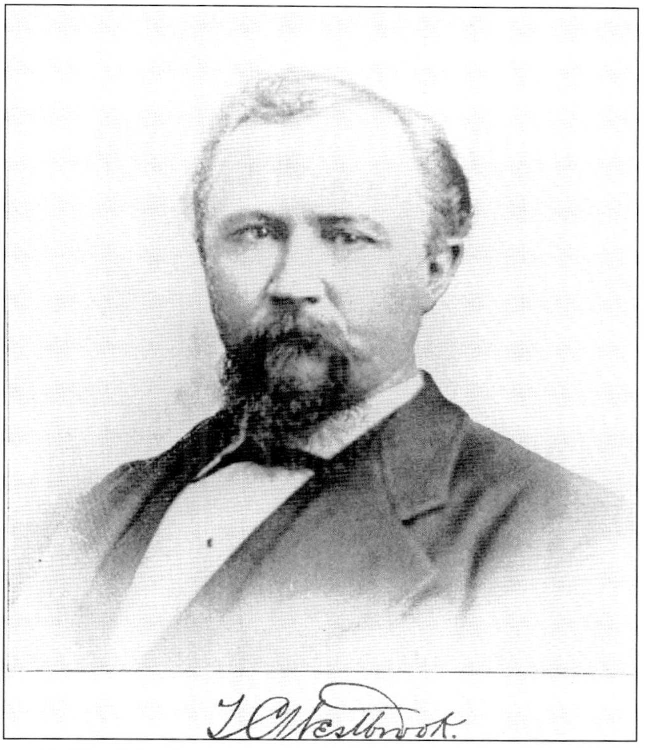

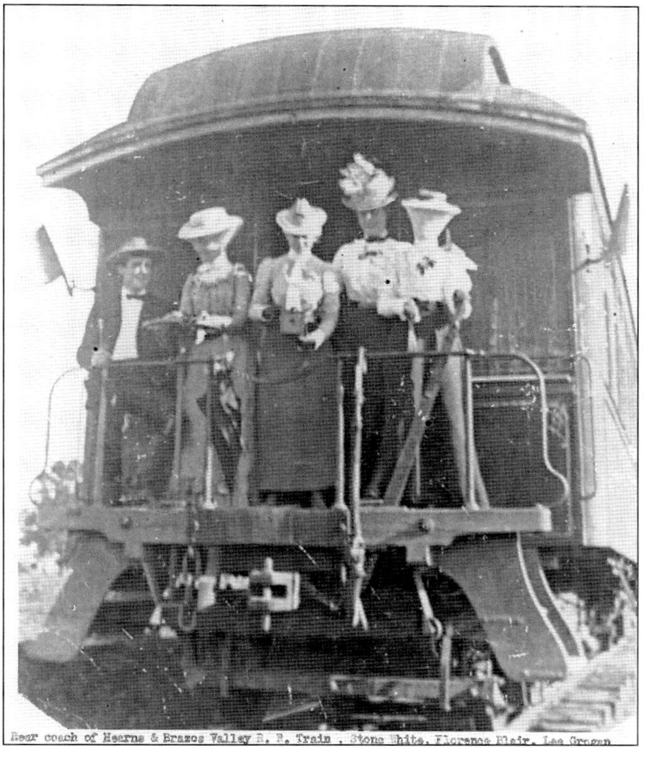

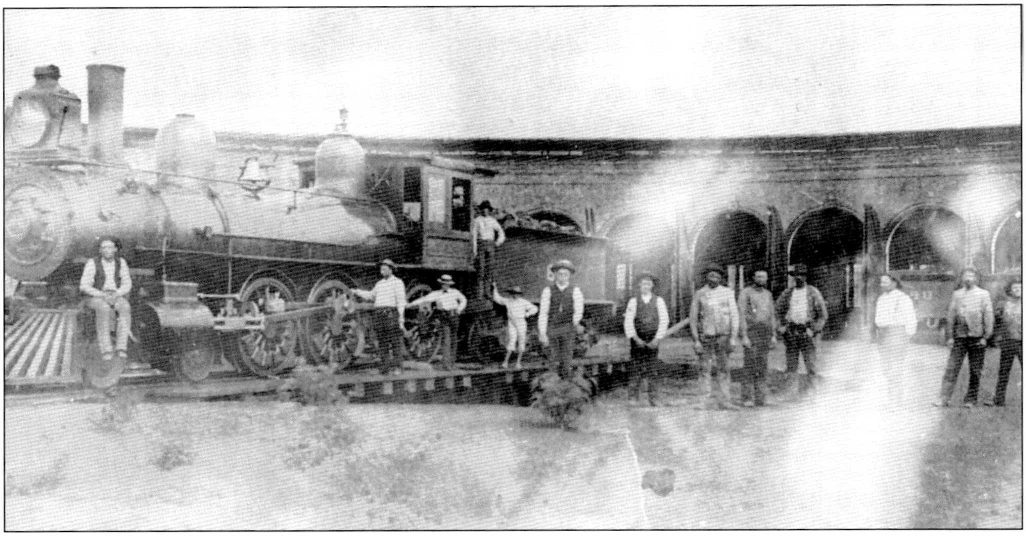

Near the Hearne depot, the two main railroad lines had offices, roundhouses, machine shops, and huge switching yards, requiring a significant workforce. "Workin' on the railroad," like these laborers who are manning a turntable, was a Hearne thing to do. (Courtesy of Hearne Chamber of Commerce.)

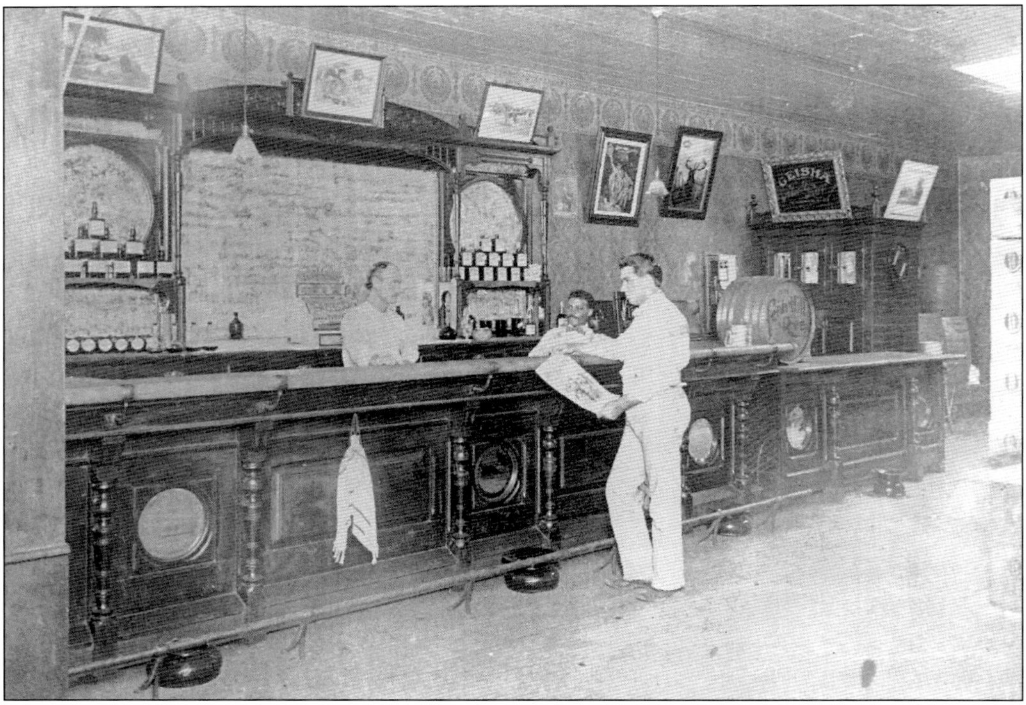

By the mid-1870s, Hearne's canvas drinking establishments had given way to genuine, Old West–looking saloons. Joe Lambert's was first, followed by Rohde's Cotton Exchange (pictured), McNutt's OK, Simmon's, Cohen's, Martin's, Later's, and Hall's—the town's largest. With construction crews gone, Hearne's saloons became somewhat genteel—no women bartenders and no minors allowed—but occasional shootings still occurred (Courtesy of Hearne Chamber of Commerce.)

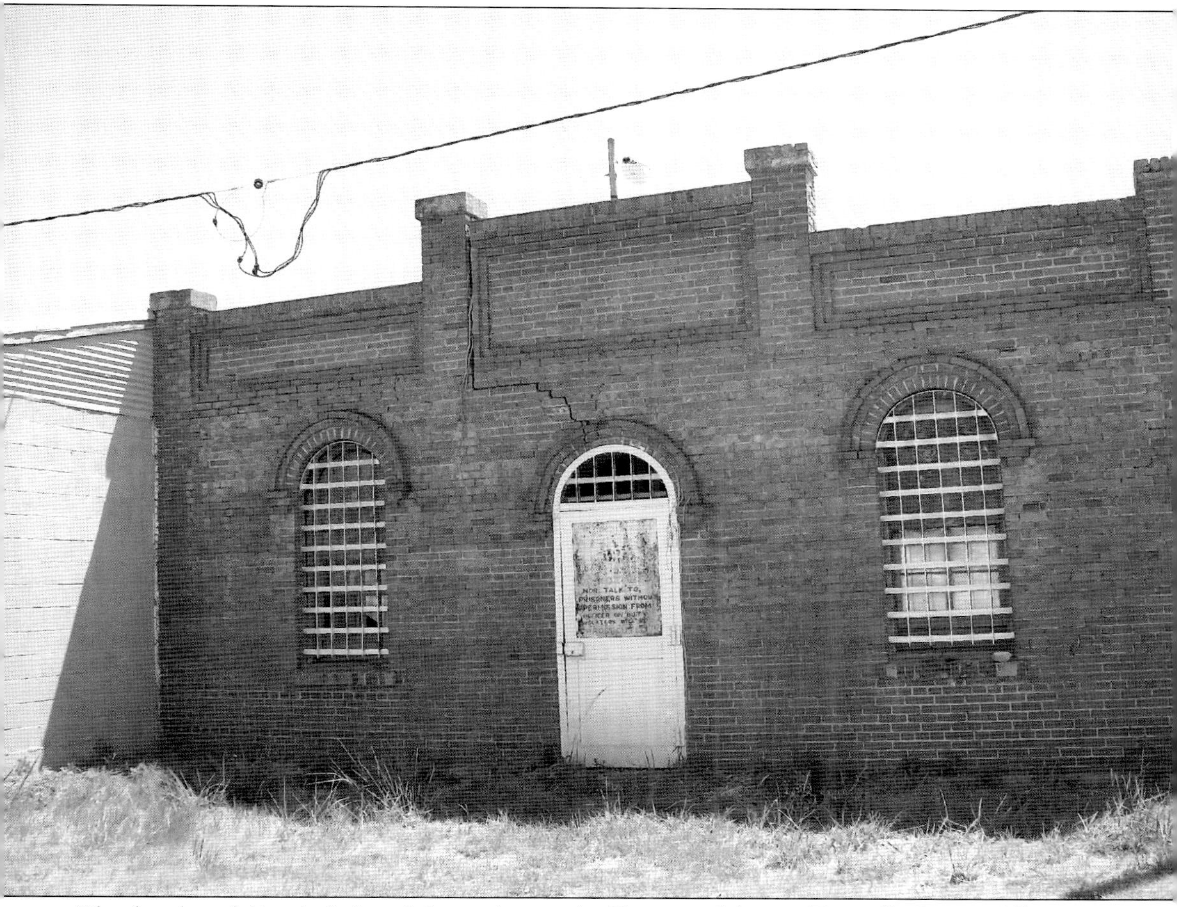

The drunk and disorderly found themselves in the Hearne calaboose. Typically, Justice Albert G. Cobb would allow no plea but "guilty." When Constable Sam Brown brought in a collar, Judge Cobb was famous for saying, "Why do you think Sam brought you in here if you were not guilty?" Cobb had served in the Confederate army as a teenager and survived to return to Texas where he spent 32 years on the bench, first in Wheelock and then as Hearne's justice of the peace. McCarver and McCarver said he exemplified the word "justice." (Courtesy of author.)

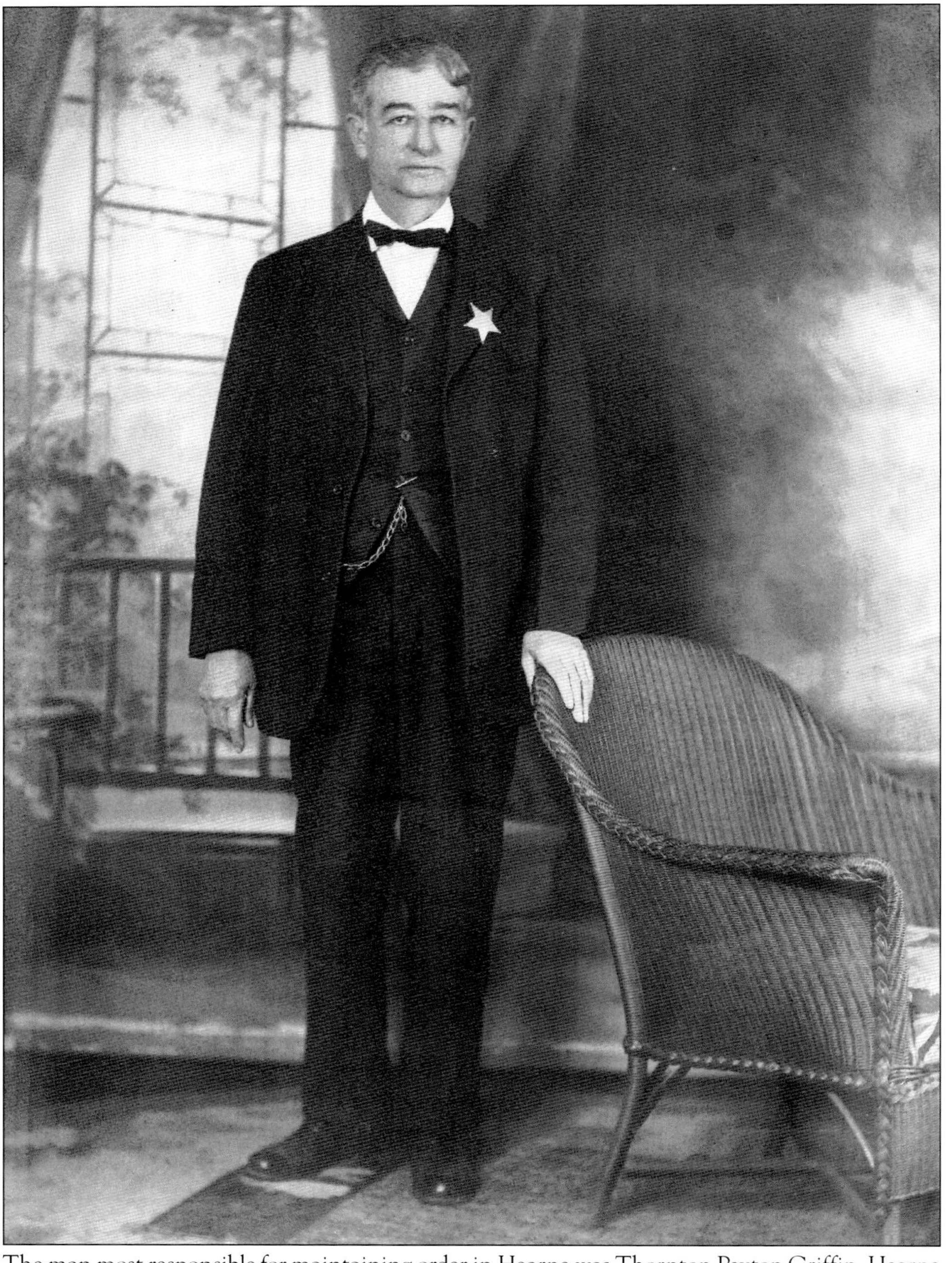

The man most responsible for maintaining order in Hearne was Thornton Peyton Griffin, Hearne city marshal for 43 years. Griffin earned such a reputation for solid police work that he received recognition as one of the best peace officers in Texas. Hearne businessmen appreciated him enough to present him with a silver-plated Colt .45—a useful gift on several occasions. (Courtesy of Carolyn Lampo.)

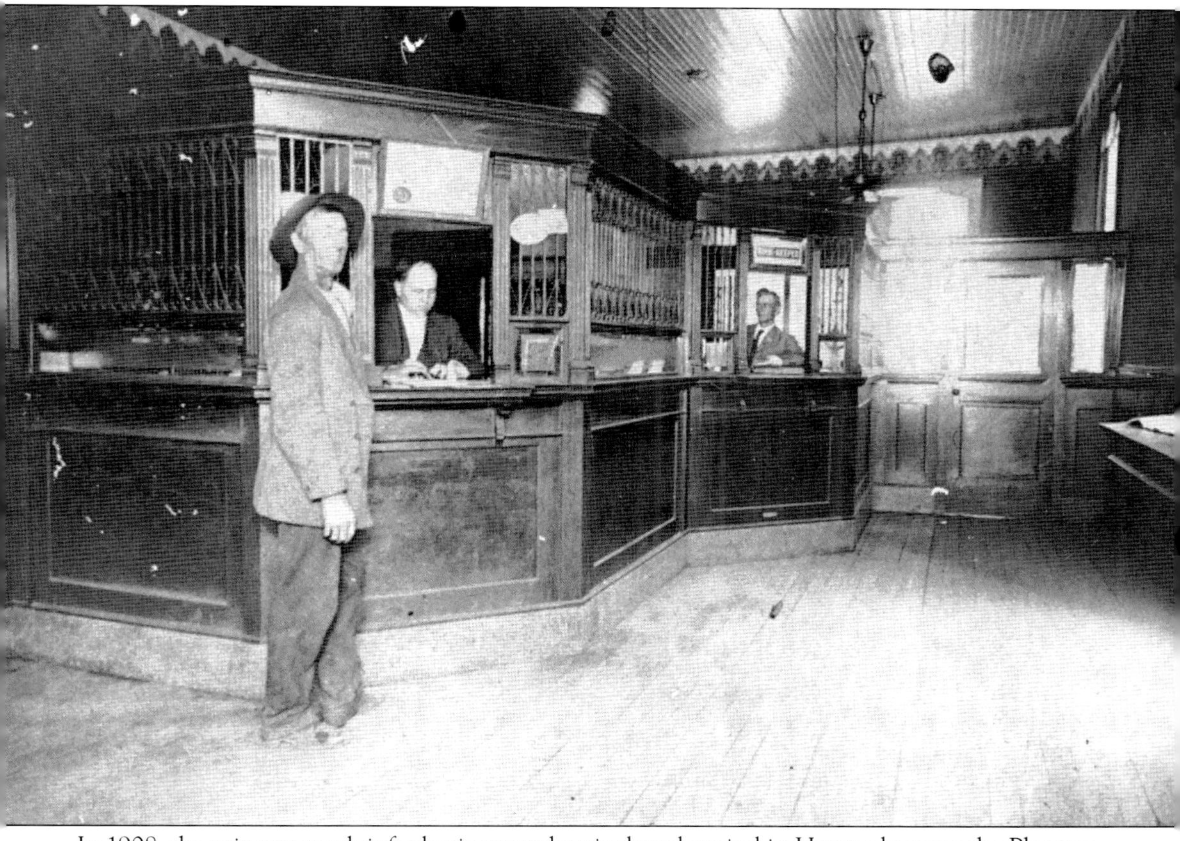

In 1908, the primary conduit for business and agricultural capital in Hearne became the Planters & Merchants Bank, the town's main money source for 100 years. The bank was organized by a group headed by Hatch Cummings (shown manning the back teller booth), who was also a local doctor and president of the Texas Medical Association that same year. As bank president from 1912 to 1927, Cummings was a champion of Hearne and of public health in Texas. (Courtesy of Hearne Chamber of Commerce.)

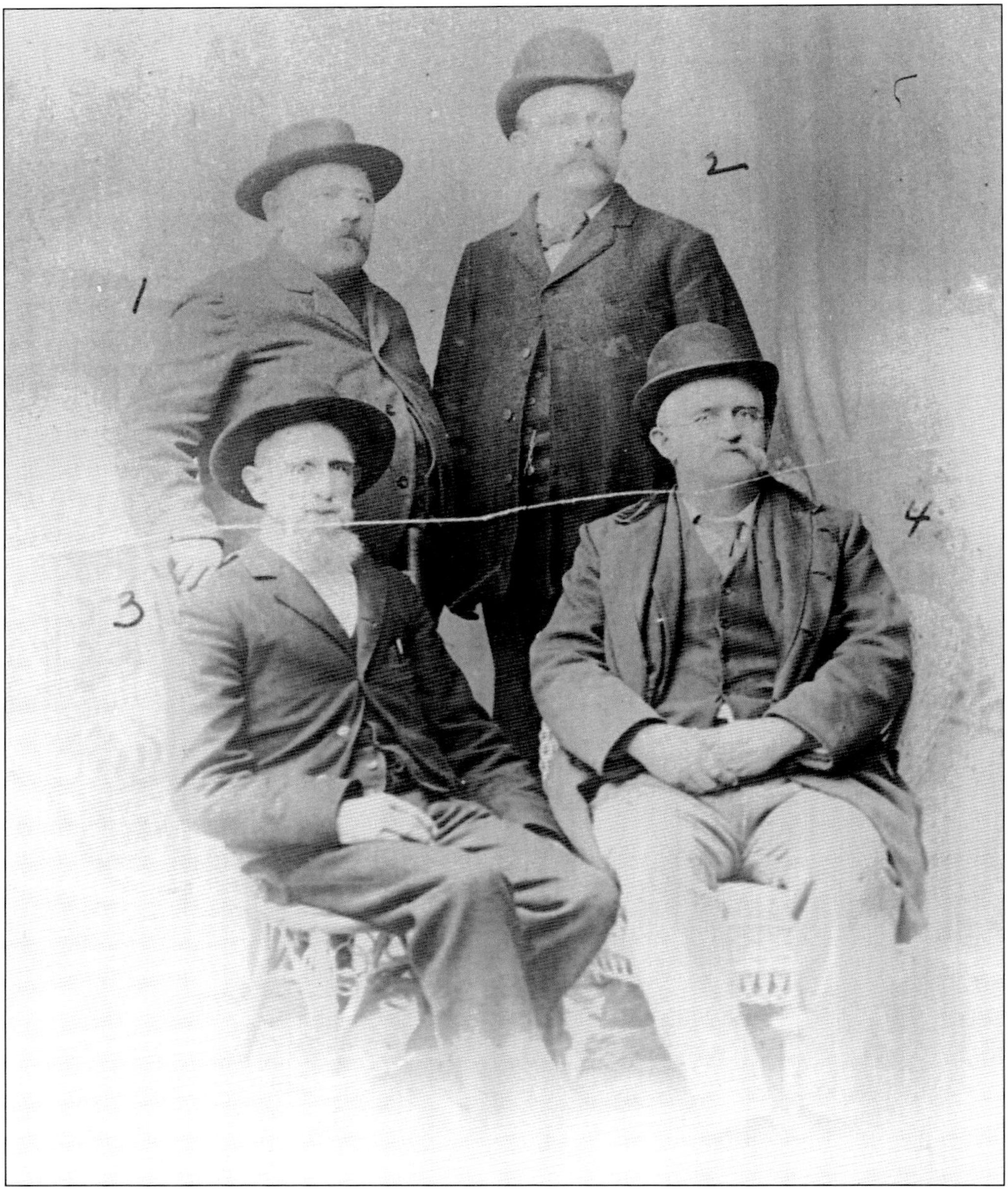

Established in 1892, the Hearne Building and Loan was one of Texas's original building and loan institutions, having received the sixth charter issued by the state. Headed by Hearne merchant and developer R.A. Allen (seated right), its board hired Irish immigrant William Crenan as its first president. With the Building and Loan, the Planters & Merchants Bank, and the First National Bank, Hearne had the capital to move forward. (Courtesy of Hearne Chamber of Commerce.)

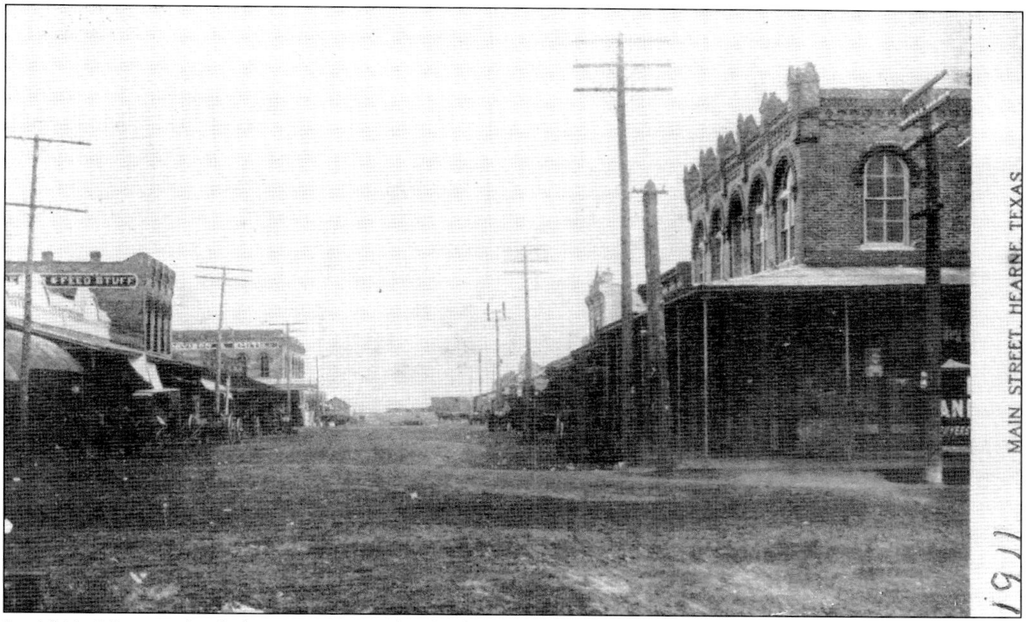

In 1911, Hearne had dirt streets and telephones, the *Hearne Democrat*—which would remain in publication for 100 years—published its first edition (at least five newspapers preceded the *Democrat*), motorized vehicles had made an appearance, and a host of stores and saloons housed in brick buildings constructed of materials from Hearne's own brick company—Robb's—graced its streets. Mayor Peter Brady would soon build a privately owned electric plant. Merchandise packed the shelves in grocery (pictured) and hardware stores, and whatever residents needed could probably be found in Hearne. (Both, courtesy of Hearne Chamber of Commerce.)

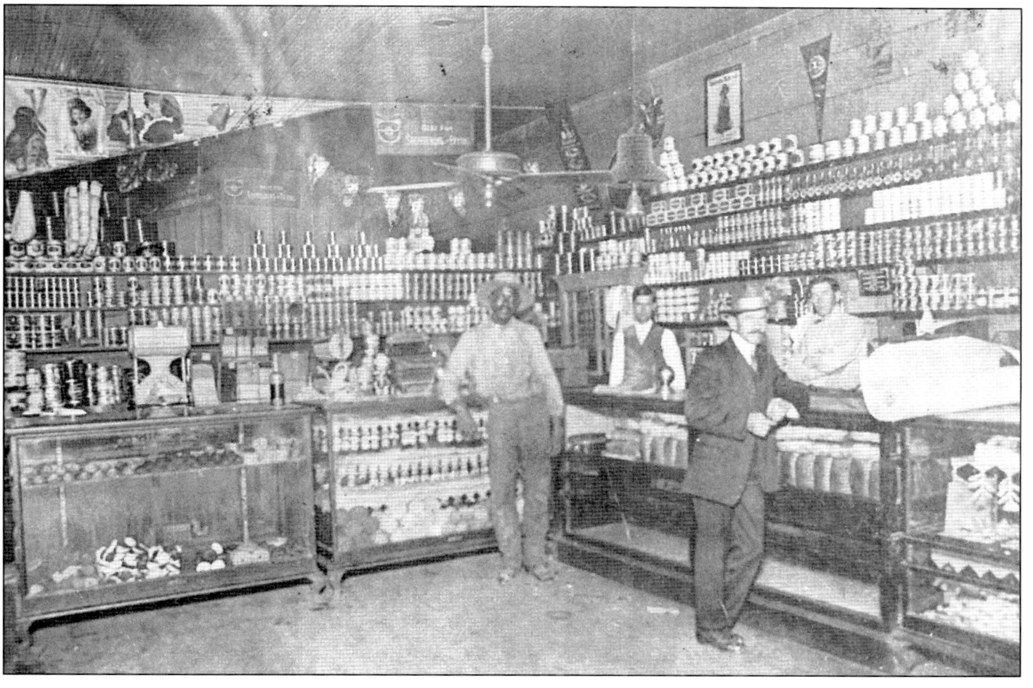

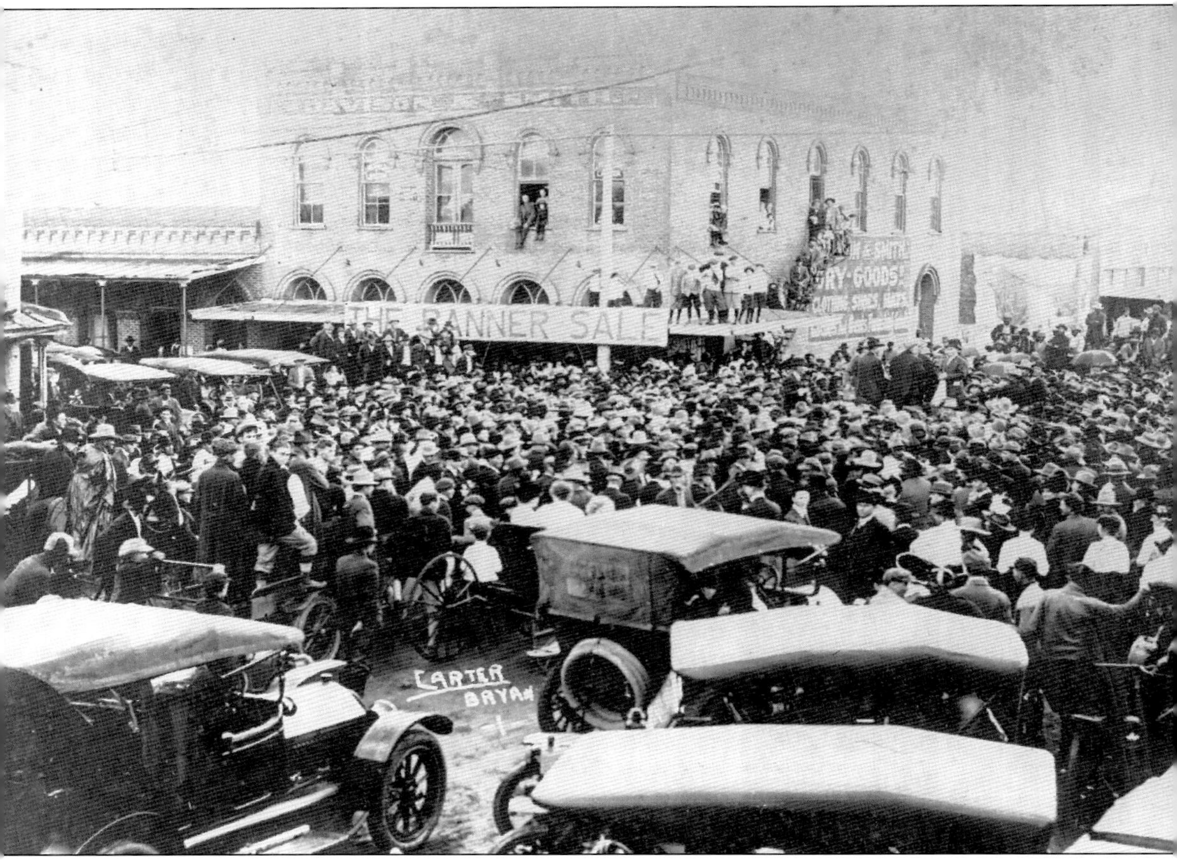

In 1916, business was good, and Hearne's annual "trade days" had begun. Downtown business owners hoped to attract shoppers county-wide with great deals and prizes. A lucky shopper would win a new car that year. Naturally, the crowds around Hoyt's Store (formerly the Davison building) were big, as residents waited to see if they would drive home in new-car style. (Courtesy of Hearne Chamber of Commerce.)

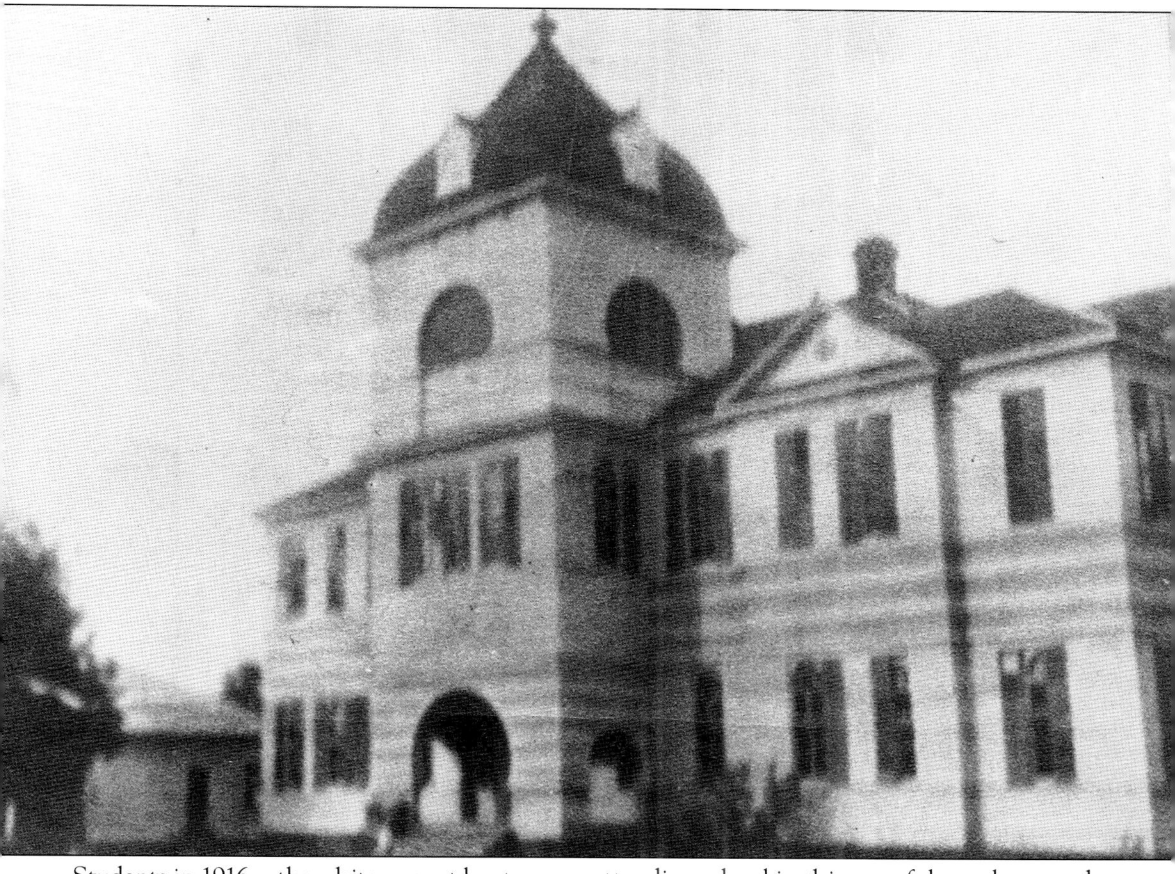

Students in 1916—the white ones at least—were attending school in this graceful cupola-topped building accommodating all grades. The wooden structure would be abandoned and a brick one built in 1920. African American students were learning catch-as-catch-can, often in schools provided by churches. (Courtesy of Hearne Chamber of Commerce.)

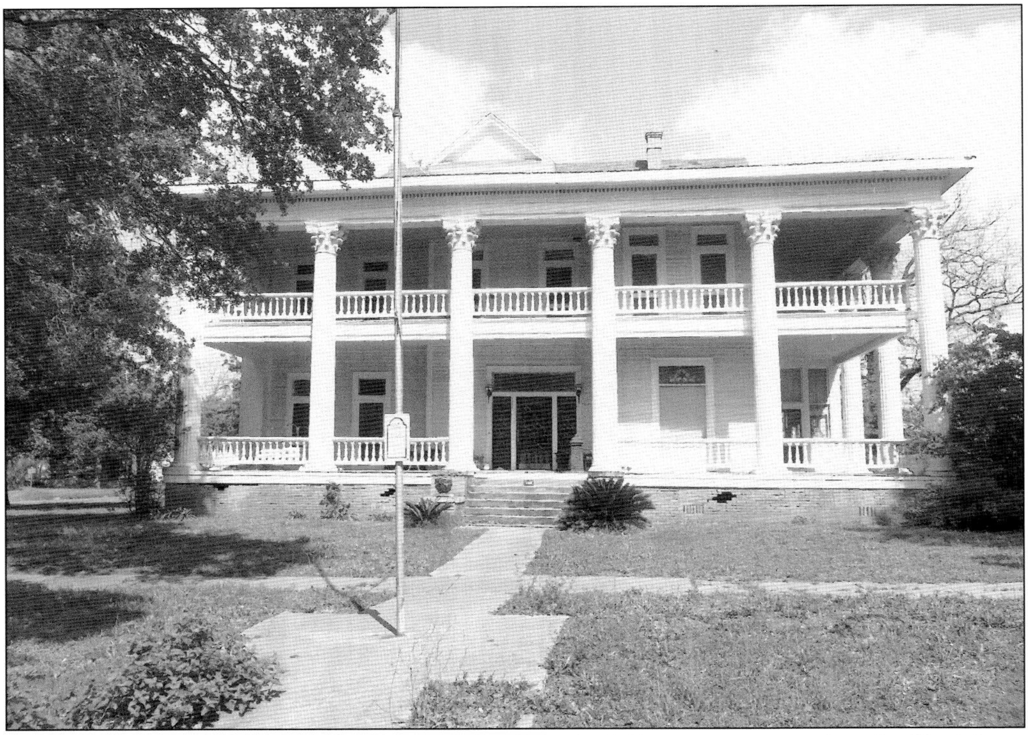

Hearne's wealth was dramatized by its houses. By the early 1900s, prominent residents had built large homes for themselves with houses and outbuildings often covering a block or half a block, like the estate known as the Columns (above), originally built by G.F. Britton in the 1890s and later owned by the Easterbrook family. The Kenneth and Janna Byrd home on Magnolia Street (below) was built by Jeannie Westbrook after the death of her husband, Titus. (Both, courtesy of author.)

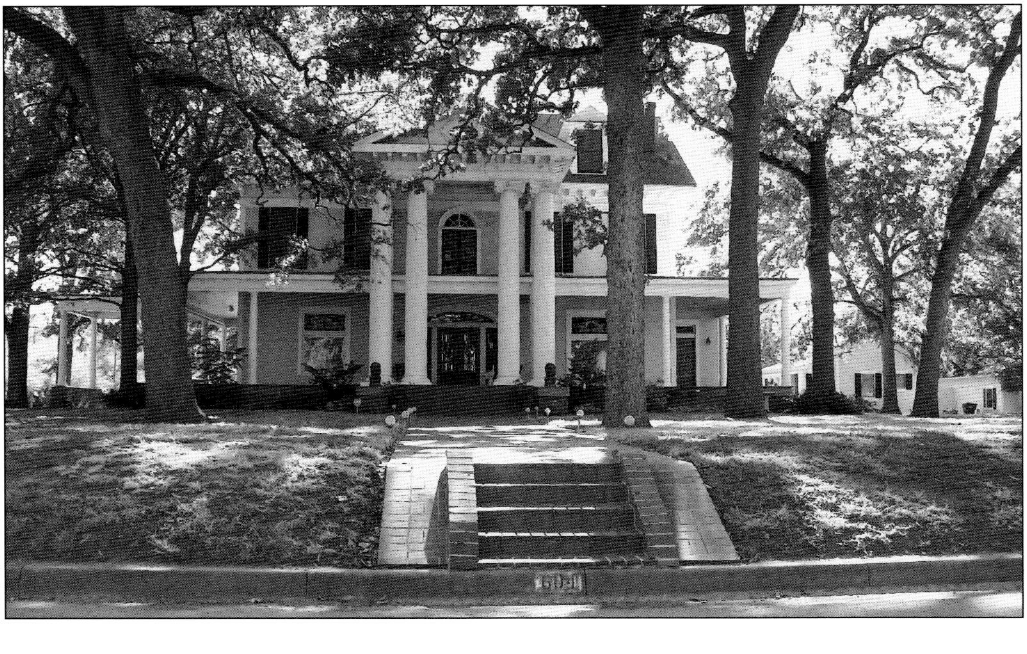

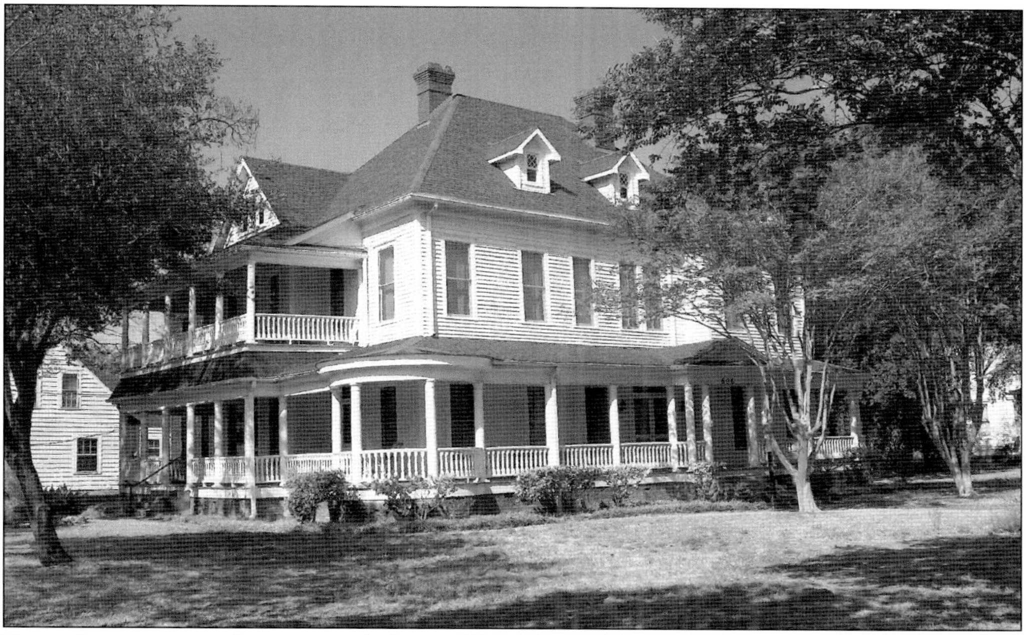

Two other expansive beauties include the Wood home (above), built around 1900, which later became the McCarver home (with 10 children, Centennia McCarver needed the space), and Hearnewood (below), the Allen-Holloway home, built by hardware dealer Robert C. Allen and now owned by Jack and Norma Holloway. (Both, courtesy of author.)

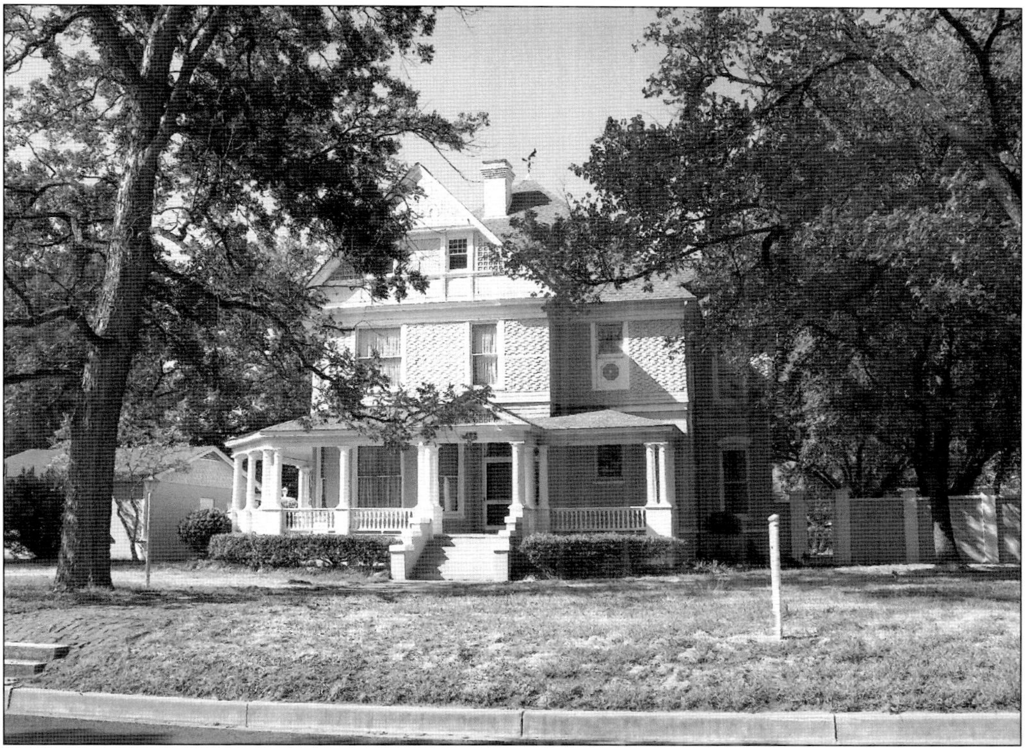

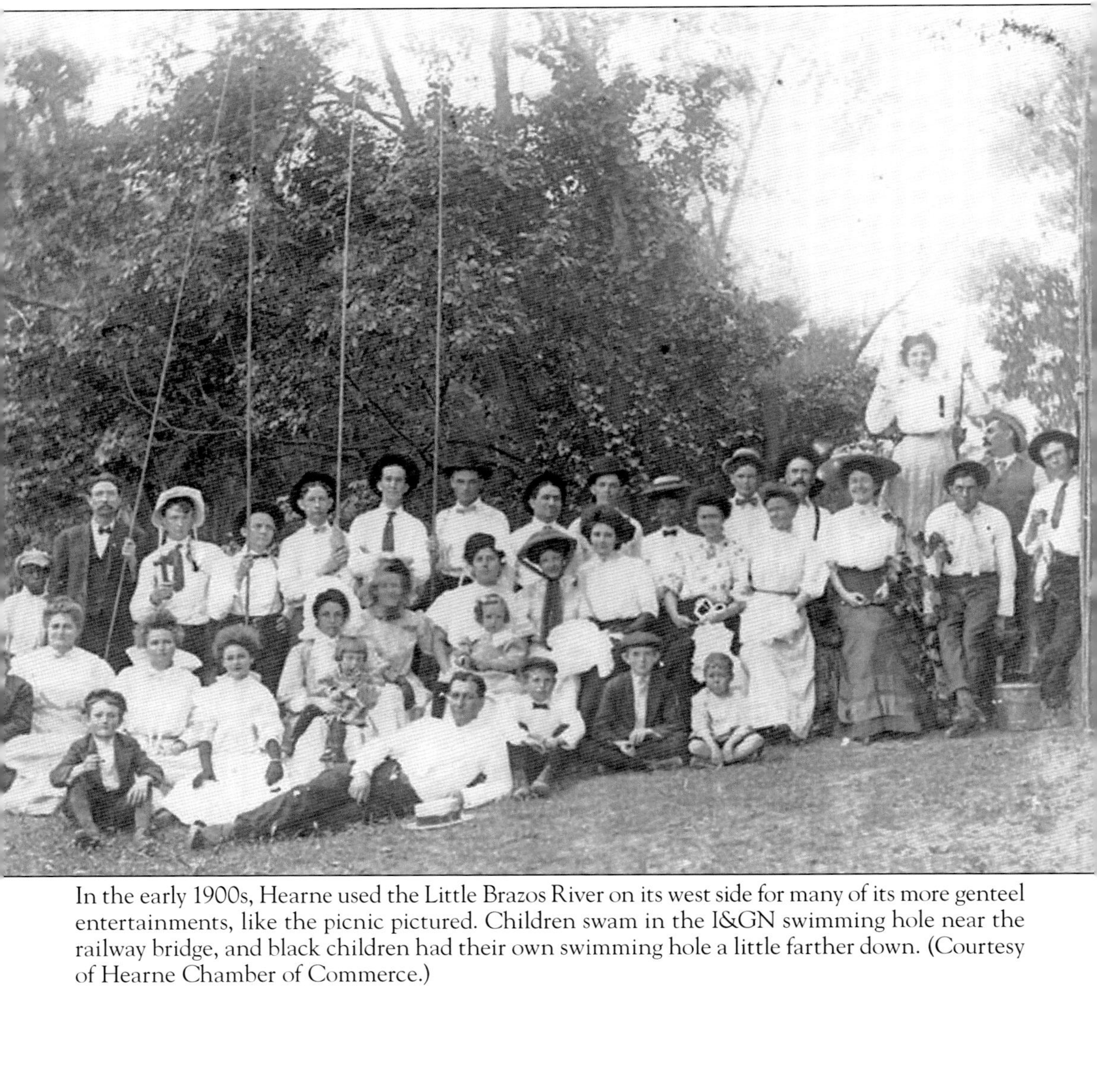

In the early 1900s, Hearne used the Little Brazos River on its west side for many of its more genteel entertainments, like the picnic pictured. Children swam in the I&GN swimming hole near the railway bridge, and black children had their own swimming hole a little farther down. (Courtesy of Hearne Chamber of Commerce.)

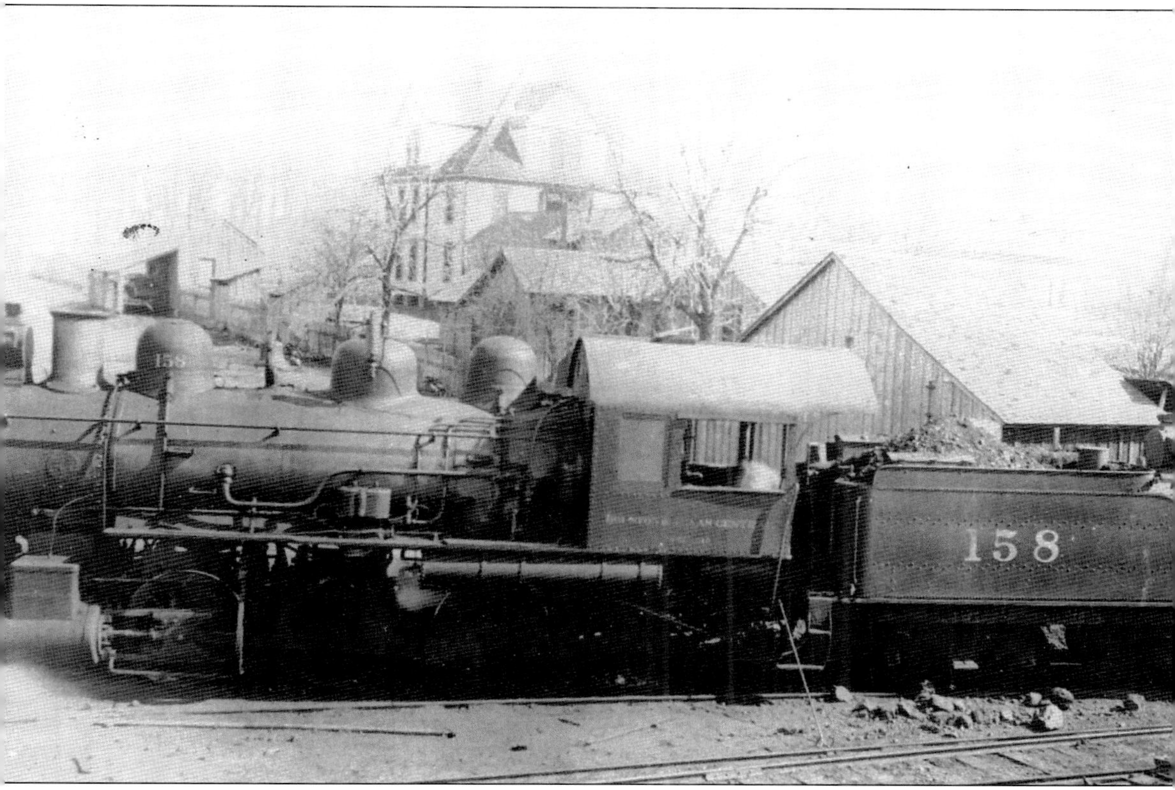

In 1916, Hearne was vibrating with heavy train traffic and with optimism born of good times and wide-open economic opportunity. (Courtesy of Hearne Chamber of Commerce.)

Farewell to the open saloon.
Why have we tolerated you so long?
You have built in our midst an awful den
And blighted the prospect of many men.
Mothers and wives in deepest despair
Have the burdens of shame to bear.
Farewell to the open saloons,
Den of the vice that thrives in the slum.
The pride of the thief, gambler and bum.
We consign you to the places that you so well,
Mumford, Hearne and h . . . .

But three years later, with plantations still heavily mortgaged as a result of the 1913 flood, Hearne's downtown businesses suffered another setback—Prohibition. Alcoholic beverages had already been banned from the eastern side of the county, and the east-side teetotalers were disparaging the habits of unruly west-siders as indicated by this poem, which appeared in local newspapers. With saloons closed and plantations struggling to pay their bank notes, Hearne was poised for a big blow. (Courtesy of McCarver and McCarver.)

Four

Boom and Bust Between the Wars

Hearne was minimally affected by World War I and the 1918–1919 influenza pandemic, though the city did suffer loss, such as the death of Pvt. Miles Scrivener. Scrivener died not under fire but stateside, one of a relatively small number of Hearne's influenza victims. Most of Hearne's veterans returned from the Great War relatively unscathed. Hearne had dodged the Yellow Fever epidemic earlier and had sent financial aid to neighboring Calvert, devastated by the disease.

The real disaster came in the form of Hearne's third great flood. In 1921, the Bottoms suffered the most economically devastating deluge to date. With the cotton almost ready to be picked, water raged over the plantations. Planters, mortgaged to the hilt, packed it in. The days of the big plantation were over. Within the next few years, Italian farmers bought out the Robertson County Bottoms, bringing Hispanic field workers with them. People with names like DeStefano and Cotropia replanted the cotton, introduced better farming practices, and bought homes in town. People with names like Gomez, Montelongo, and Aguirre were poised to make their own impact on Hearne.

Also in the 1920s, a young Texas A&M student working for the USDA found a tiny pink worm in a Brazos Bottom cotton boll. It was a pink bollworm, and the entire crop had to be eradicated.

Despite economic losses from 1920 to 1940, Hearne saw growth in its educational, religious, and social institutions. Schools were built, and social and civic clubs like the Hearne Shakespeare Club, Hearne Music Club, Rotary, PTA, and Hearne Chamber of Commerce, flowered or were established. The "rough" town was taking on some polish.

When the Great Depression (1929–1940) hit Hearne, several factors made it bearable. First, Hearne was essentially a farming community; people knew how to raise and hunt for food. Hearne native Frank Adams's father said to him, "It's time to go huntin'." Second, Hearne was tight-knit; people helped each other. Third, said Adams, local businessmen carried people on credit or gave food away until their economic situation improved. Fourth, Hearne had a city manager who knew how to take advantage of federal programs to improve the city. Adams said, "I've never had a hungry day in my life."

Still, racial divisions were sharp and sometimes violent—at least one lynching of a black man strung up by a prominent white man occurred while random acts of racial violence were common. Determined to stop the lawlessness, Marshal Griffin appointed Wesley Adams, a black man respected in both communities, to be his constable. The situation slowly improved. Despite problems, hard times promoted cohesion and determination within disparate groups.

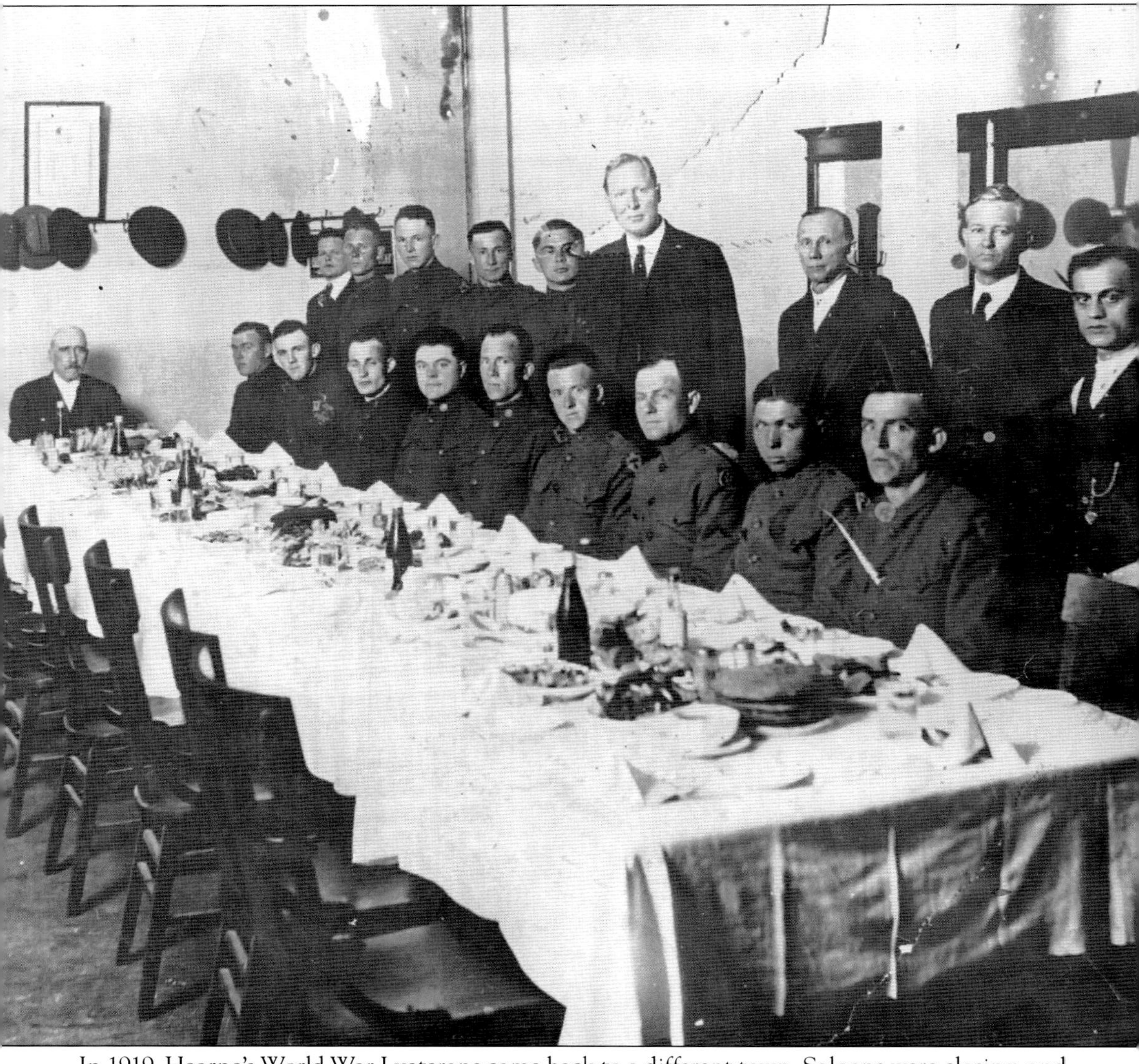

In 1919, Hearne's World War I veterans came back to a different town. Saloons were closing, and the town was redefining itself—something it would have to do again and again. But veterans were happy to be alive and enjoying a good dinner. They are shown with Hearne city officials at the City Café as the invited guests of proud business owner George Palmos. Hearne's mayor and councilmen welcomed back these young men that one day would lead Hearne. (Courtesy of Carolyn Lampo.)

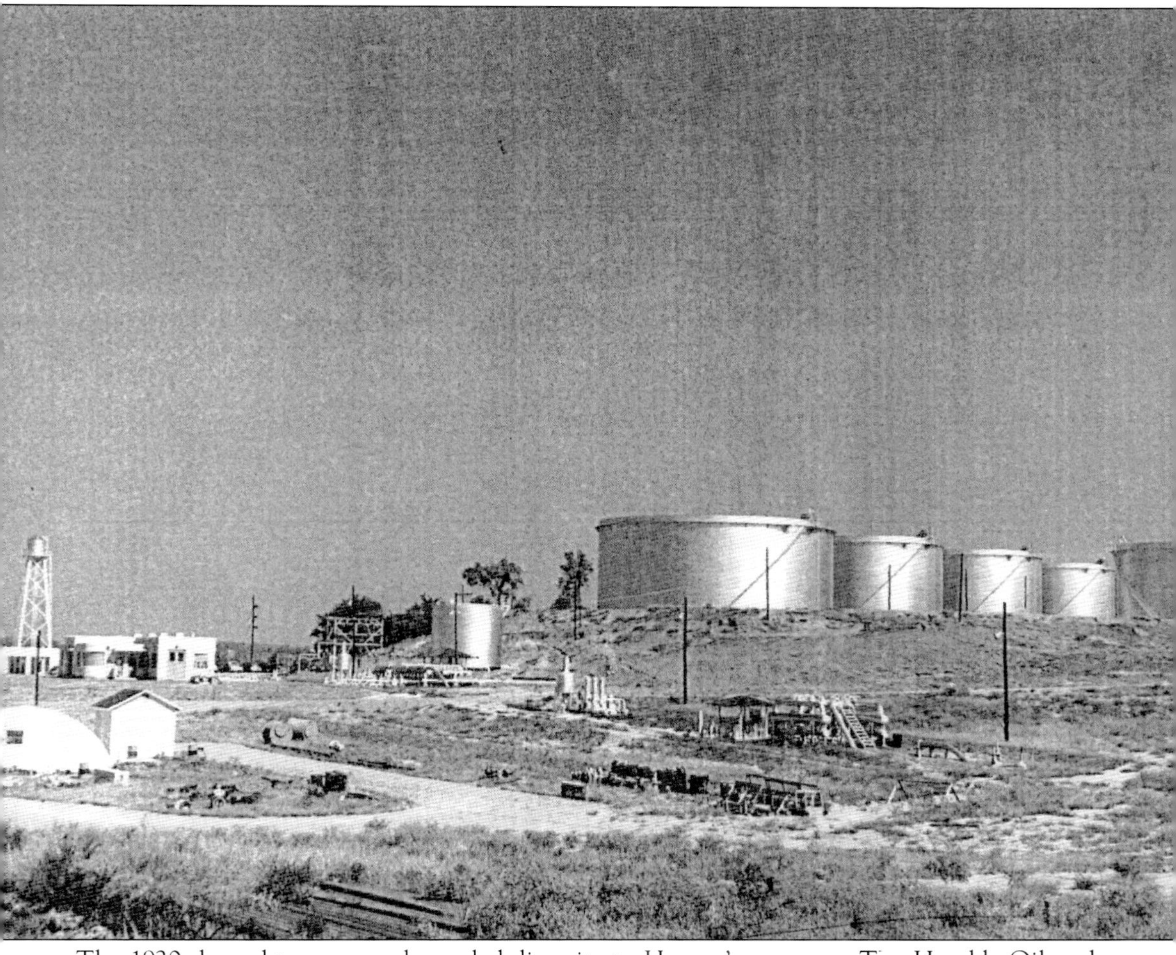

The 1920s brought some much-needed diversity to Hearne's economy. The Humble Oil and Petroleum pump station south of town offered jobs, as did new cattle ranches on either side of Hearne. Cattle pens were constructed near rail yards, and Hearne's was no longer a one-crop economy. (Courtesy of Dorothy Starkey.)

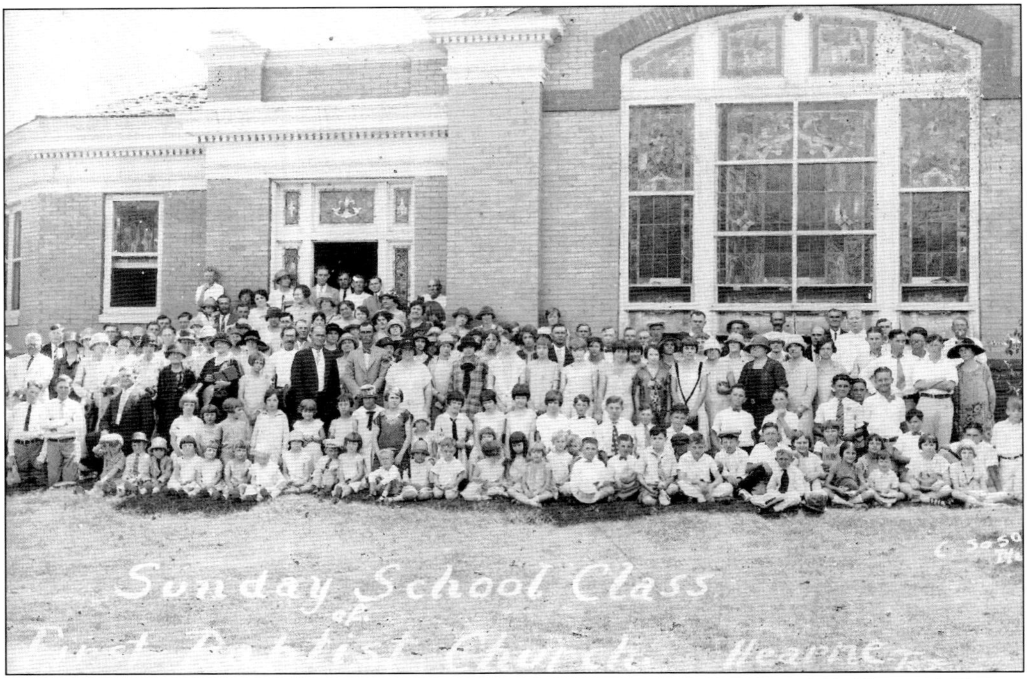

From 1907 to 1960, Hearne's First Baptist Church was worshiping in an octagon-shaped sanctuary with striking stained-glass windows. Sadly, only one of those windows was later transferred to its current facility. The church was experiencing steady growth—mirroring the growth of the city—under a deacon board that often looked somewhat like the city's governing board. (Courtesy of First Baptist Church of Hearne.)

Program

FEBRUARY FOURTH

Hamlet

"The play 's the thing"

Hostesses: Mrs. Easterwood-Mrs. Boguskie

Roll Call: Characteristic Passages.

Give Hamlet's soliloquy.

Comments.

Hamlet—A Study in Psychology.

Study: Act III.

Leader, Mrs. Boguskie.

Established in 1911, the Hearne Shakespeare Club was the town's literary society and enjoyed growth and prestige in the 1930s. The club offered literary study and polite conversation for those with a prominent place in Hearne society. Ladies with a hankering for culture attended its meetings. For men, the Hearne Music Club provided the city's gentlemen opportunities to play and enjoy music. (Courtesy of Cushing Library, TAMU.)

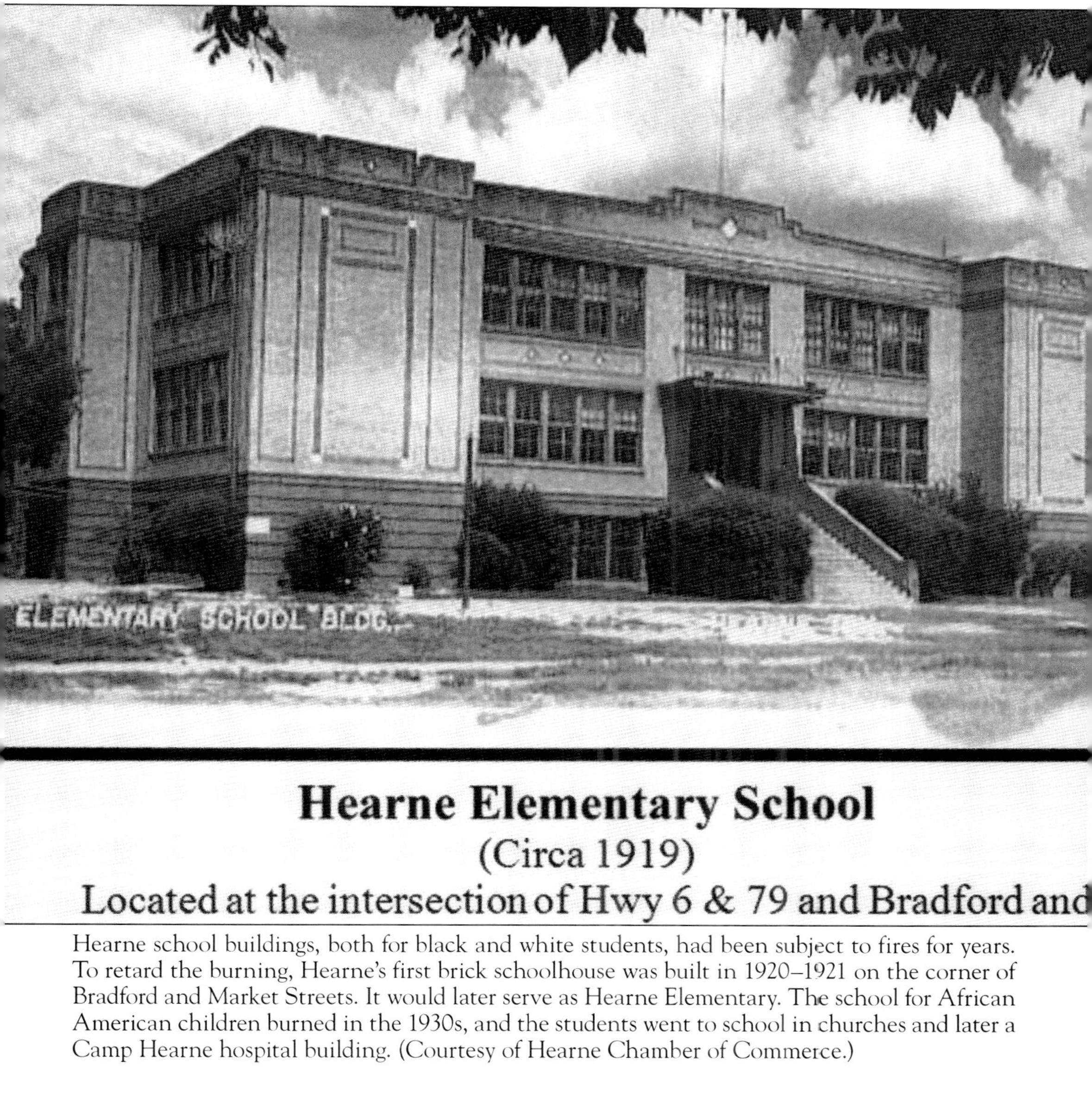

Hearne school buildings, both for black and white students, had been subject to fires for years. To retard the burning, Hearne's first brick schoolhouse was built in 1920–1921 on the corner of Bradford and Market Streets. It would later serve as Hearne Elementary. The school for African American children burned in the 1930s, and the students went to school in churches and later a Camp Hearne hospital building. (Courtesy of Hearne Chamber of Commerce.)

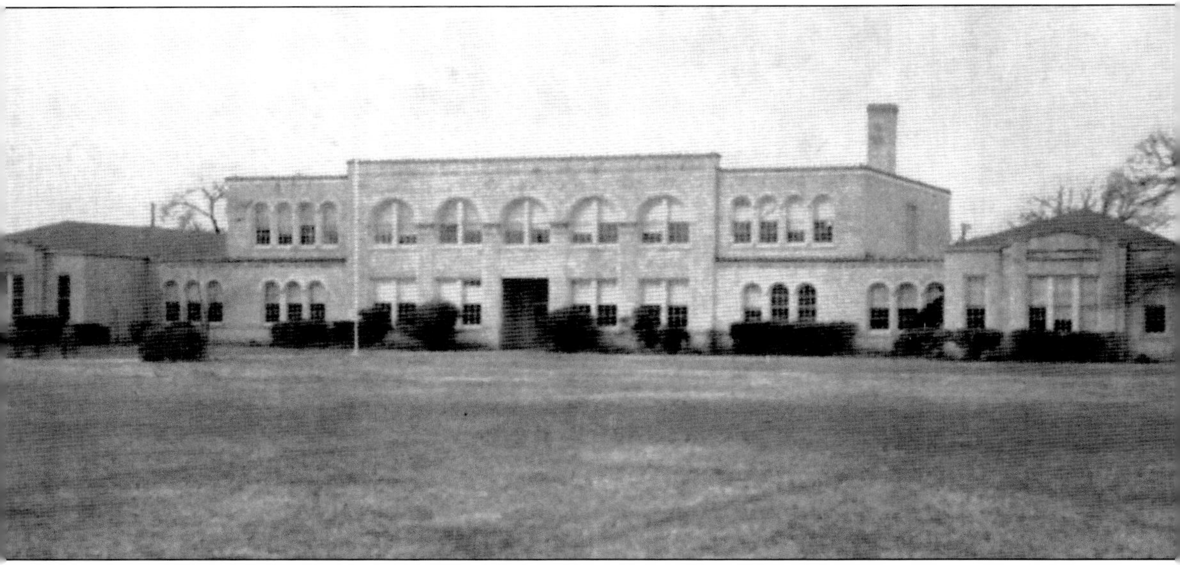

In 1929, just before the stock market crash ushered in the Great Depression, Hearne Independent School District (ISD) began construction of Hearne High School, an amazing brick building enhanced with Spanish tile roof and porcelain tile facade inlays. Though the old Hearne Elementary has passed into history, the 1930 Hearne High School on Wheelock Street is now home to the Robertson County Boys & Girls Club. (Courtesy of Hearne Chamber of Commerce.)

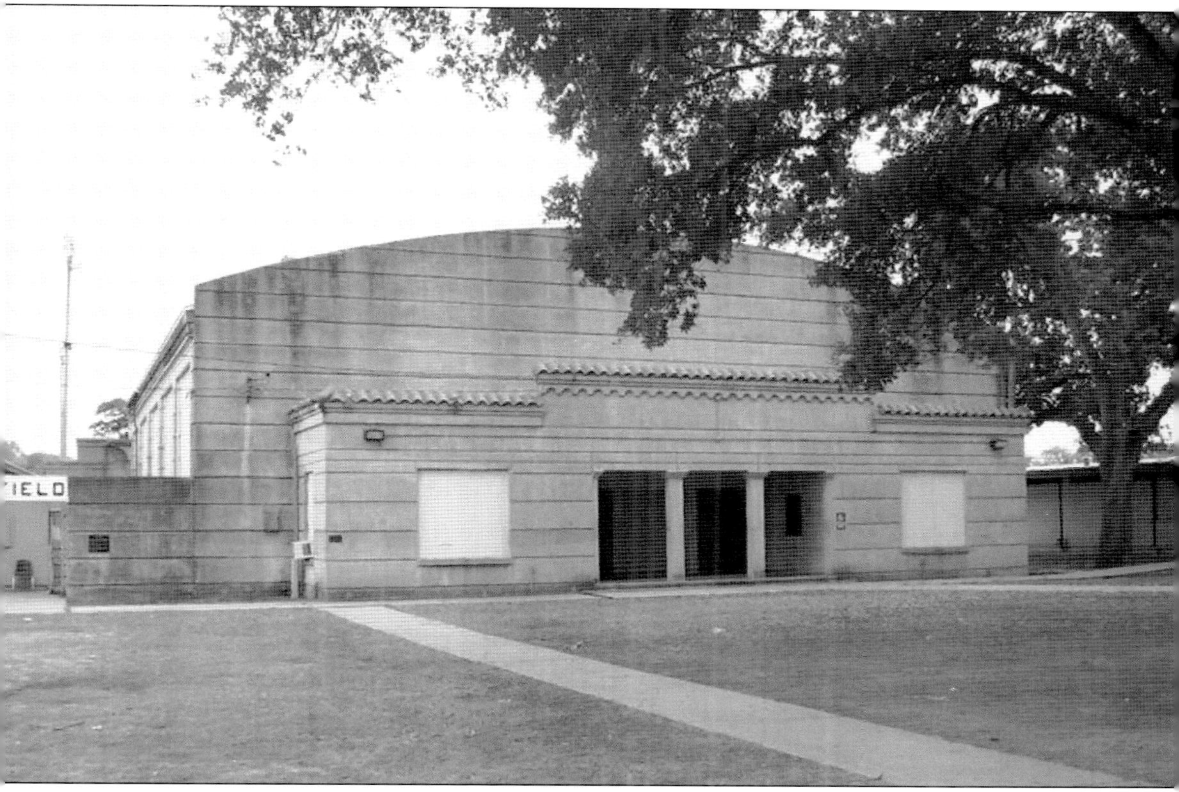

By 1940, the Hearne ISD had added an attractive, state-of-the-art gym to its high school campus, also with the aid of Pres. Franklin D. Roosevelt's Depression-era WPA program. Both the school district and the Boys and Girls Club still use the gym today. (Courtesy of author.)

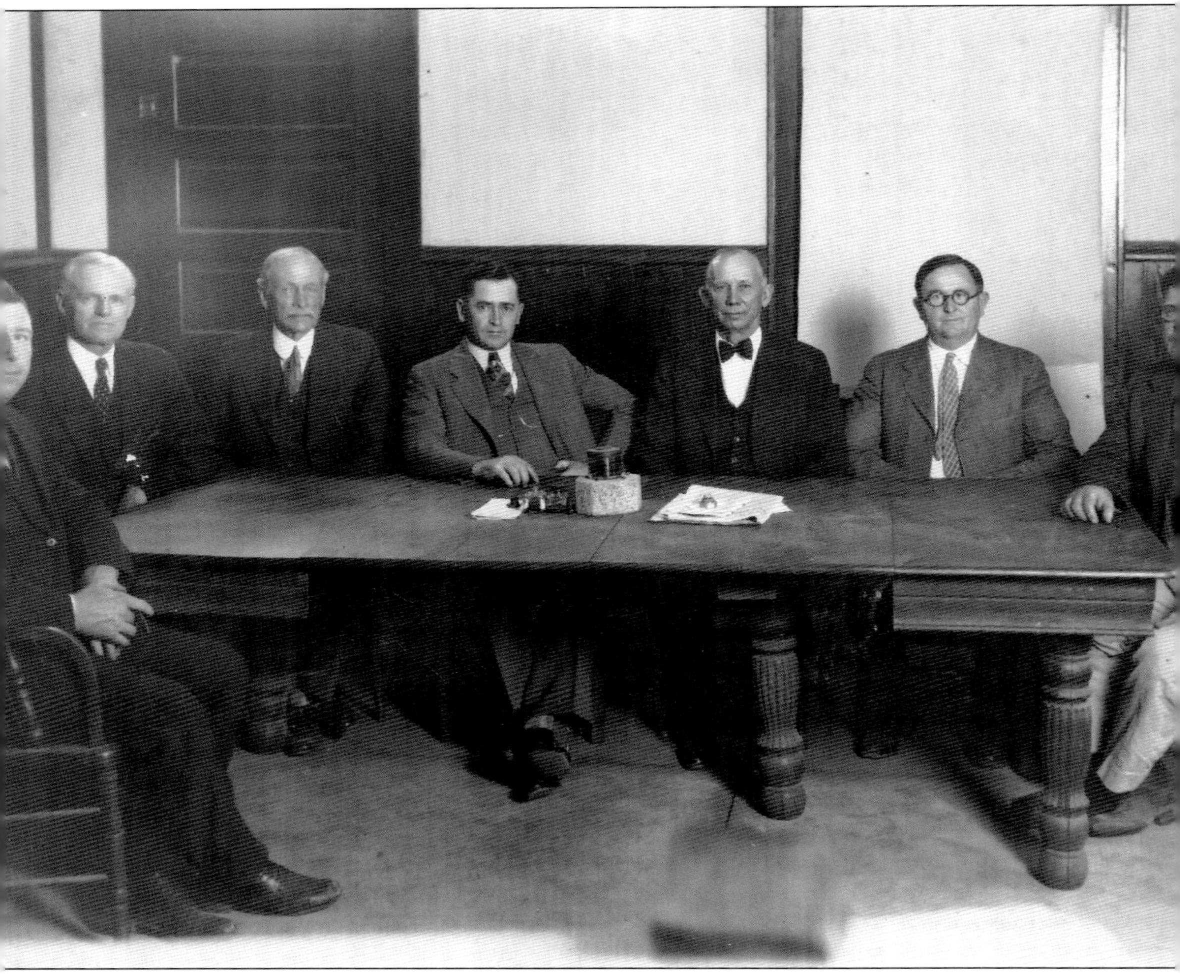

Much credit for Hearne's progress in the 1920s and 1930s goes to city secretary and manager W.A. Wilkerson (second from left), backed by Mayor W.H. Ely (seated center). In two decades, streets were paved, a volunteer fire department was established (1922), the city-owned power plant was modernized, and natural gas and water systems were established. The tax department, alleys, and city hall were all Wilkerson "babies." During the Depression, Wilkerson used federal programs to help finish the job. (Courtesy of City of Hearne.)

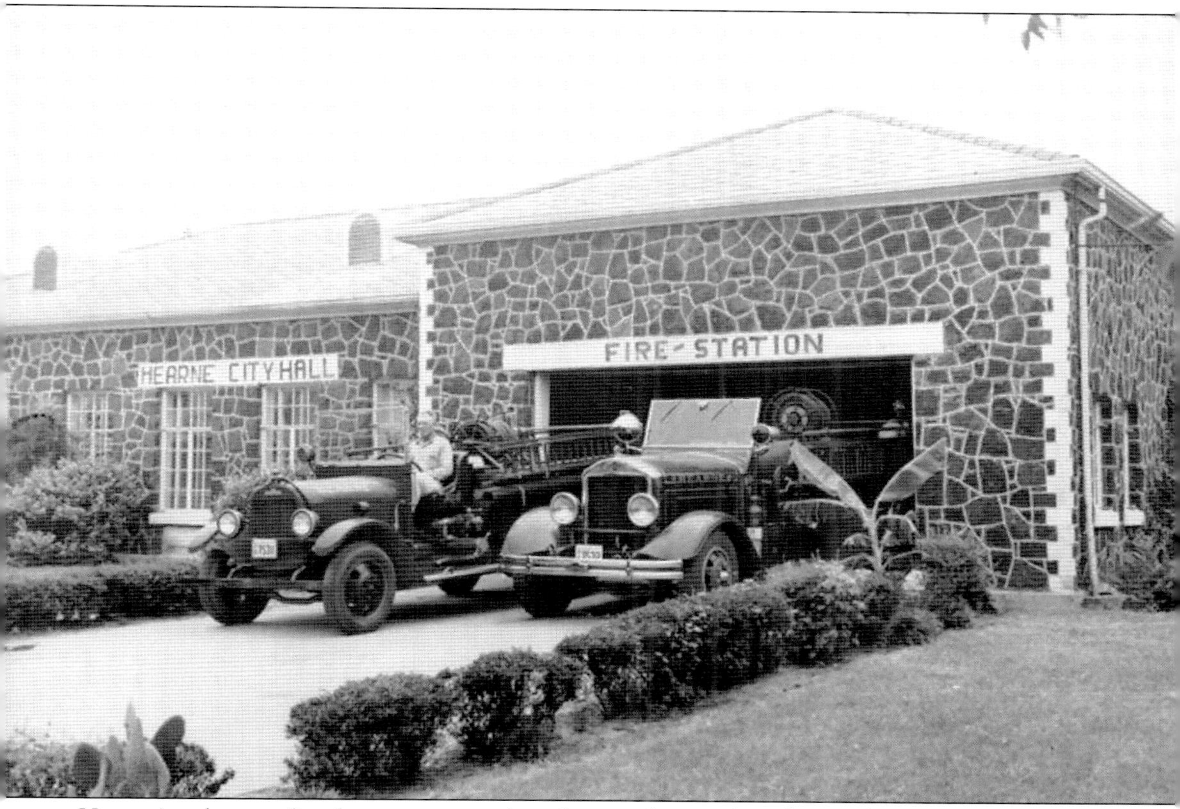

Hearne's volunteer fire department purchased a new fire truck and moved into new facilities in 1941, despite bad economic times. Again, Wilkerson's foresight and ingenuity seemed to have a lot to do with Hearne's continuing progress when money was tight. (Courtesy of City of Hearne.)

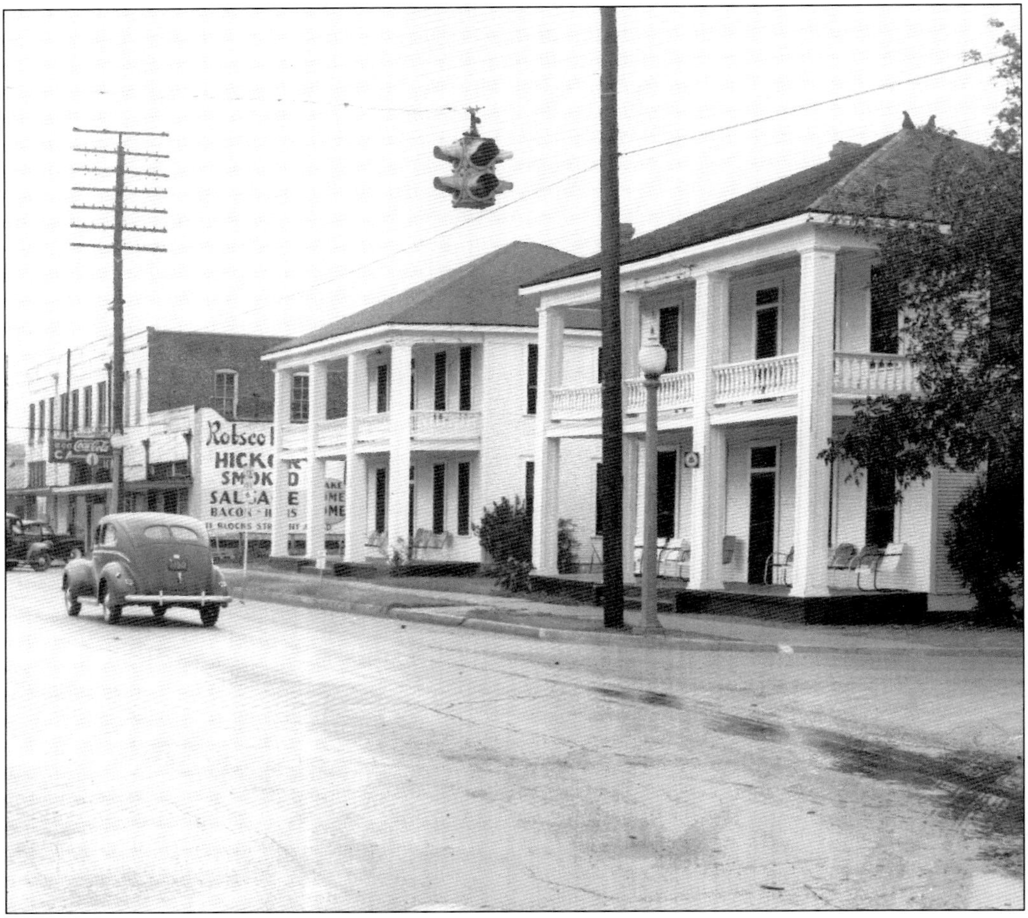

Even in hard times, Hearne has had the hospitality business to fall back on. For the 170 years of its existence, travelers have had no trouble finding accommodations in Hearne. The matching structures of the Oxford Hotel stood throughout the 1920s and 1930s, along with several others, until modern hotels took their places. (Courtesy of Hearne Chamber of Commerce.)

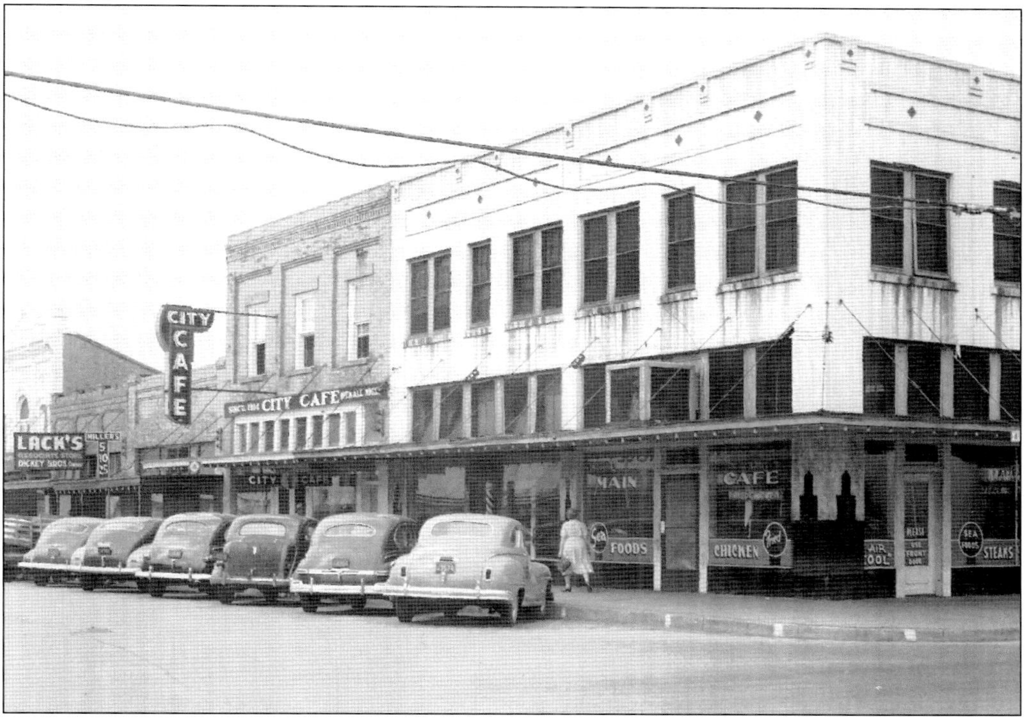

Finding a place to eat in Hearne has never been a challenge—not even during the Depression. When young Bill Palmos came to Hearne in 1915, he was surprised to find three 24-hour restaurants—something one would associate with a larger city. After his father bought the City Café, he had to compete with the Vannoy and Hall's for downtown business. The City Café continued to prosper in the 1920s and 1930s to become a Hearne institution. Rumor even has it that Bonnie Parker and Clyde Barrow ate at the City Café on their final trip through Texas before being gunned down in Louisiana. (Both, courtesy of Hearne Chamber of Commerce.)

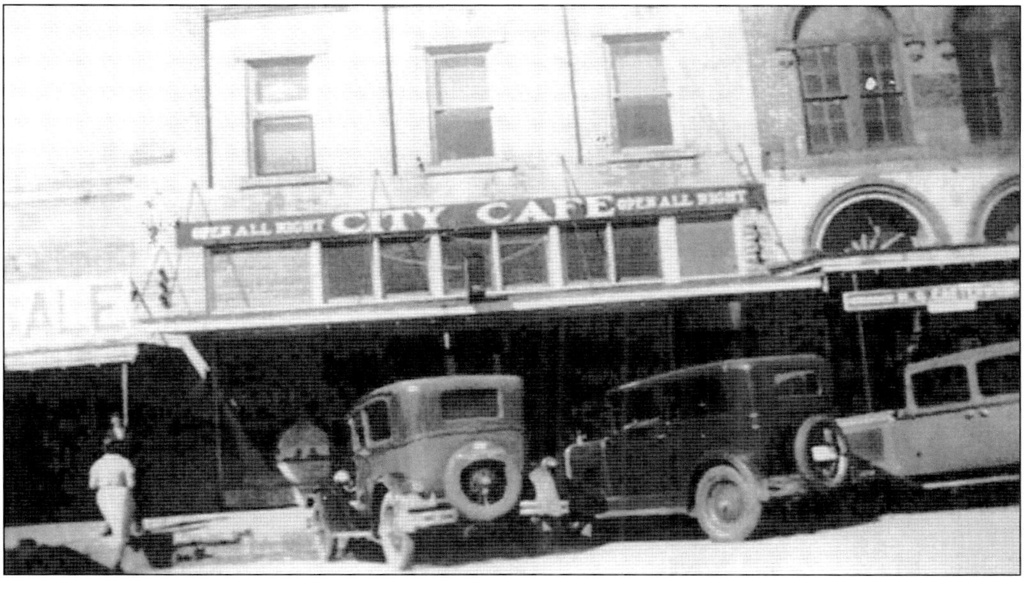

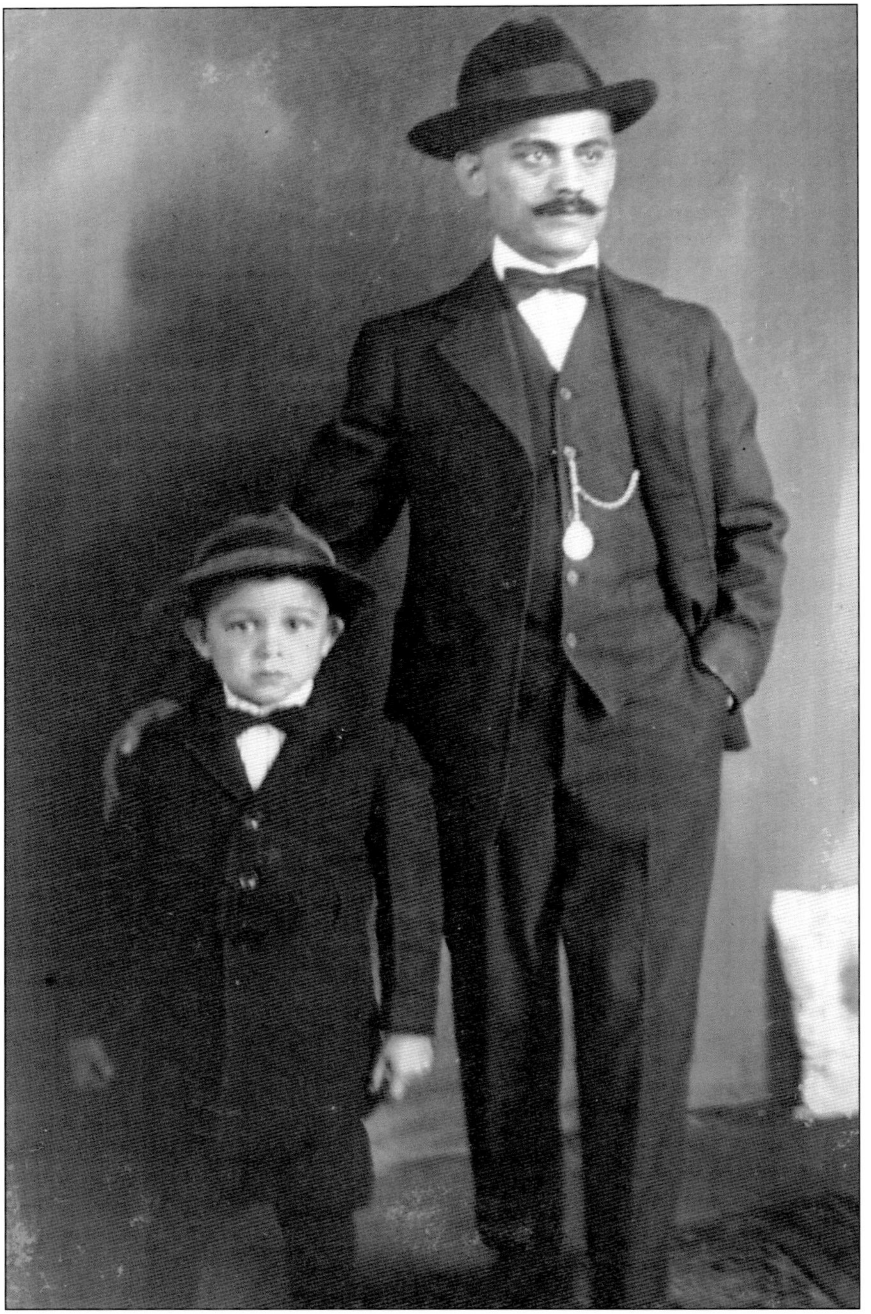

In truth, Hearne has always been a welcoming town. The Palmos family, the Chatmus family, the Brazos River Bottoms Italians, and many others have found Hearne to be a place that will "take you in" for a visit or for a lifetime. Others who remembered how hard things had been in the old country and how good they became in Hearne were Simon Cohen, Sam Lipsitz, and Isaac Levine, central European Jews, and Alex Silverman, who used to recall bad times in Russia. Pictured is young Bill Palmos with his father, George, owner of the City Café. (Courtesy of Carolyn Lampo.)

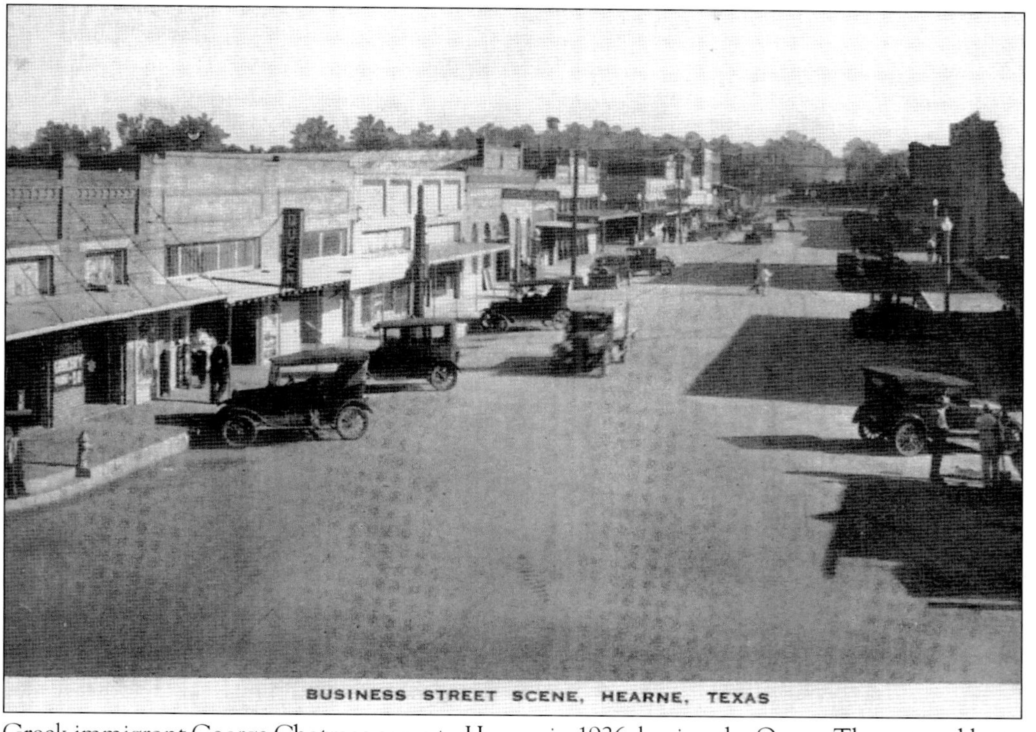

Greek immigrant George Chatmas came to Hearne in 1926, buying the Queen Theatre and later, in 1936, building his own, the Chatmas—a Hearne entertainment institution for the next four decades. In addition to the Queen, Hearne had enjoyed other silent movie theaters, but it was George Chatmas who brought the first "talkie" to Hearne. He would become one of the oldest, most respected movie retailers in Texas. (Both, courtesy of Hearne Chamber of Commerce.)

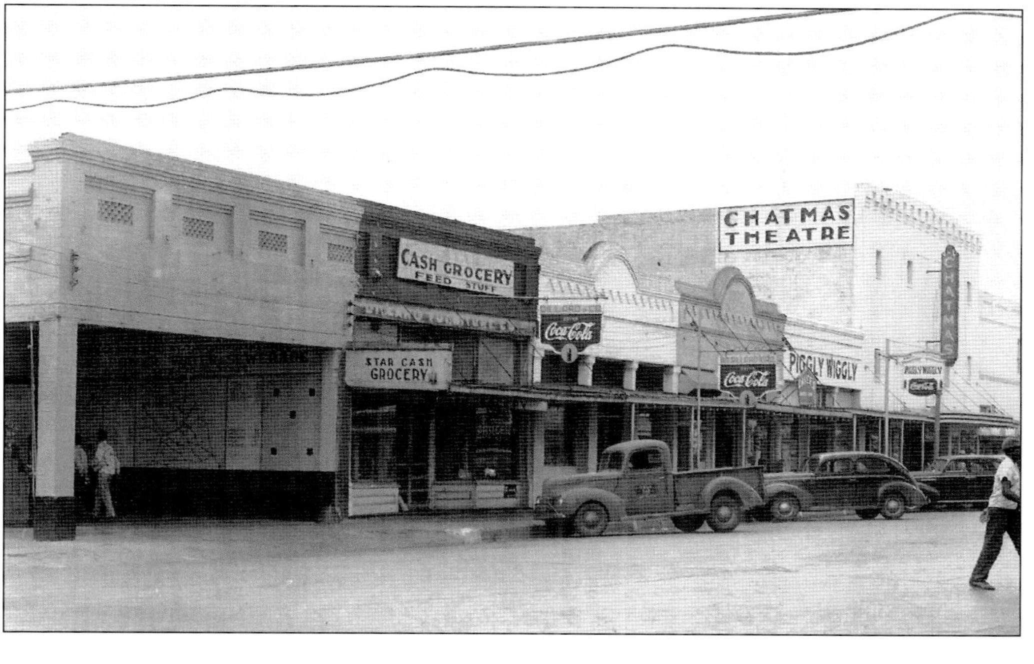

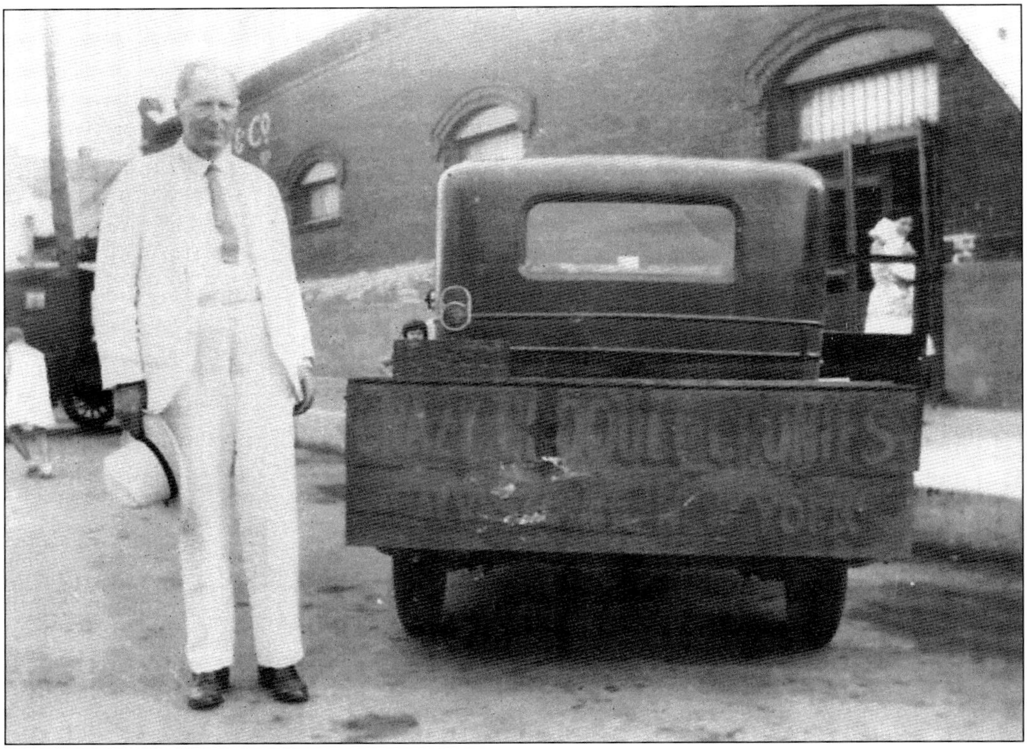

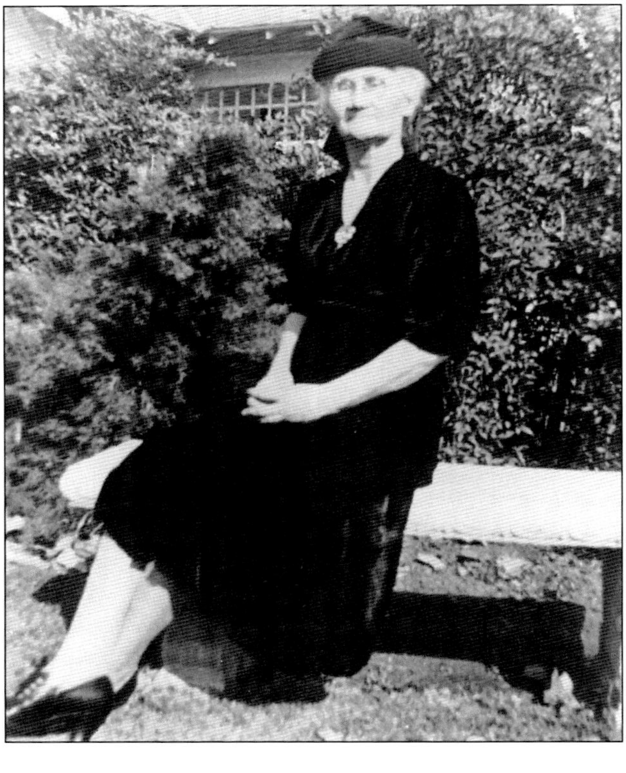

Hearne weathered the Depression with an exceptionally strong newspaper, the *Hearne Democrat*, an exceptionally large editor, Judge Felton Lane (the "Tall Sycamore of the Brazos"), and a skilled society columnist and editor, Annie Laurie Bishop. Bishop wrote for the paper until the 1950s, parlaying a local career into a statewide feature-writer career. (Above, courtesy of Carolyn Lampo; left, courtesy of Hearne Chamber of Commerce.)

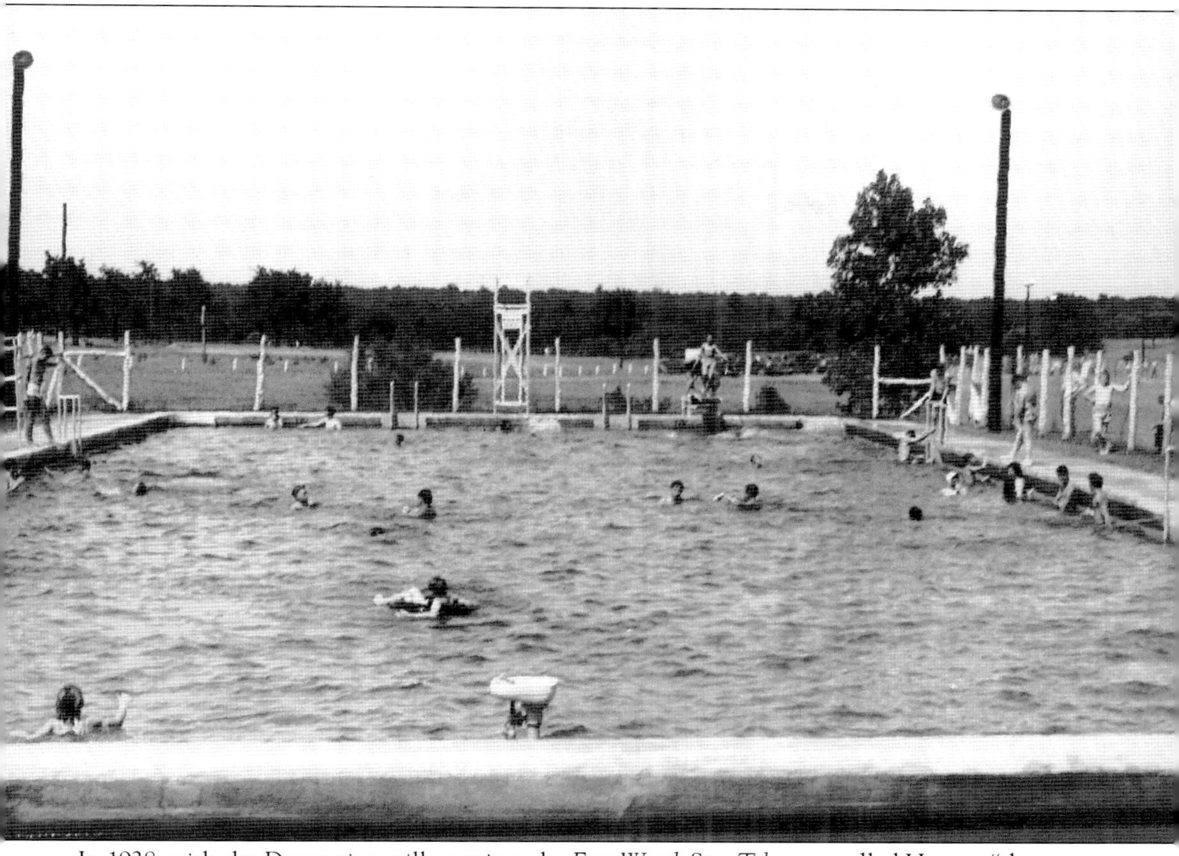

In 1938, with the Depression still ongoing, the *Fort Worth Star Telegram* called Hearne "the town with bright lights and sparkling artesian water," a phrase generated by Wilkerson. That year, the city purchased 81 acres to build a large park, appealing to the Works Progress Administration to help with construction of a pool and clubhouse. (Courtesy of Hearne Chamber of Commerce.)

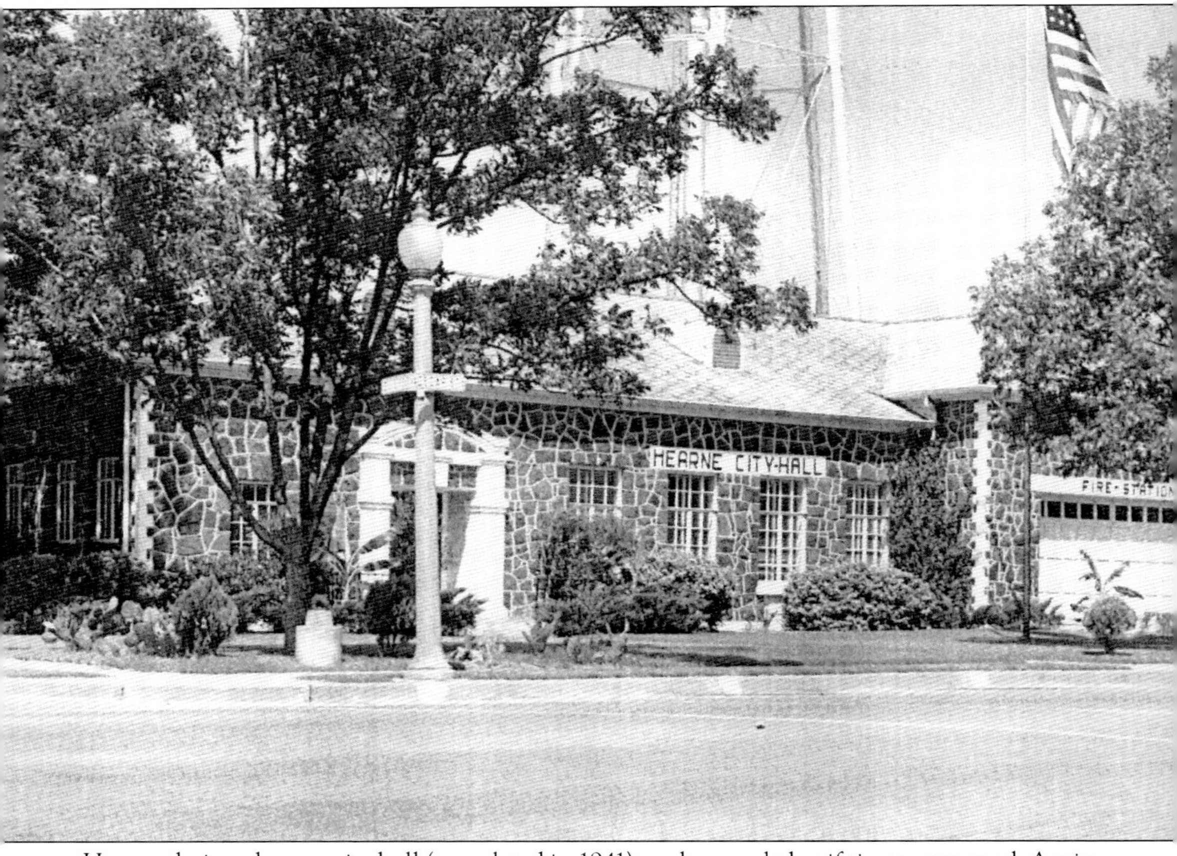

Hearne designed a new city hall (completed in 1941), and expanded as if times were good. Again, the city utilized federal programs to help, and what is now City Hall A emerged with a typical federal WPA look: a natural rock facade. The Hearne Fire Department occupied the other half of the building. (Courtesy of City of Hearne.)

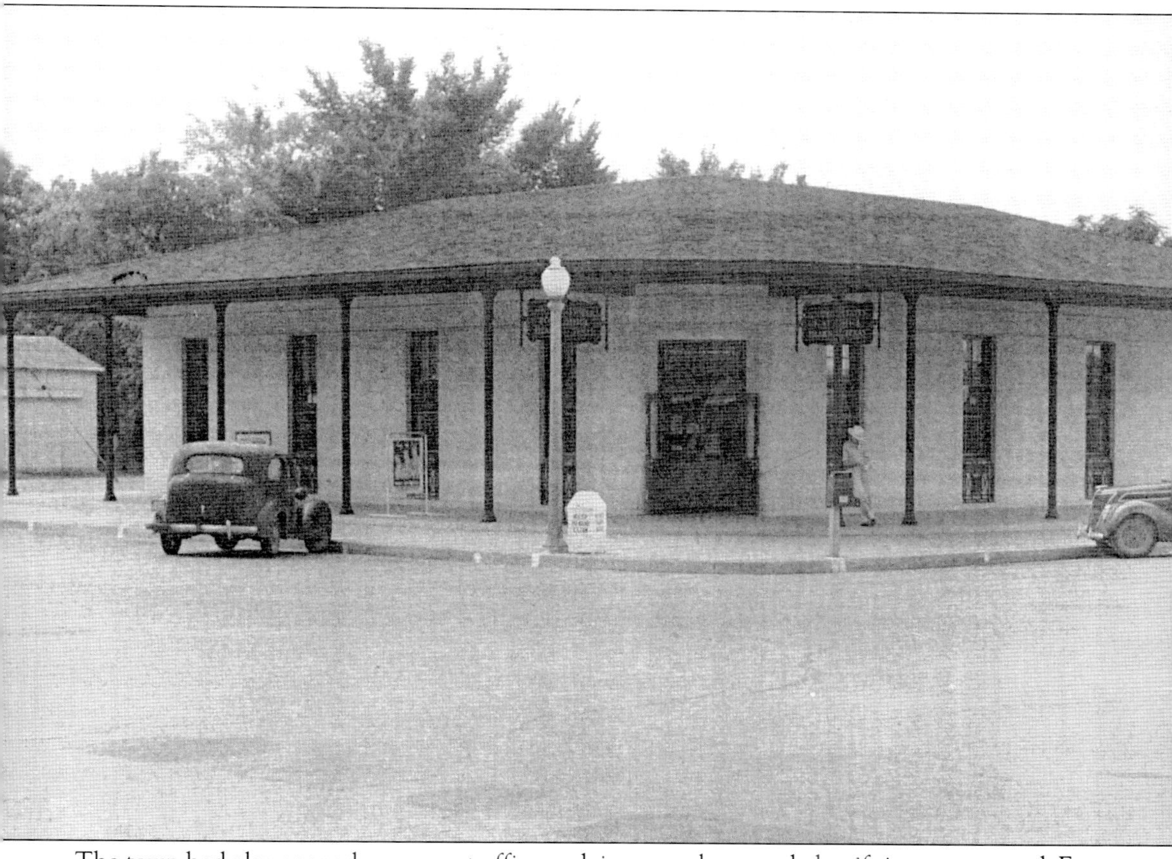

The town had also opened a new post office and, in general, expanded as if times were good. For Hearne, they were good enough. (Courtesy of Hearne Chamber of Commerce.)

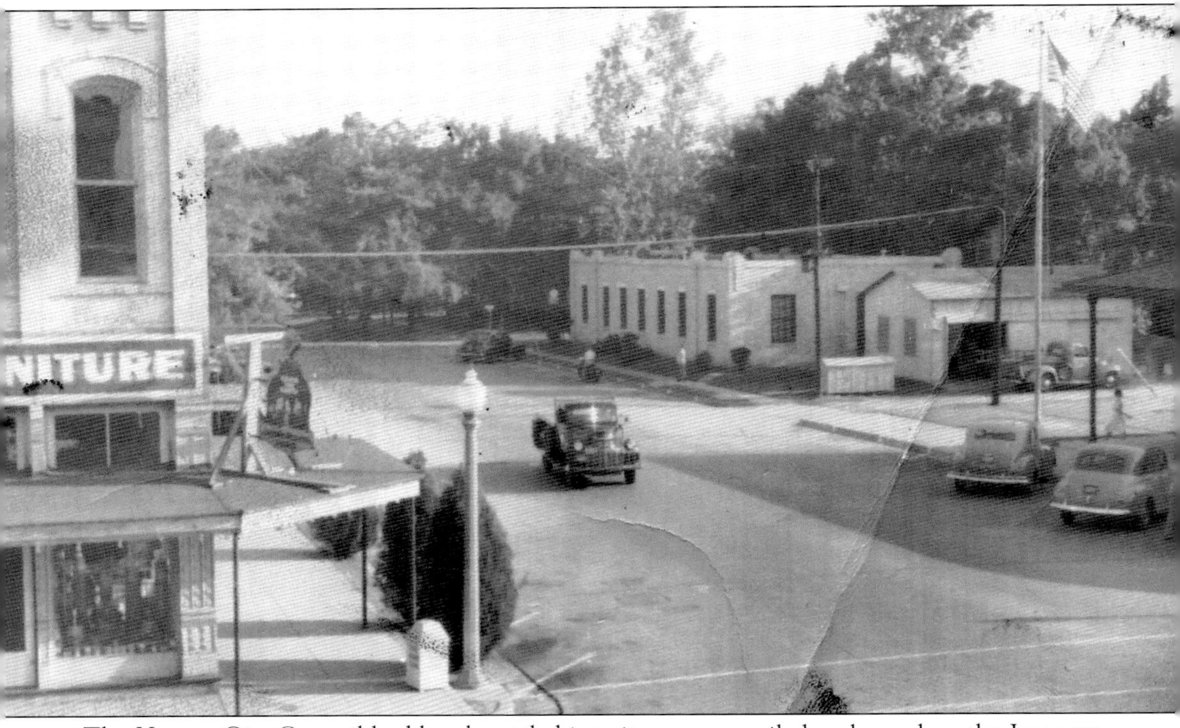

The Hearne City Council had barely settled into its new council chambers when the Japanese bombed Pearl Harbor on December 7, 1941, and the Depression was over. The new challenge for the peaceful-looking little town that had weathered the Depression was finding ways to help win the war. With military bases already assigned to other cities, the city decided to build a camp. (Courtesy of Hearne Chamber of Commerce.)

Five

Hearne Fights World War II

During World War II, Hearne sent over 70 of its sons and daughters into both the Pacific and European theaters of combat. On the home front, Hearne residents pitched in to rubber drives, paper drives, and scrap metal drives; they bought War Bonds and rationed goods and services. But that was not enough for Hearne. The city wanted to do more to win the war and boost its own economy in the process. Hearne Chamber of Commerce director Roy Henry went to Washington and asked for an internment camp. He got it.

Hearne was ideally suited to host prisoners of war. Its two rail lines—by then the Southern Pacific and Missouri Pacific—made getting POWs to Hearne easy. Local farmers had plenty of land to sell (the US government bought over 700 acres to house the camp), the nearest large city was over 100 miles away, and the Gulf Coast was several miles farther. "Nowhere to run," was an apt description of Hearne's location—at least from a German's point of view.

The US Army Corps of Engineers arrived in 1942, hired local labor, and within six months, in December of 1942, a POW camp with 250 buildings and complete water, sewer, electrical, and heating systems was ready. About five months later, the German Afrika Korps surrendered, and in June 1943, Camp Hearne became one of the first occupied of over 500 POW camps in the United States.

For Hearne, the POW camp was a windfall as well as a way to help the war effort. The camp, which at its largest held 4,800 POWs, purchased its electricity from Hearne, which had a population of just over 3,500. Generators ran at full capacity, and the US government paid. Also, Hearne residents took jobs building, maintaining, and staffing Camp Hearne; some worked for its professional fire department—a job they could not have in town where all firemen were volunteers.

For German prisoners, stays at Camp Hearne would be the best or, in a few cases, the worst of times.

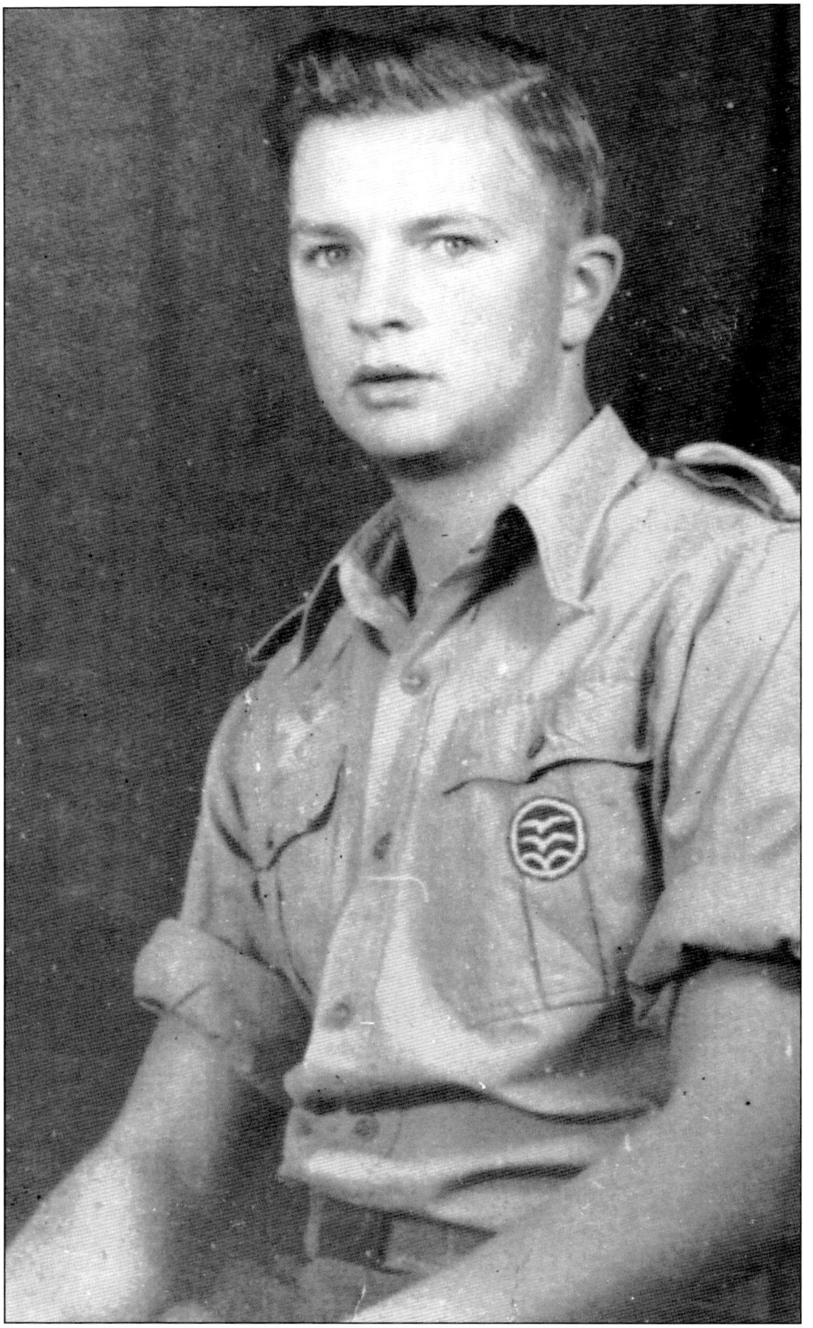

When German prisoners like Walter Fricke arrived after a long trip in Pullman train cars, they were marched to camp and treated to hygiene items, showers, and a good meal. The anticipated harsh treatment never came. They settled into military barracks, and since most were noncommissioned officers (NCOs) and not required to work, they entered a life of leisure pursuing their interests: art, theatre, music, education, or sports—Camp Hearne had it all. (Courtesy Dr. Michael Waters, TAMU Camp Hearne Collection.)

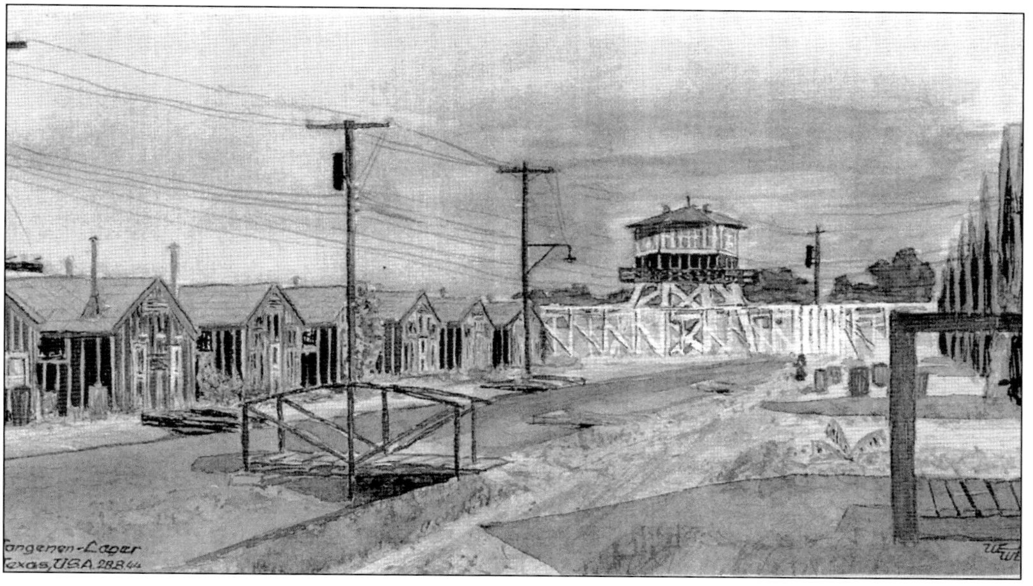

Camp Hearne (pictured in this POW painting) adhered to the 1929 Geneva Conventions to the letter—meaning POWs had comparable food, housing, and clothing to American soldiers. They were paid in Camp Hearne coupons (below), redeemable in the camp canteen. Privates, which were about 20 percent of the population, were required to work, but they received a coupon an hour while the unemployed NCOs received a coupon a day—making the lowly, cotton-picking private a rich man. (Both, courtesy Dr. Michael Waters, TAMU Camp Hearne Collection.)

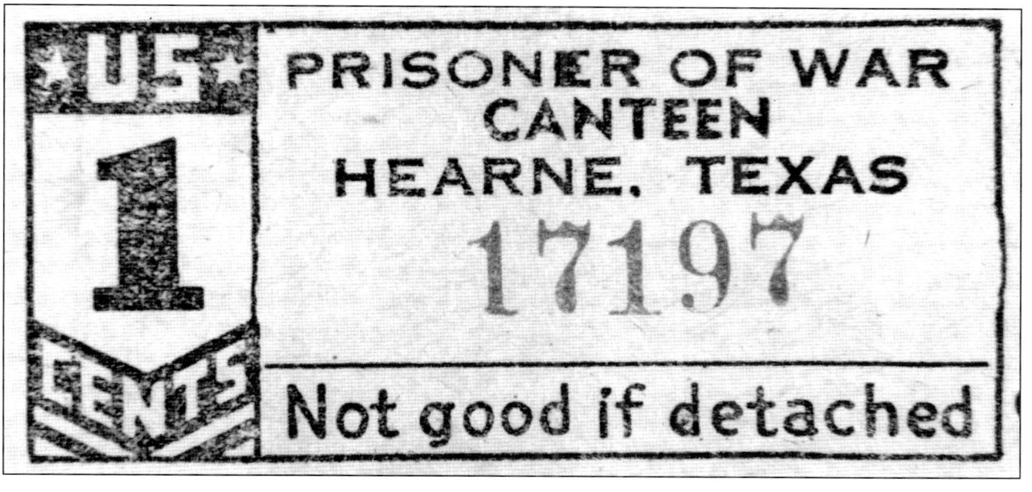

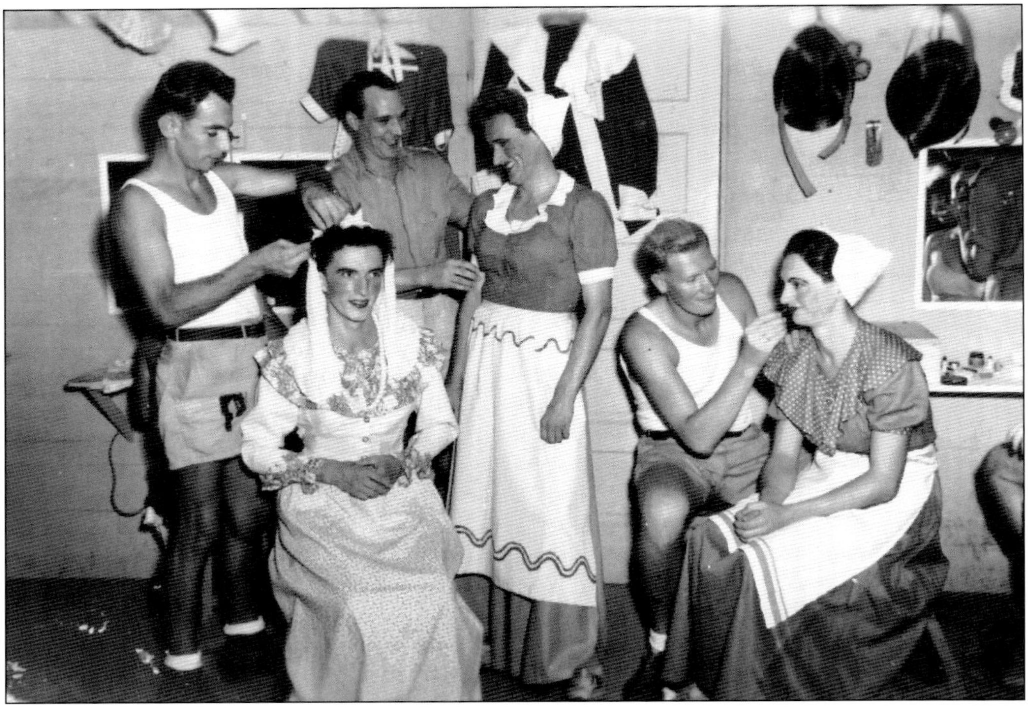

POWs converted extra buildings into theaters in all three compounds, and large-scale productions ensued. Compound 3 boasted the best theater, complete with tiered seating, a stage, and an orchestra pit—all POW made. (Both, courtesy Dr. Michael Waters, TAMU Camp Hearne Collection.)

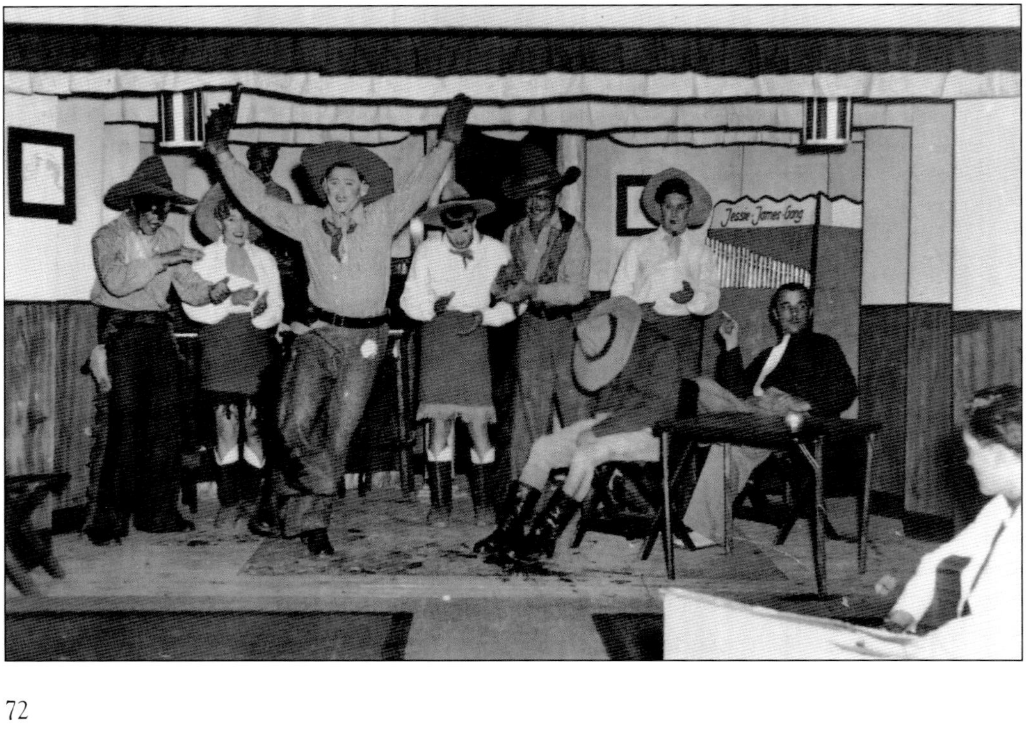

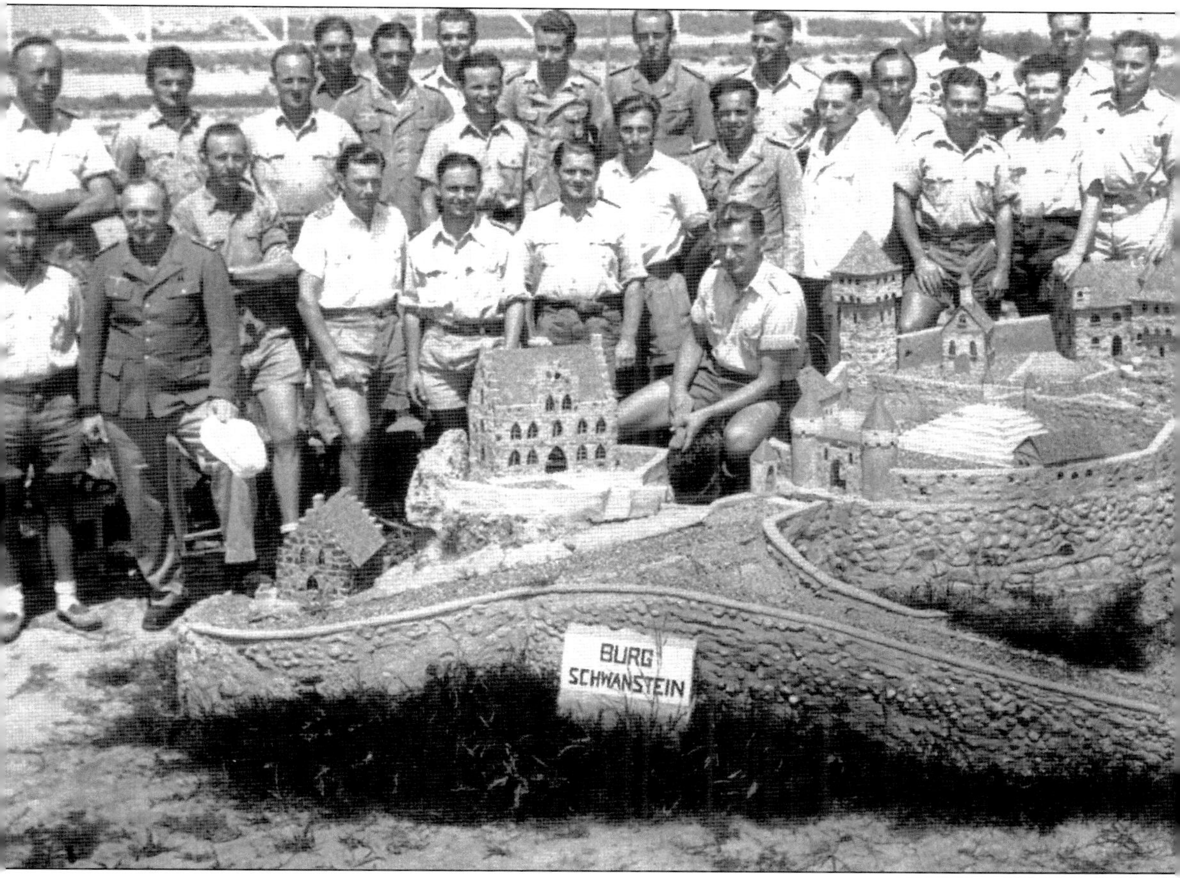

Germans also built elaborate, European-style fountains, and Hearne's excellent water supply found new expression in German waterworks like the castle fountain, a European castle complex in miniature. (Courtesy Dr. Michael Waters, TAMU Camp Hearne Collection.)

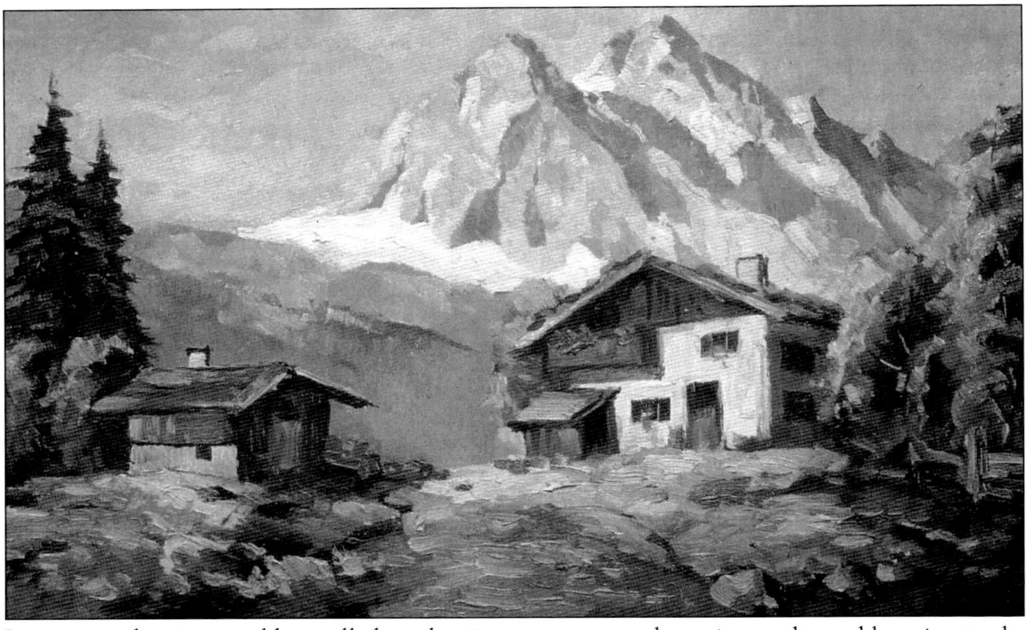

Incarcerated artists could get all the oil paint, canvas, wood-carving and wood-burning tools, concrete, and construction equipment they needed from the camp or the Sears Roebuck catalog. They painted Camp Hearne scenes and scenes from their minds on canvas and on boards. (Courtesy Dr. Michael Waters, TAMU Camp Hearne Collection.)

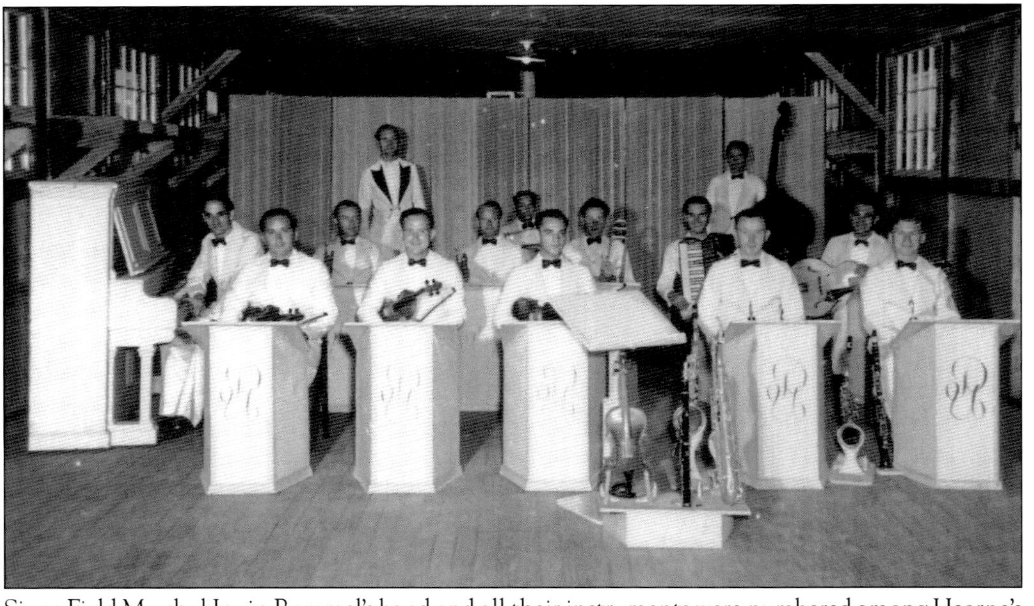

Since Field Marshal Irwin Rommel's band and all their instruments were numbered among Hearne's POWs, music ensembles were easy to put together. Additional instruments were provided by the YMCA, and small orchestras developed. POW-built music venues, like the band shell pictured, popped up in each compound. On Sundays, all three compound orchestras united, and Hearne residents came out to enjoy the music. During the weekends of the war years, one could almost talk about a Hearne Philharmonic. (Courtesy Dr. Michael Waters, TAMU Camp Hearne Collection.)

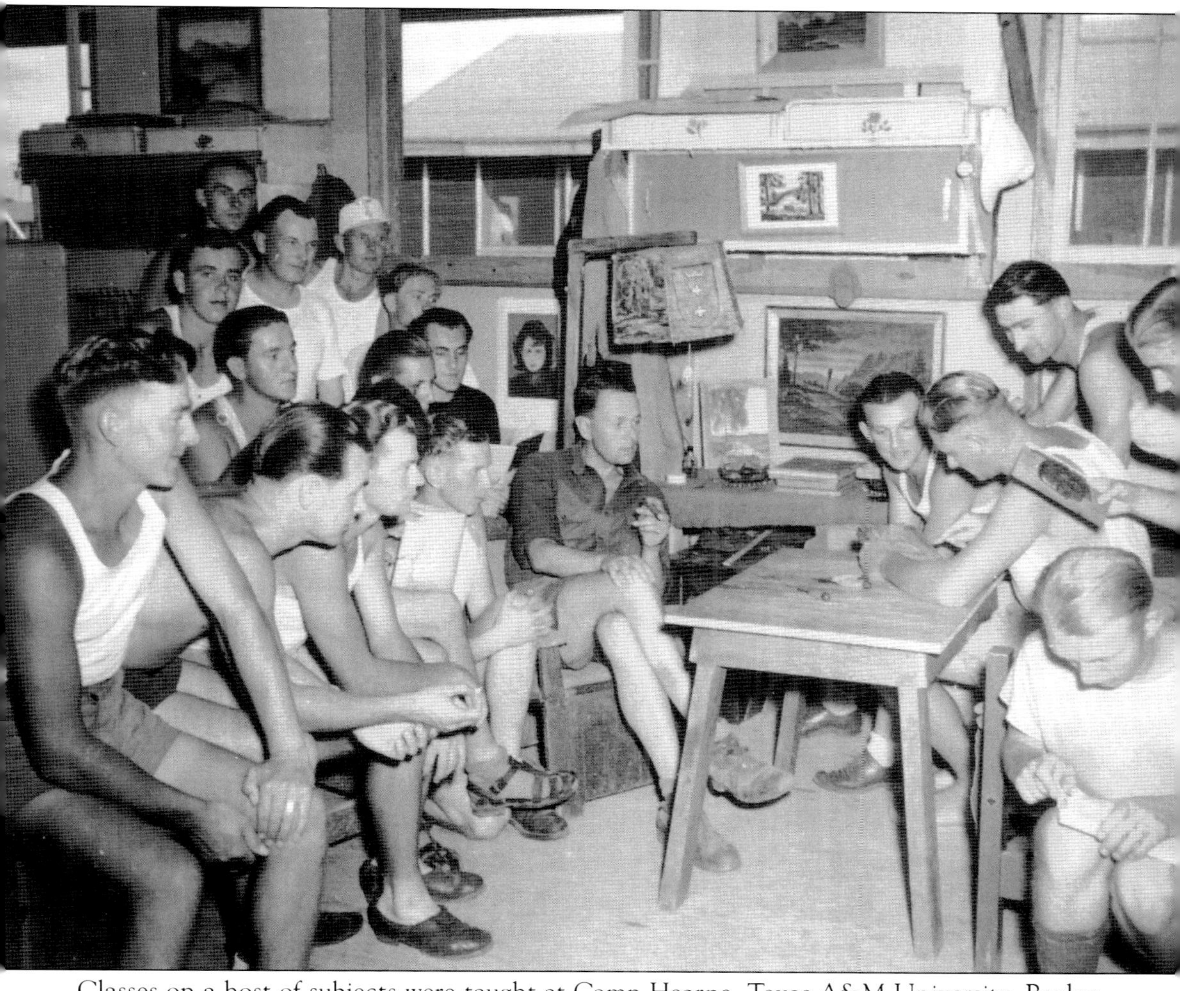

Classes on a host of subjects were taught at Camp Hearne. Texas A&M University, Baylor University, and the POWs themselves offered courses, though only Baylor awarded college credit. However, when the POWs finally returned to Germany, many of the German universities gave credit for academic courses no matter who taught them. POWs were receiving a free college education whether they realized it or not. (Courtesy Dr. Michael Waters, TAMU Camp Hearne Collection.)

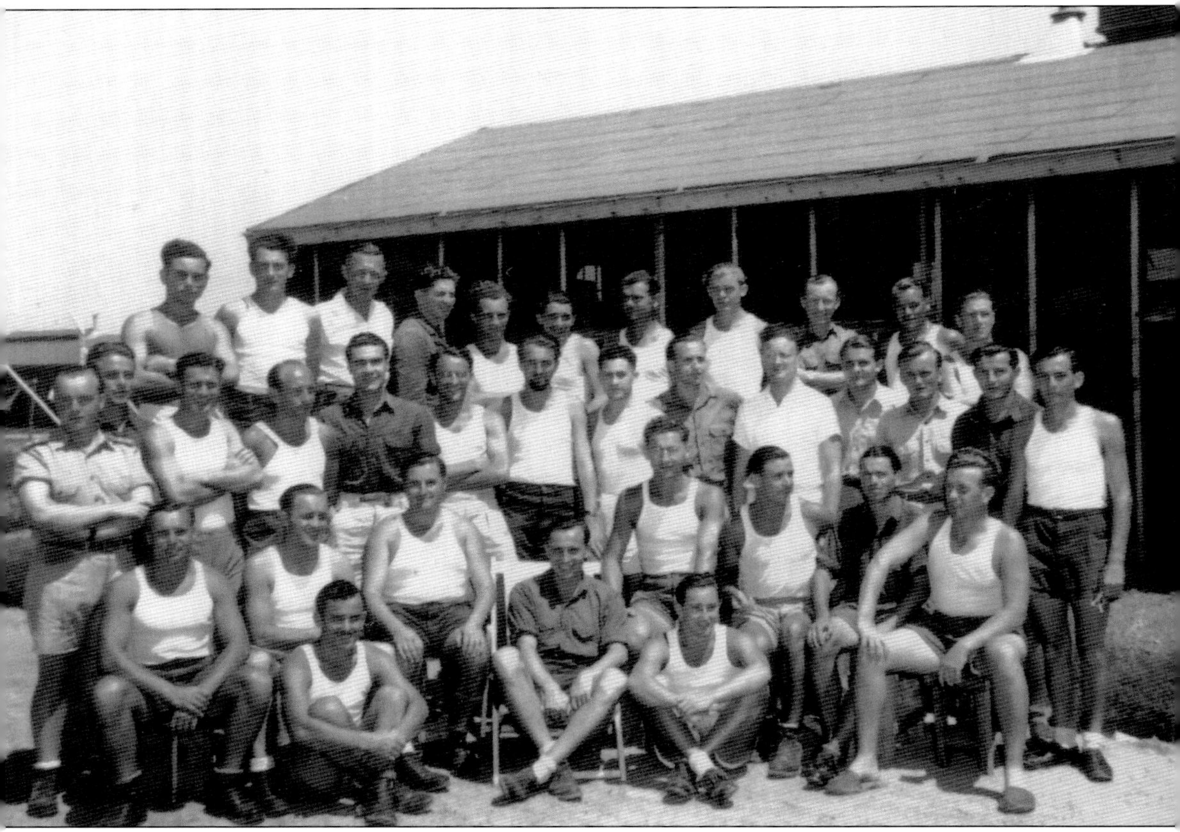

POWs at Camp Hearne changed from thin and war-weary to well-fed and healthy in short order. While meat and sugar were rationed throughout the United States, German prisoners were not subject to rationing. They made thousands of sugar cookies for their first in-camp Christmas, and when they ran out of chalk for soccer boundaries, they used sugar. The reason? The Geneva Conventions stipulate that countries must feed their POWs as well as they feed their own troops. Meat, bread, vegetables, and dessert graced every table. Recreation fields and halls provided ample space for exercise. (Courtesy Dr. Michael Waters, TAMU Camp Hearne Collection.)

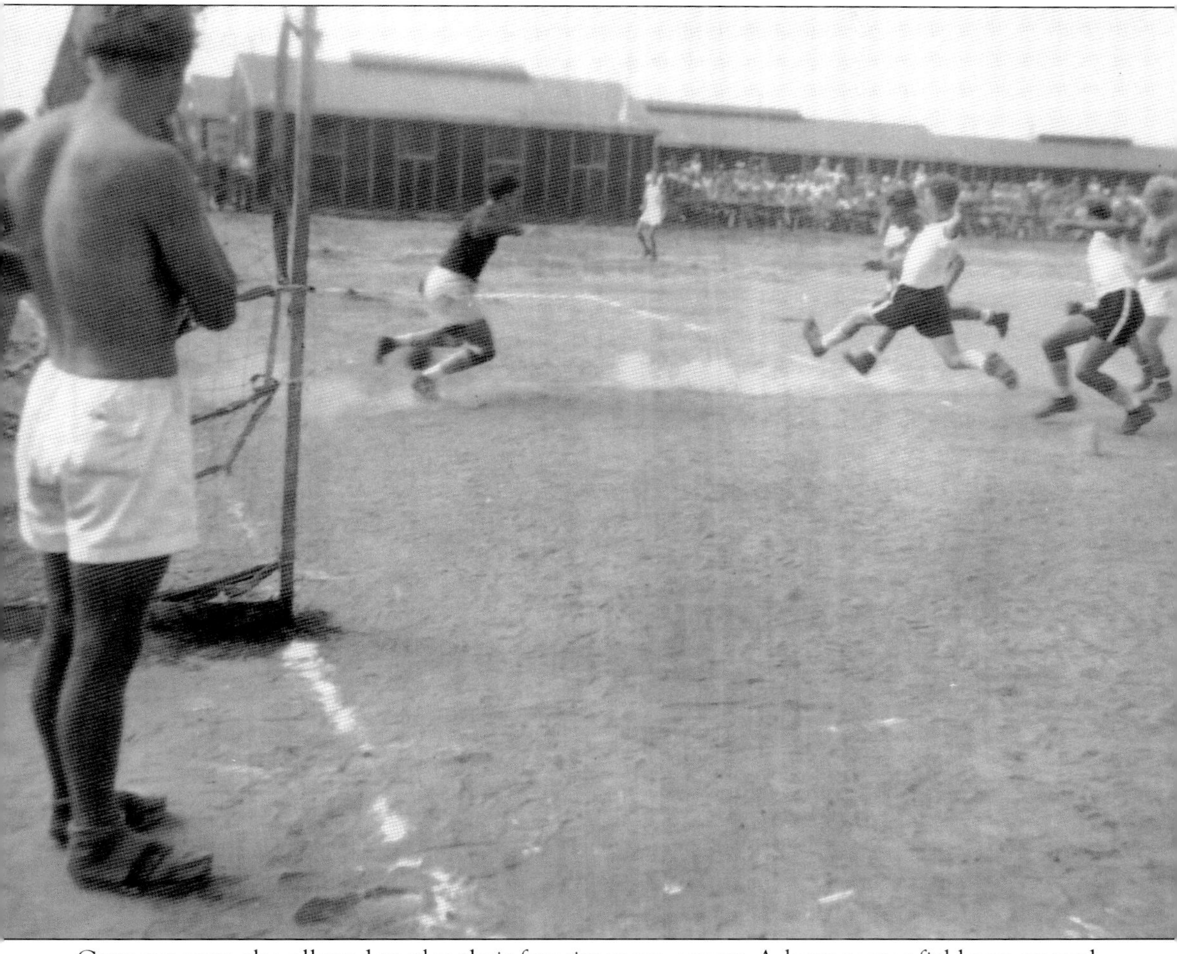

Germans were also allowed to play their favorite sport, soccer. A large soccer field was created behind the three compounds, leagues were formed, and competition was stiff. Camp Hearne guards—Army Military Police—were playing football. They were not particularly successful, but they were a better reflection of Hearne, where soccer has never caught on. (Courtesy Dr. Michael Waters, TAMU Camp Hearne Collection.)

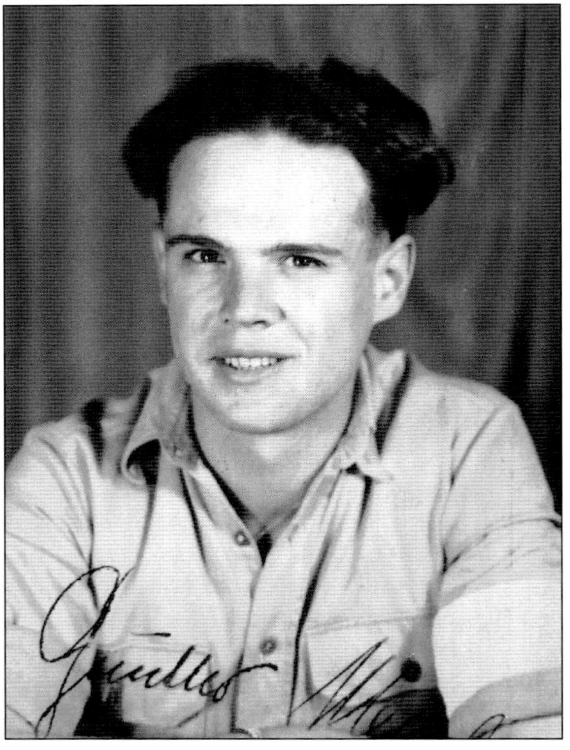

Despite these diversions, fear soon gripped the camp. In December 1943, Nazi hardliners, including Guenther Muensel (left), held a kangaroo court, convicting Cpl. Hugo Krauss, a German who had spent part of his childhood in America, of treason for saying that the Allies deserved to win. He was beaten, dying later in a Temple hospital. Pvt. Heino Erichsen (below) witnessed the brutal murder and promptly asked to be transferred to another camp. He, like Krauss, was a camp translator. Men who spoke to their captors were suspect. During other night raids, Nazis beat POWs with nail-studded two-by-fours—tightening their iron grip on the prisoner compounds. (Both, courtesy of Dr. Michael Waters, TAMU Camp Hearne Collection.)

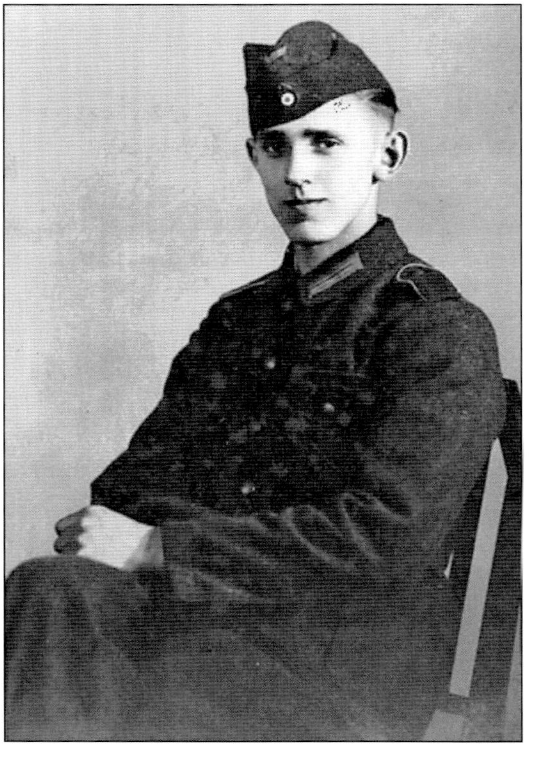

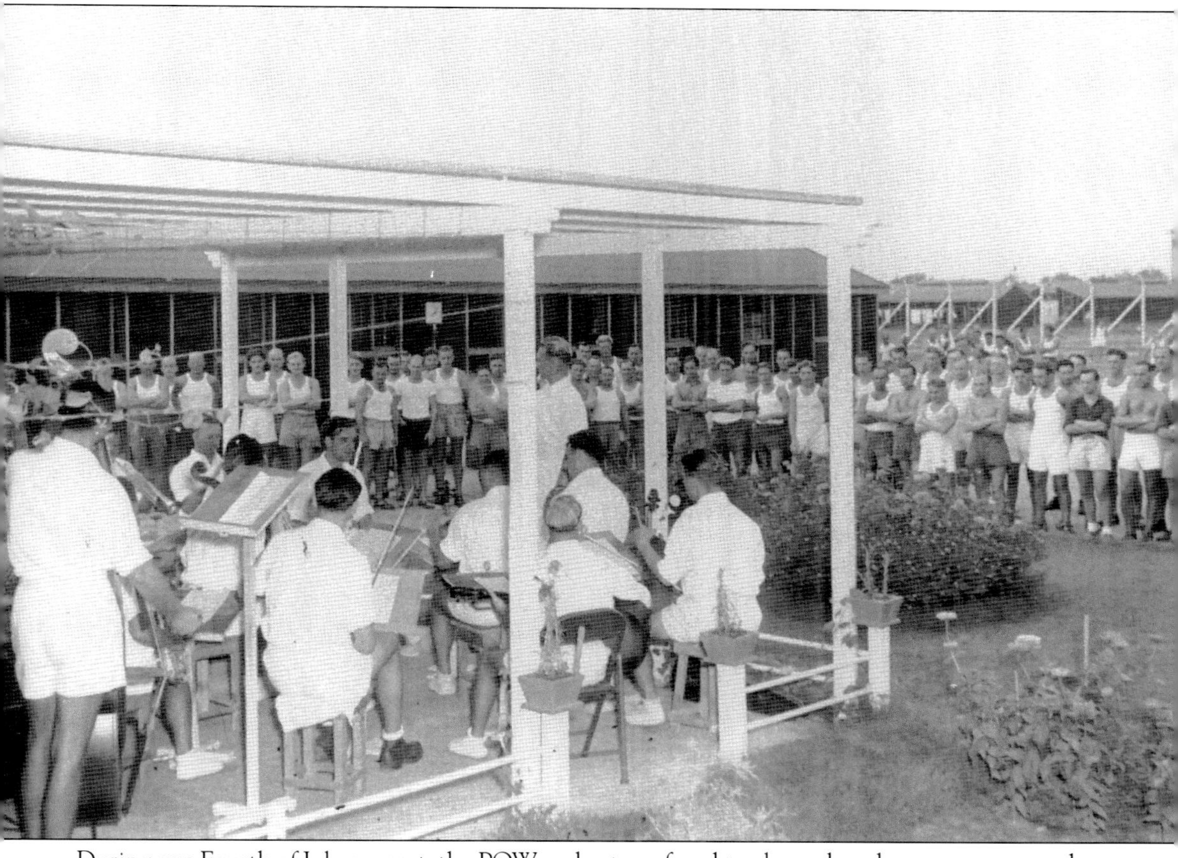

During one Fourth of July concert, the POW orchestra refused to play unless the camp commander lowered the US flag flying near the stage. It was lowered. The German camp spokesmen had also convinced camp officials to limit the military police guards' weapons to nightsticks when guarding POWs at work or conducting them to and from the camp. Though peace was usually maintained and no escapes were successful, the power within the POW compounds probably wore hidden swastikas. (Courtesy of Dr. Michael Waters, TAMU Camp Hearne Collection.)

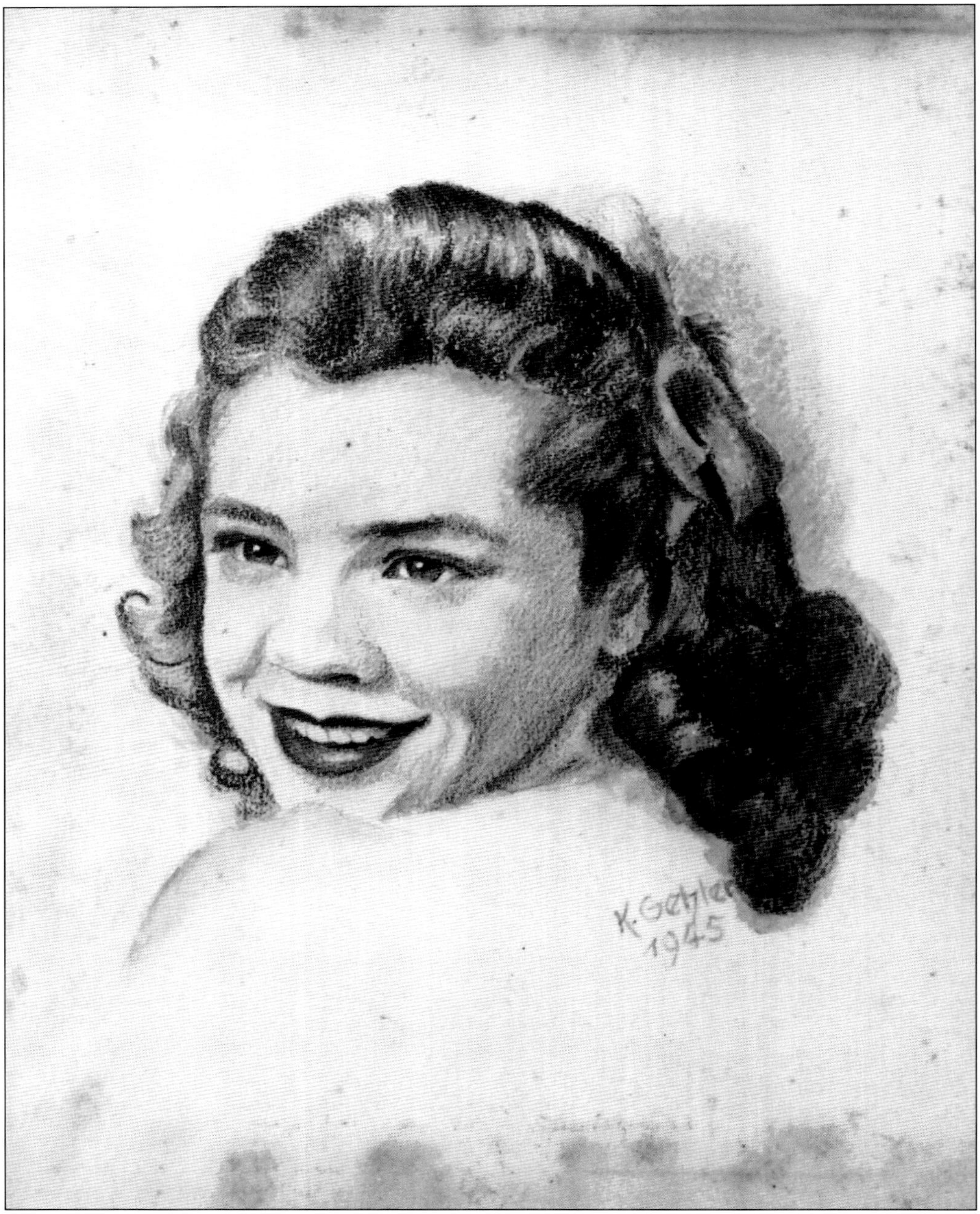

Despite the initial violence that lessened as troublemakers were removed, most POWs enjoyed their stay at Camp Hearne. After all, they had time—maybe for the first time in their lives—to pursue their interests, even long-distance romantic ones. (Courtesy of Dr. Michael Waters, TAMU Camp Hearne Collection.)

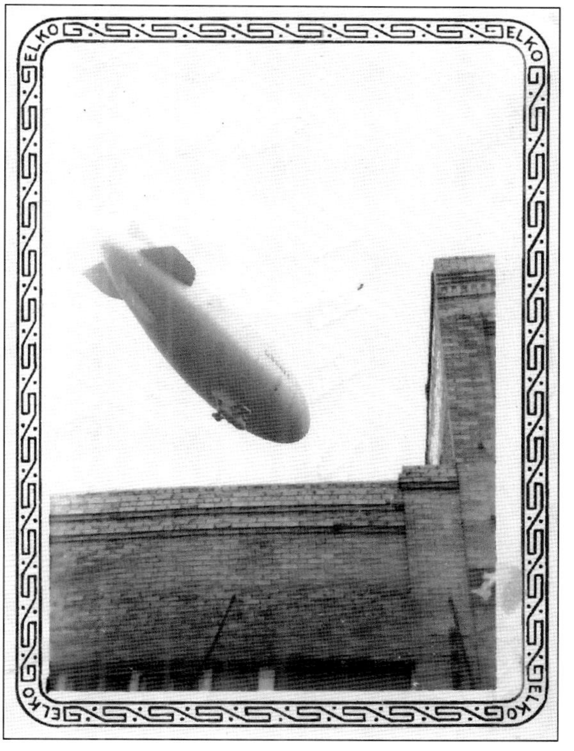

In Hearne, camp threats had little impact. In fact, two months before the murder of Corporal Krauss, the town had a big war-related laugh. Blimp pilot and German U-boat tracker Bill Palmos found himself flying over Hearne after a storm diverted his course. Never missing a chance for fun, Bill dropped a message to his little brother on to the football field. Shortly after, both would mourn the loss of their brother Paul, pictured below, who went down with his ship. (Courtesy of Carolyn Lampo.)

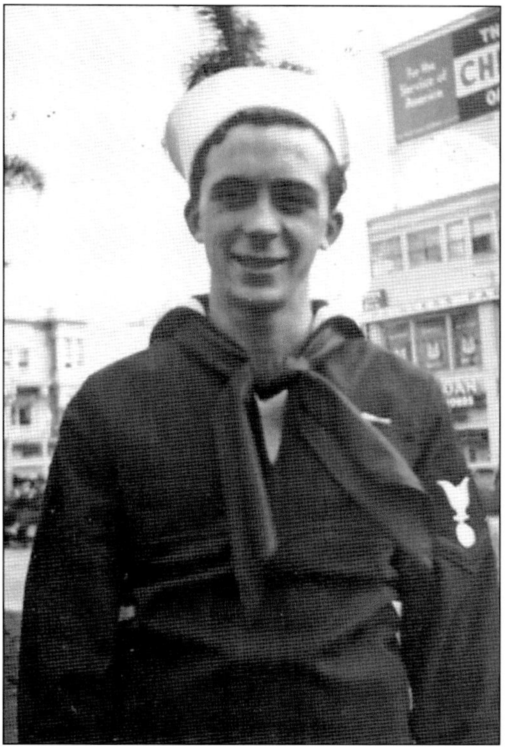

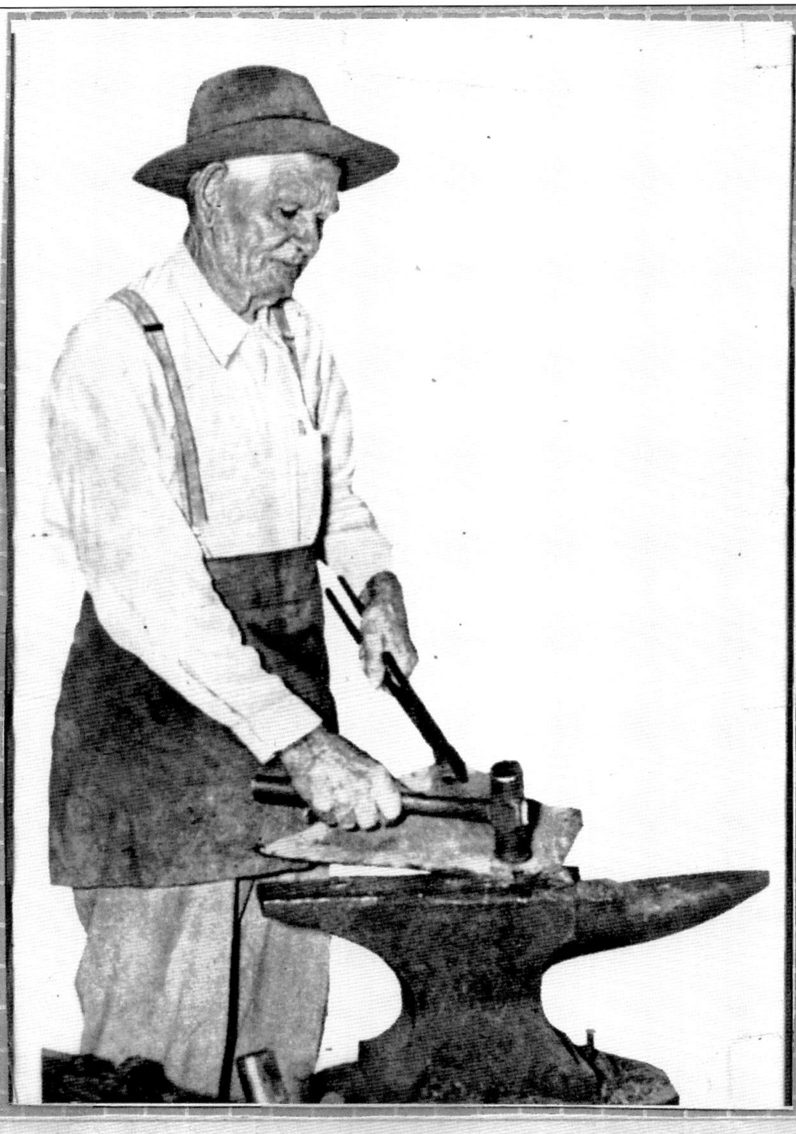

J.E. Mooney, 1875-1967. "Justice of Anvil" John Mooney, blacksmith's hammer in hand, opens a smoky session of his Precinct 2 court in Hearne, Texas where he has forged hot steel and cold justice for more than a quarter of a century.

Throughout the war years and the decade before, people eager to get married without the trouble of a church wedding could be wed "before the anvil" by Judge John E. Mooney, justice of the peace, Precinct 2. Mooney, whose court was also his blacksmith's shop on the corner of Cedar and Magnolia Streets, meted out "justice before the anvil" as well as nuptials and was known as one of Hearne's most colorful and friendly residents. (Courtesy of Robertson County Clerk's office.)

In 1945 and 1946, Hearne again welcomed back its veterans, and beginning in January 1946, Camp Hearne was dismantled. Veterans who had graduated from Hearne High School, like C.J. Allen and George Sisson (pictured), were honored in the 1944 *Eyrie*, the high school yearbook. These men returned to secure places in 1945–1946 Hearne society. (Right, courtesy of Hearne High School; below, courtesy of Hearne Chamber of Commerce.)

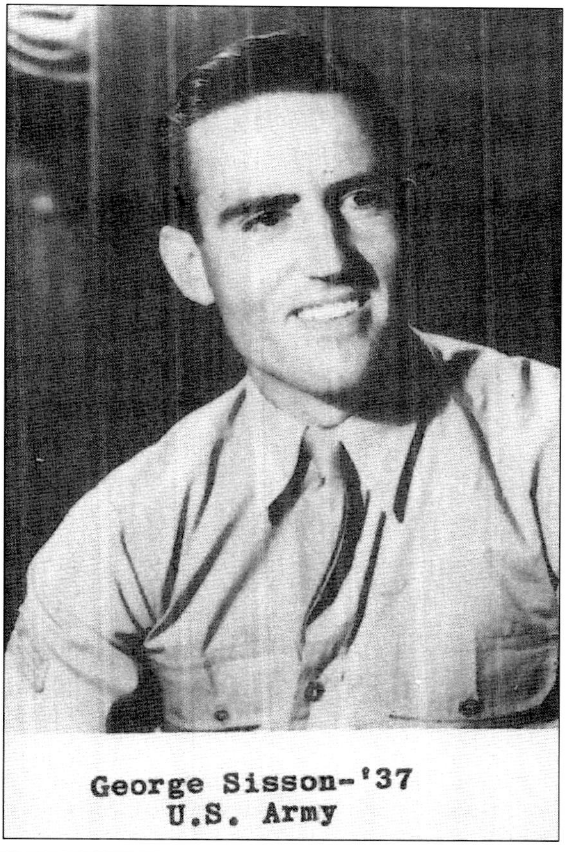

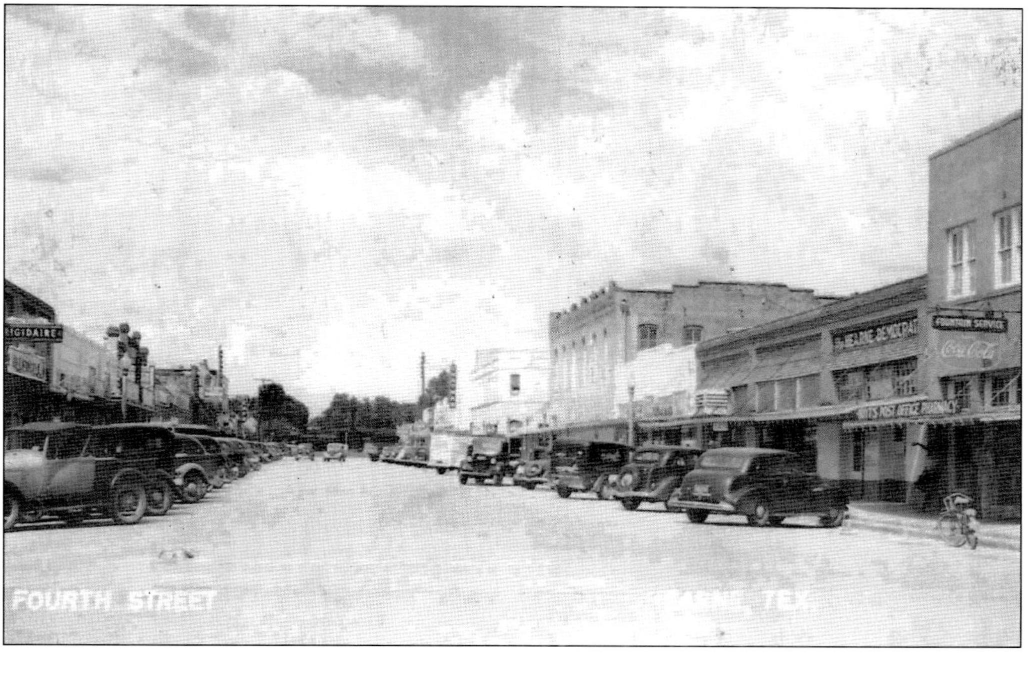

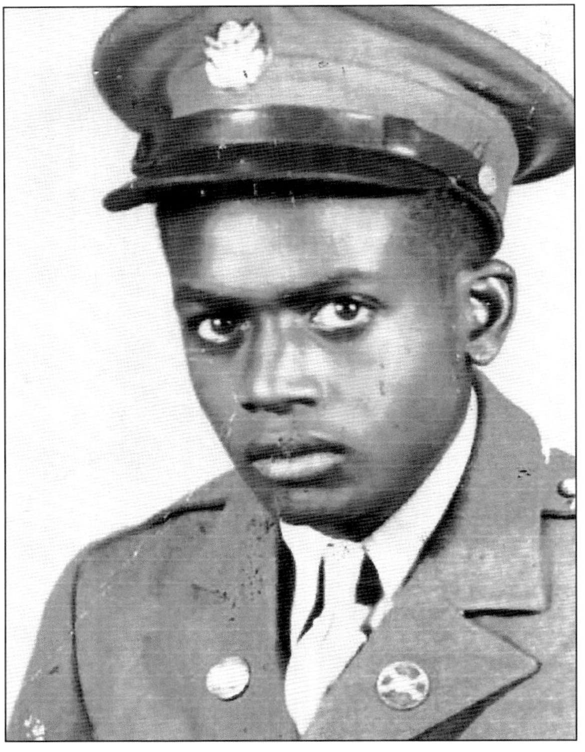

Guys like future reverend O.W. Mack (left) and Adrian Cordova (below, right) did not make the yearbook in a segregated Hearne, even though Cordova had been involved in some of the toughest fighting of the war. However, despite local segregation, both Mack and Cordova did make their way back; Mack became a minister and educator, and Cordova became a downtown business owner in postwar Hearne. (Both, courtesy of Cathy Lazarus.)

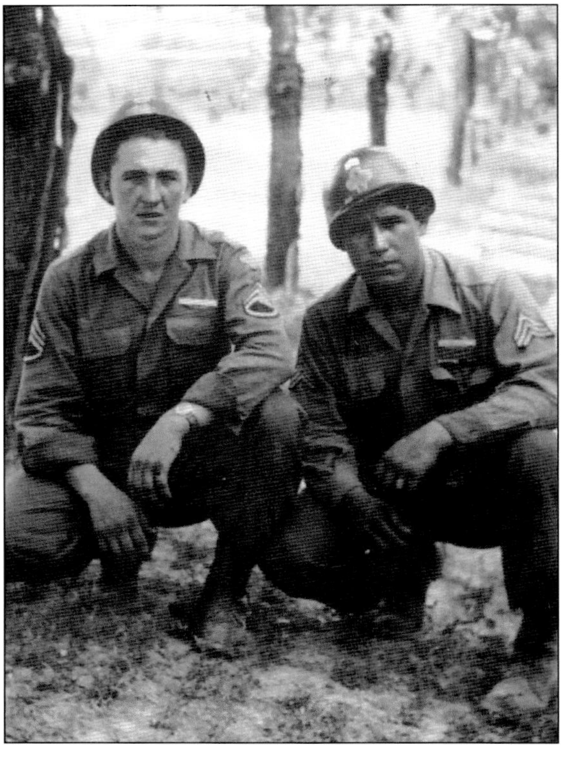

Six

Postwar Bustle

The closing of Camp Hearne in December 1945, three years after its completion, heralded the beginning of unprecedented growth and prosperity for the city of Hearne. Many believe that the years from 1946 to 1969 were Hearne's best. Under the management of Norman McCarver, Hearne city manager for over three decades, the town's government became of model for small cities (*Kansas Publisher: Official Publication of the Kansas Press Association*, June 1950) and its power plant the poster child for Cooper-Bessemer gas-diesel engines (*Wall Street Journal*, June 17, 1954). The city was growing and showing revenue surpluses. Its utilities—particularly the municipal power plant—were making profits for the city.

However, Hearne's African American population was still denied an equal place in society despite the military service in World War II of many—O.W. Mack and James Satchell, for example. Hearne's Hispanic community did not fare much better.

After being shifted from one temporary building to another, Hearne's black children finally got their own substantial school building in 1957, housing the Blackshear School, named after an educator at Prairie View A&M College under which many of Blackshear's teachers earned their degrees.

In the 1950s, Cayce Moore put Hearne on the map when the *Saturday Evening Post*, probably the most popular magazine in America, put the Hearne barber on its front cover. The *Post* declared Cayce the "nation's most famous barber" and the best storyteller in America—also one of the funniest. When he was not cutting hair in Hearne, Moore was traveling across the nation as its favorite after-dinner speaker. Despite his fame and fortune, he continued to barber in his Fourth Street shop next to the Chatmas Theatre.

Into the 1960s, Hearne's retail and industrial base remained strong. But in one sense, its economic and social health was a veneer covering 100 years of racial inequality and segregation—a veneer that would soon be stripped away.

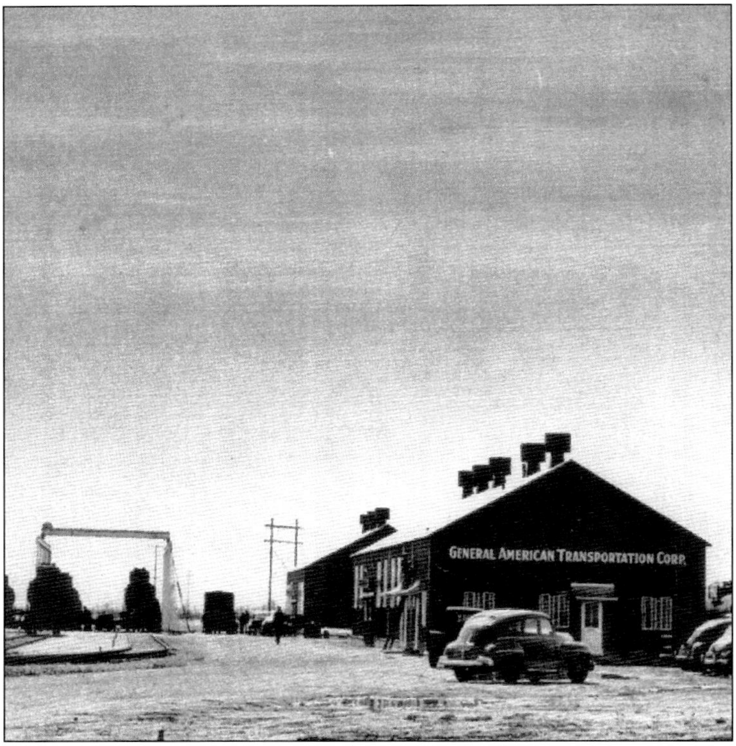

In 1948, GATX—a rail car company—established a large plant in Hearne and became one of its primary employers. The plant manager, a serious golfer, used the company's resources to expand the municipal course's amenities. The Hearne Golf Association had been established in 1942 with the course opening sometime after. (Left, courtesy of Hearne Chamber of Commerce; below, courtesy of author.)

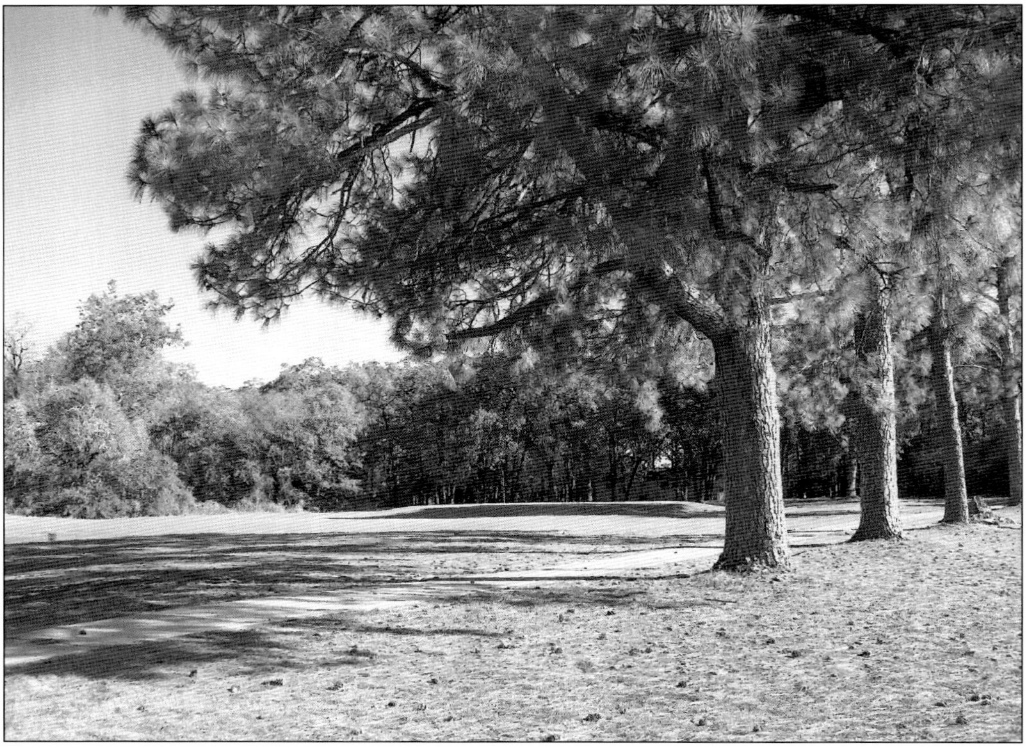

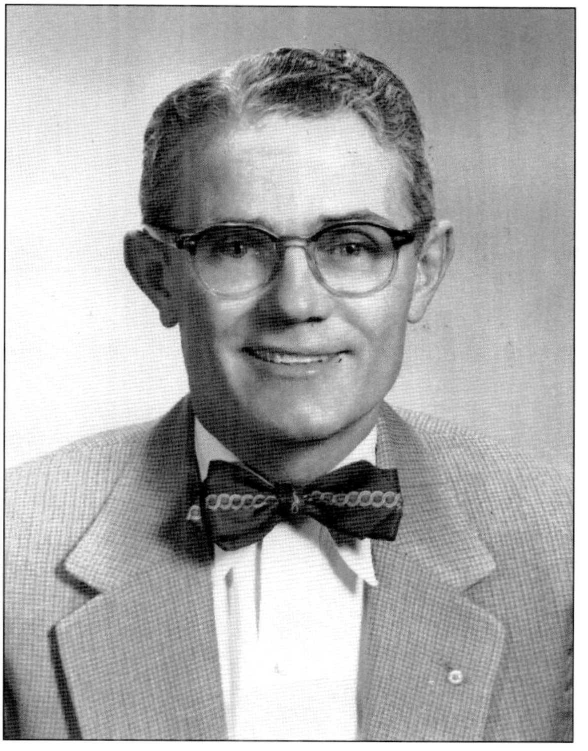

A primary reason for Hearne's "model city" status in the 1950s was the profit it was making from its own power plant and electric sales. Hearne was able to pay its bills, continue to improve its infrastructure, and enjoy a surplus in its bank accounts from power sales for several years. City Manager Norman McCarver (pictured), the man who prepared the meticulous reports, also gained a reputation for municipal management, a reputation that led to his election as president of the International City Managers Association. (Both, courtesy of City of Hearne.)

CITY OF HEARNE, TEXAS
MUNICIPAL UTILITIES FUND
Statement of Changes in Surplus
Year Ended March 31, 1963

Schedule 29

Balance, April 1, 1962	$1,125,868.87
Add net income for the year less transfers to other funds (Sch. 30)	15,185.97
Balance, March 31, 1963	$1,141,054.84

CITY OF HEARNE, TEXAS
MUNICIPAL UTILITIES FUND
Statement of Operations
Year Ended March 31, 1963

Schedule 30

	Electricity	Water	Sewer	Garbage	Total
Sales and connection charges	$314,038.94	$55,395.46	$11,389.12	$ 16,735.59	$397,559.11
Direct costs					
Production costs	$ 92,483.09	$ 484.16	$ --	$ --	$ 92,967.25
Distribution costs	36,418.38	15,904.98	8,256.17	--	60,579.53
Garbage contract	--	--	--	17,749.92	17,749.92
Total direct costs	$128,901.47	$16,389.14	$ 8,256.17	$ 17,749.92	$171,296.70
Gross profit on sales	$185,137.47	$39,006.32	$ 3,132.95	($ 1,014.33)	$226,262.41
Operating expenses					
Customer accounting and collecting	$ 10,568.30	$ 9,668.73	$ --	$ --	$ 20,237.03
Administrative and general	17,975.20	4,860.05	3,038.63	178.88	26,052.76
	$ 28,543.50	$14,528.78	$ 3,038.63	$ 178.88	$ 46,289.79
Gross profit less operating expenses (exclusive of depreciation and interest on revenue bonds)	$156,593.97	$24,477.54	$ 94.32	($ 1,193.21)	$179,972.62
Other income					
Reconnect charges				$ 292.00	
Recovery of bad debts				164.40	
Interest income				600.00	
State sales tax fee				54.97	1,111.37
Net revenues as defined in the bond indenture					$181,083.99
Other expenses					
Revenue bond interest				$ 9,298.10	
Depreciation - electric			$33,762.08		
Depreciation - water			11,285.23		
Depreciation - sewer			8,252.61	53,299.92	62,598.02
Net income					$118,485.97
Less transfer to other funds					
General Fund				$100,350.00	
Curb and Gutter Fund				2,950.00	103,300.00
Net increase in surplus					$ 15,185.97

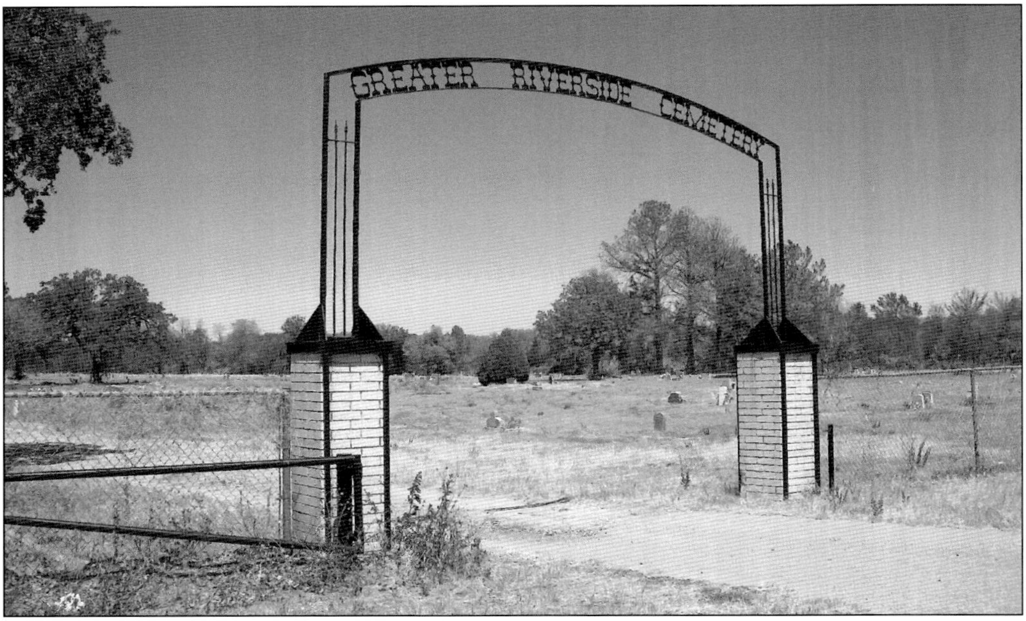

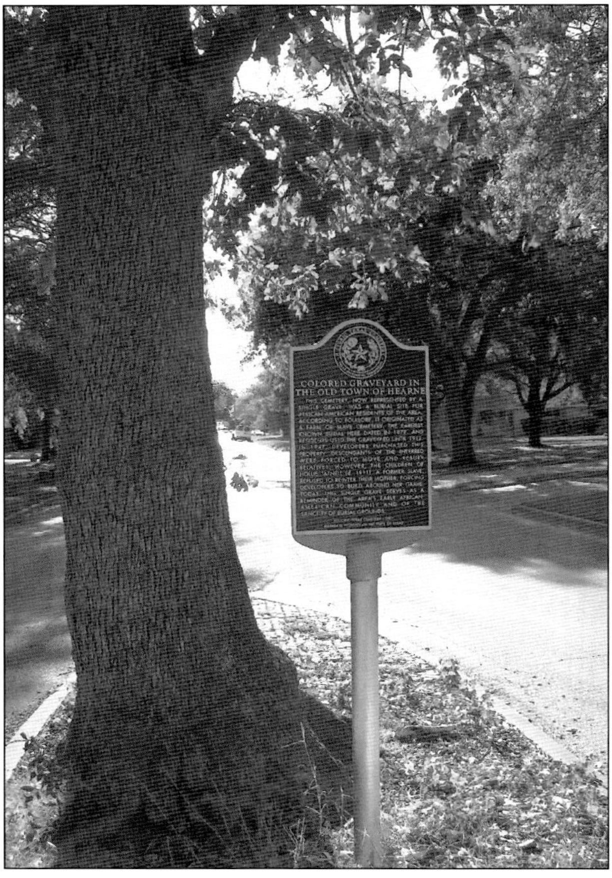

The grave in the middle of Wheelock Street is one indisputable Hearne distinction. In 1947, developers bought a two-and-a-half-acre tract near Hearne High School as part of Hearne's rapid residential expansion. Two previous surveys of Hearne had failed to show that part of the plot, purchased from Manuel Baptist Church, had been the church cemetery, abandoned in 1911. Developer Tim Thames gave the church two-and-a-half acres near the Little Brazos River on which to move the graves—creating Riverside Cemetery (above). But one grave, then enclosed in an iron fence, stayed put. The mother of Marlin doctor A.L. Hunter was buried there, and he took the city to court to keep his mother, born in slavery, right where she was. In 1948, the district court ruled that the grave would stay in the middle of Wheelock Street. Currently, Riverside Cemetery holds the graves of more military veterans than any cemetery in Robertson County. (Both, courtesy of author.)

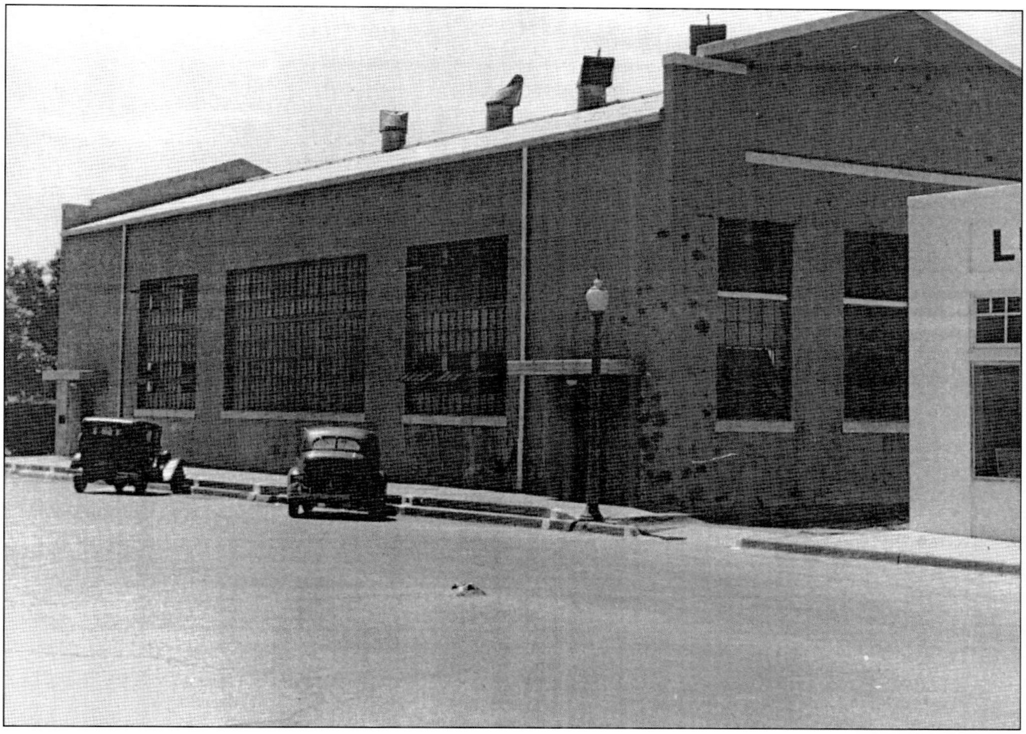

Hearne industry, both private and public (the Hearne Municipal Power Plant), had made it a very prosperous little town in the 1950s and 1960s. Car dealerships and repair shops were springing up on every corner of Market Street. The city's annual statements typically showed a healthy profit in the power plant's columns. Reports printed in the *Hearne Democrat* were sometimes republished in other periodicals to show what a healthy city looked like. (Above, courtesy of the City of Hearne; right, courtesy of the City of Hearne.)

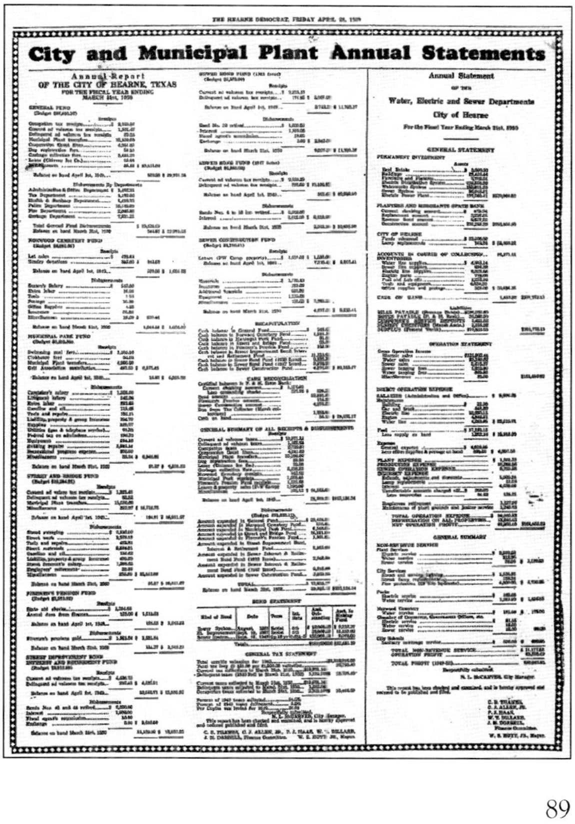

City and Municipal Plant Annual Statements

Annual Report
OF THE CITY OF HEARNE, TEXAS
FOR THE FISCAL YEAR ENDING
MARCH 31st, 1950

Annual Statement
of the
Water, Electric and Sewer Departments
City of Hearne

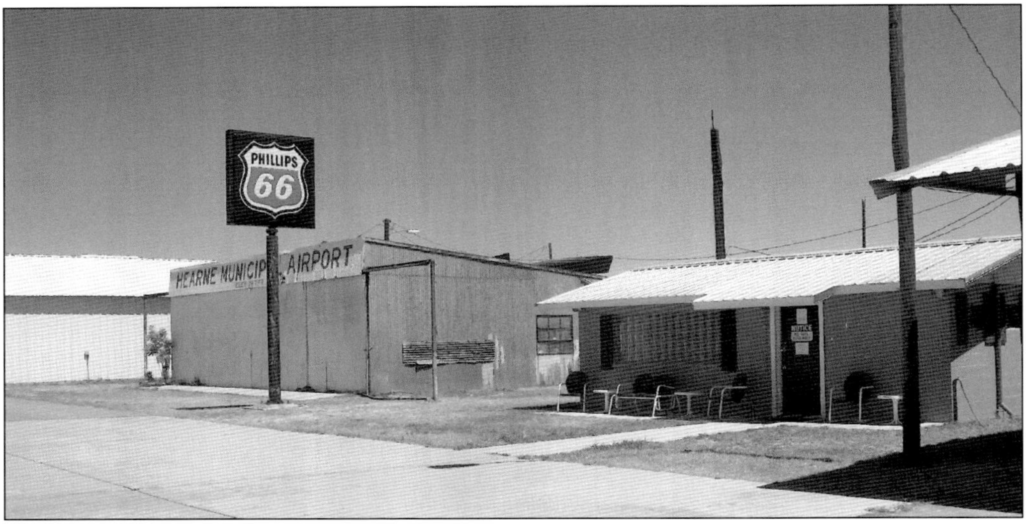

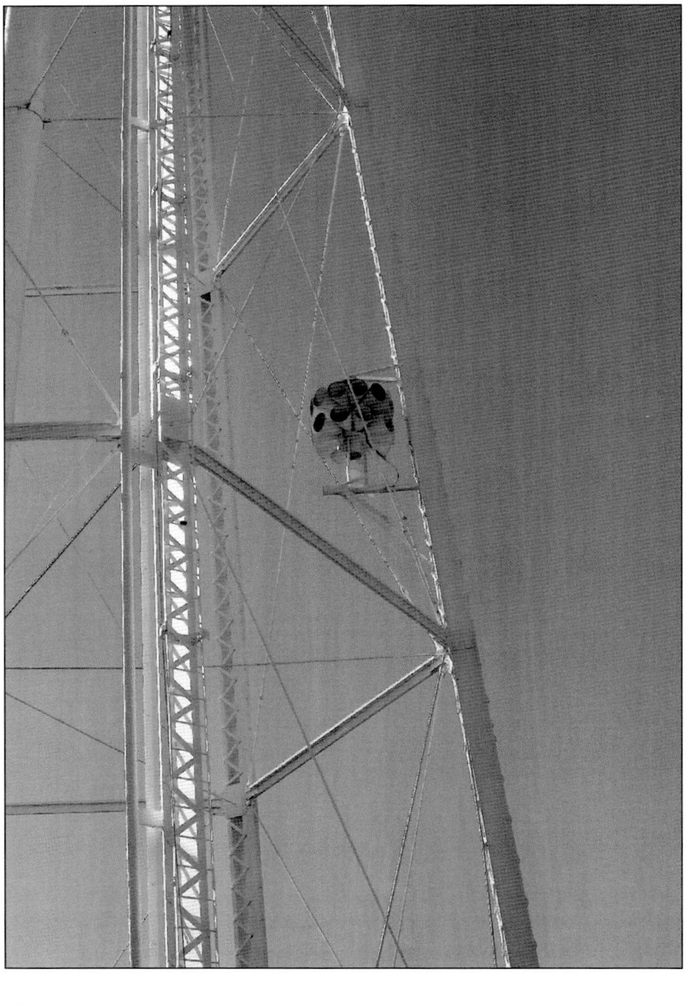

In May 1954, Hearne opened its airstrip, an auxiliary landing strip of the Bryan Air Force Base about 20 miles away. The 7,000-foot runway was used to train jet pilots. After the closing of the Bryan base, the airstrip became the key element of the new Hearne Airport—the only airport in Robertson County. (Courtesy of author.)

People moving into Hearne during the postwar years (and over 2,000 did) commented on something they had never experienced before—the Hearne dinner bell, or dinner siren, actually. Hearne played and still plays its warning siren to announce hazards (particularly approaching tornados), to summon emergency responders, and to remind folks it is time to knock off work and eat at 12:00 p.m. and 6:00 p.m. It is loud and commanding, but Hearne has always counted on its restaurant trade. (Courtesy of author.)

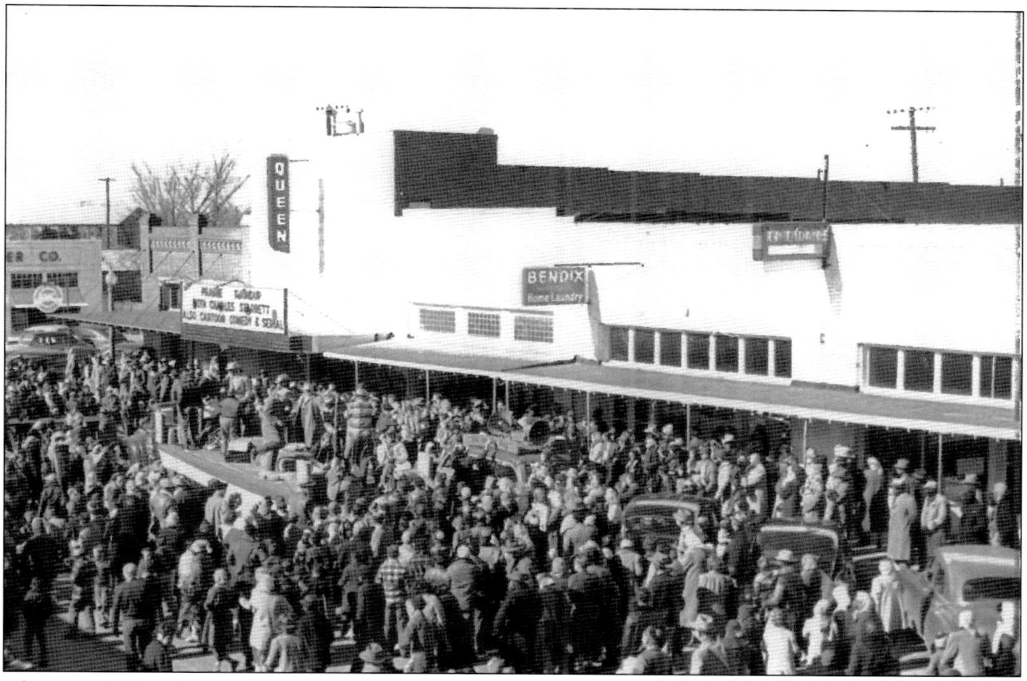

The year 1954 also marked the beginning of Hearne's annual Alfalfa Fiesta. Local farmers had introduced alfalfa to the crop rotation, and as with others crops, the Bottoms became a leading producer. That year, the festival featured a parade, agricultural events at Blackshear and Hearne High, remote radio coverage from Dallas's WFAA, a Bathing Girls Revue, and the airstrip dedication. (Above, courtesy of Hearne Chamber of Commerce; below, courtesy of Sue Gandy.)

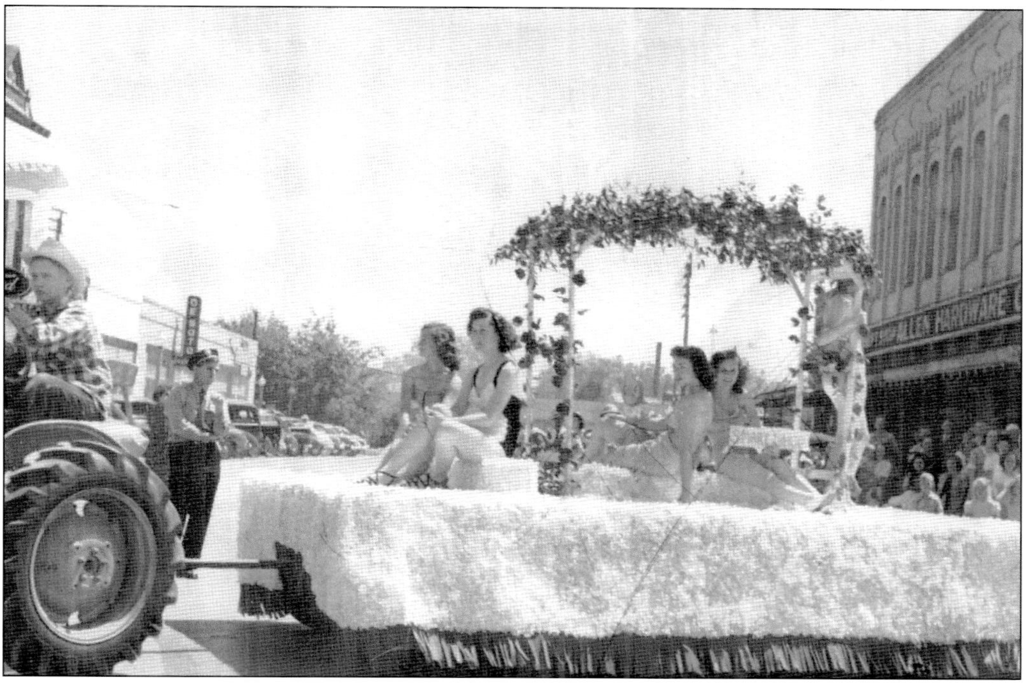

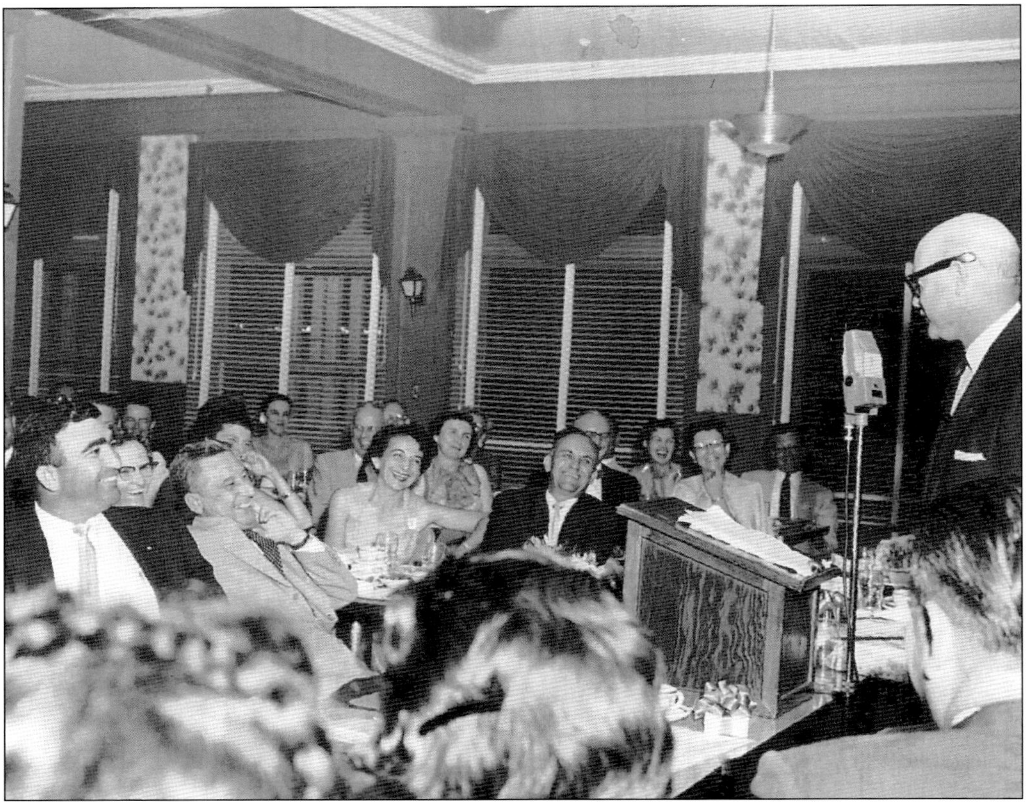

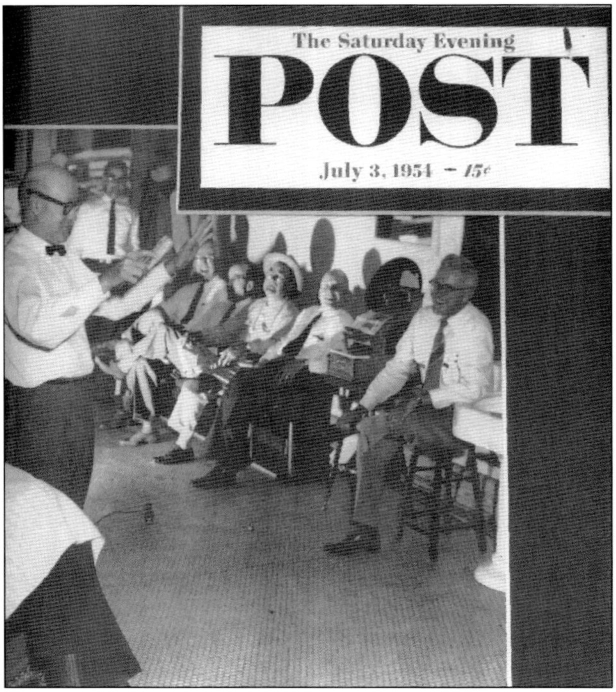

Cayce Moore, a barber with hundreds of yarns and jokes to spin, opened a shop in Hearne in 1938. In a county offering golf, music and dance venues, and movie theaters, Moore also became a primary source of entertainment in the 1950s. He was grooming while spinning yarns on Fourth Street most weekdays with one section for folks needing a hair cut and another for folks needing a good laugh. As Moore became a favorite after-dinner speaker, the *Saturday Evening Post* discovered him and put Moore on the front cover. (Both, courtesy of Hearne Chamber of Commerce.)

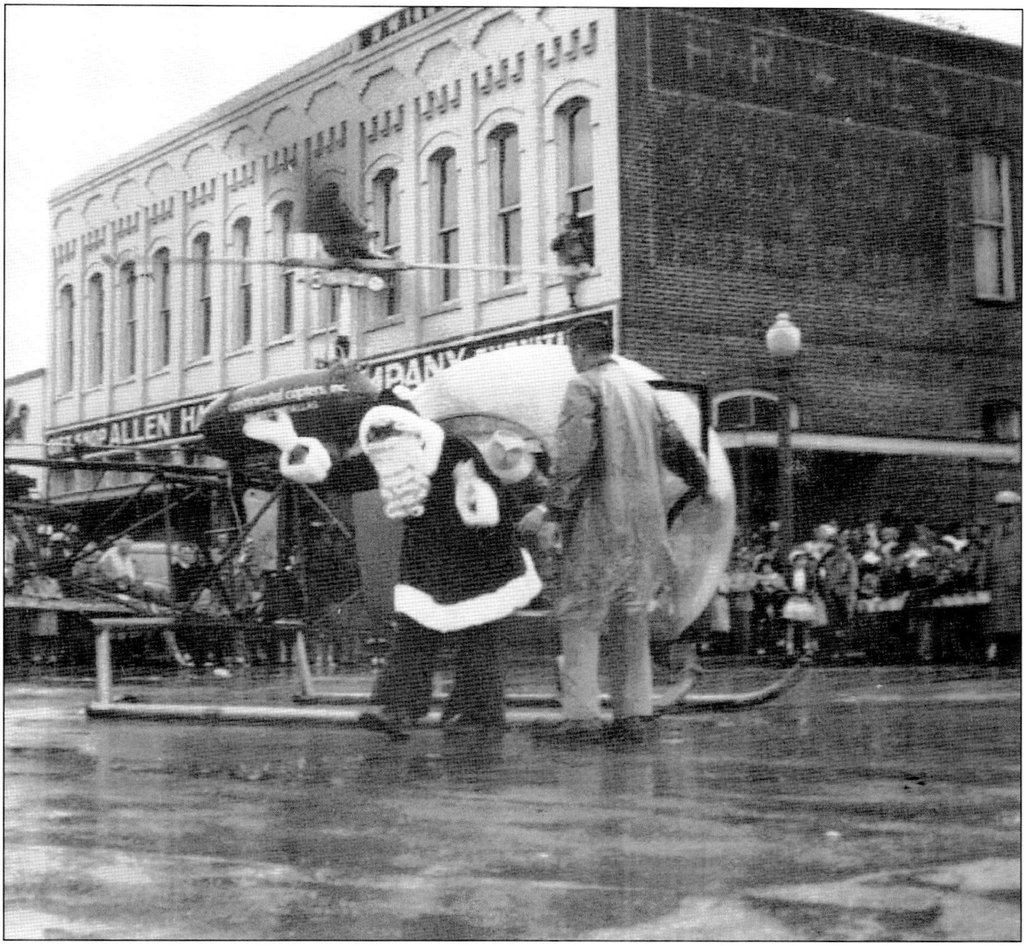

As children living in one of the Brazos Valley's more prominent towns, Hearne youngsters received visits from Santa via a "snow"-encrusted helicopter that landed in the middle of Magnolia and Third Streets during Hearne's annual Christmas Parade in the 1950s. (Courtesy of Martin family.)

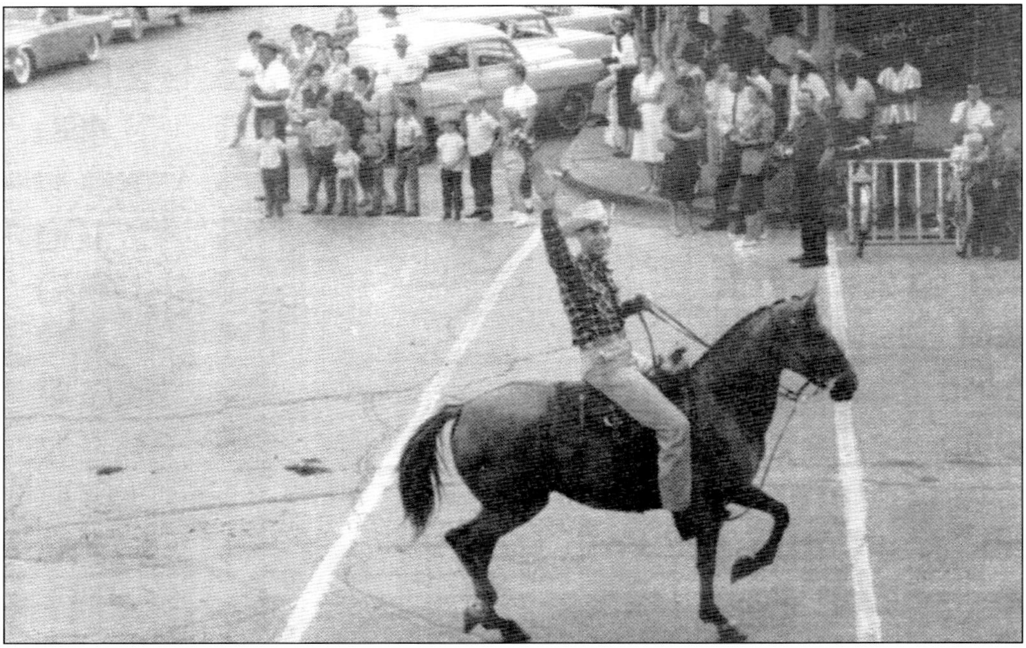

The Robertson County Youth Fair developed from Hearne's Western Day, the brainchild of Hearne car dealer Marvin Jentsch. Jentsch thought the town needed some livening up, and he believed that a trail ride, parade, and youth livestock auction would be just the thing. In the mid-1960s, after much cajoling of city officials, he pulled it off, leading the parade. Here he is leading the trail ride into Hearne. (Courtesy of Marlin Jentsch.)

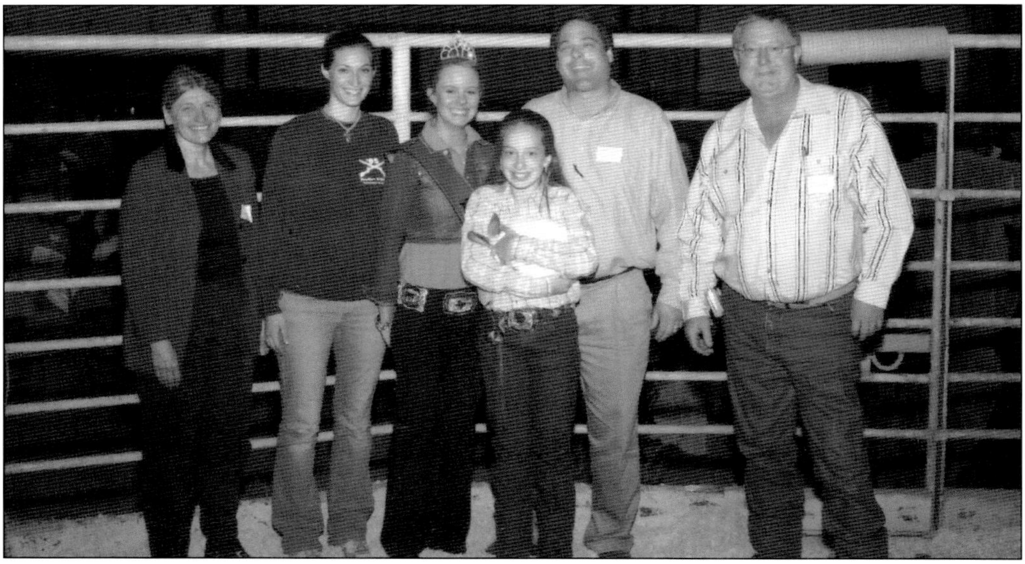

About 50 years later, the Robertson County Fair Association is probably the largest independently owned fair association with fairgrounds in Texas. The fairgrounds are currently located northwest of Hearne on part of the Camp Hearne acreage. In this photograph, the *Robertson County News* staff celebrates with 2008 Grand Champion rabbit grower Kalyn Pacely, holding her rabbit for the last time, following the fair auction. (Courtesy of *Robertson County News*.)

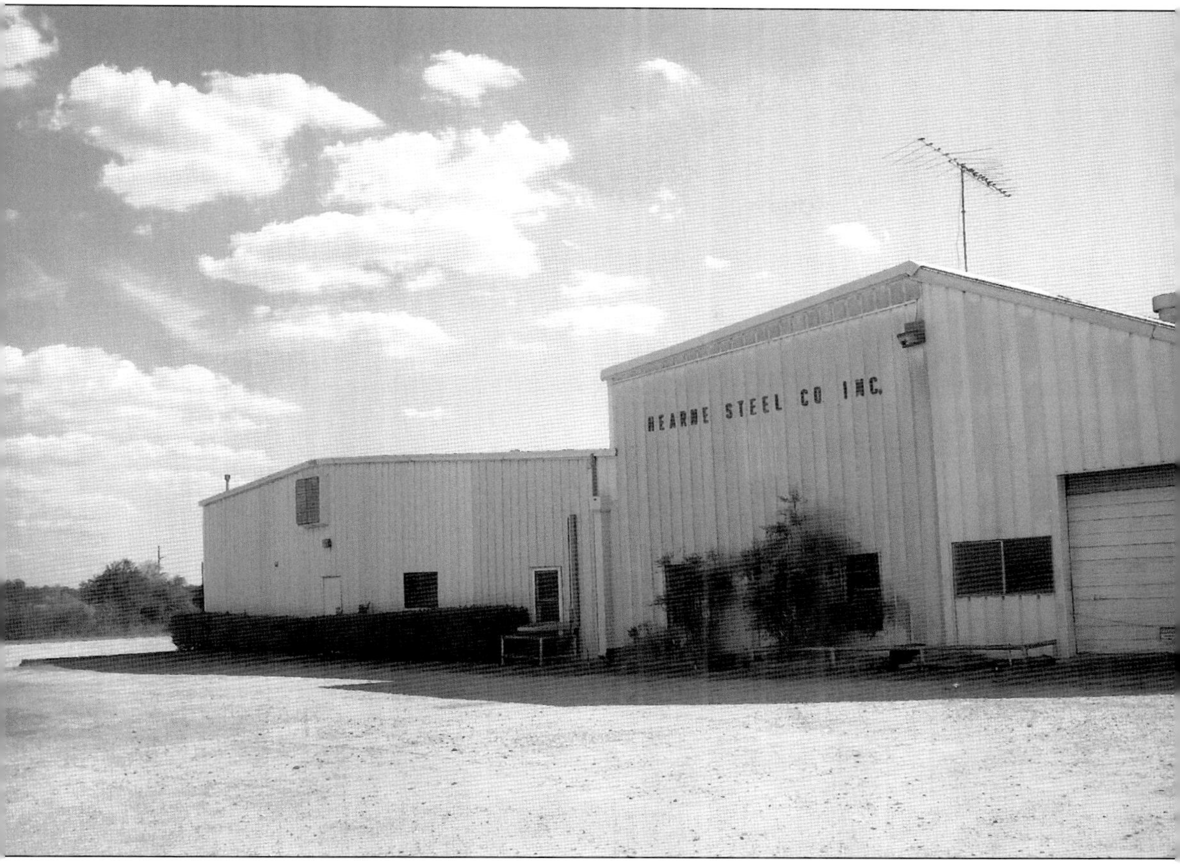

Hearne Steel Co., another bedrock of Hearne's economy, opened in 1959 and expanded in 1969. Created by the Amos family to manufacture steel and cast-iron fence parts invented by Cannon Amos, the company has one of Hearne's few remaining industrial plants and still employees over 50 people to manufacture its unique products. (Courtesy of author.)

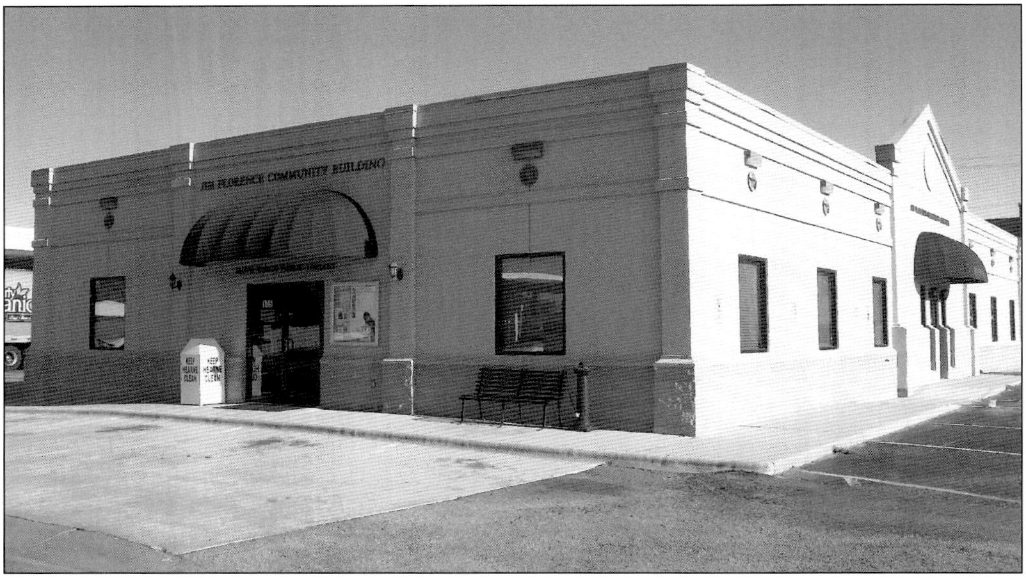

Hearne's small library expanded into the Smith-Welch Memorial Library in the late 1960s, in part as a result of large donations made by Mrs. Josie Welch, honored for the endowment bearing her name in this 1976 newspaper photograph. Today, the Smith-Welch Library offers more books and services than any other library in Robertson County, according to the state of Texas's library governing board. (Above, courtesy of author; below, courtesy of *Robertson County News*.)

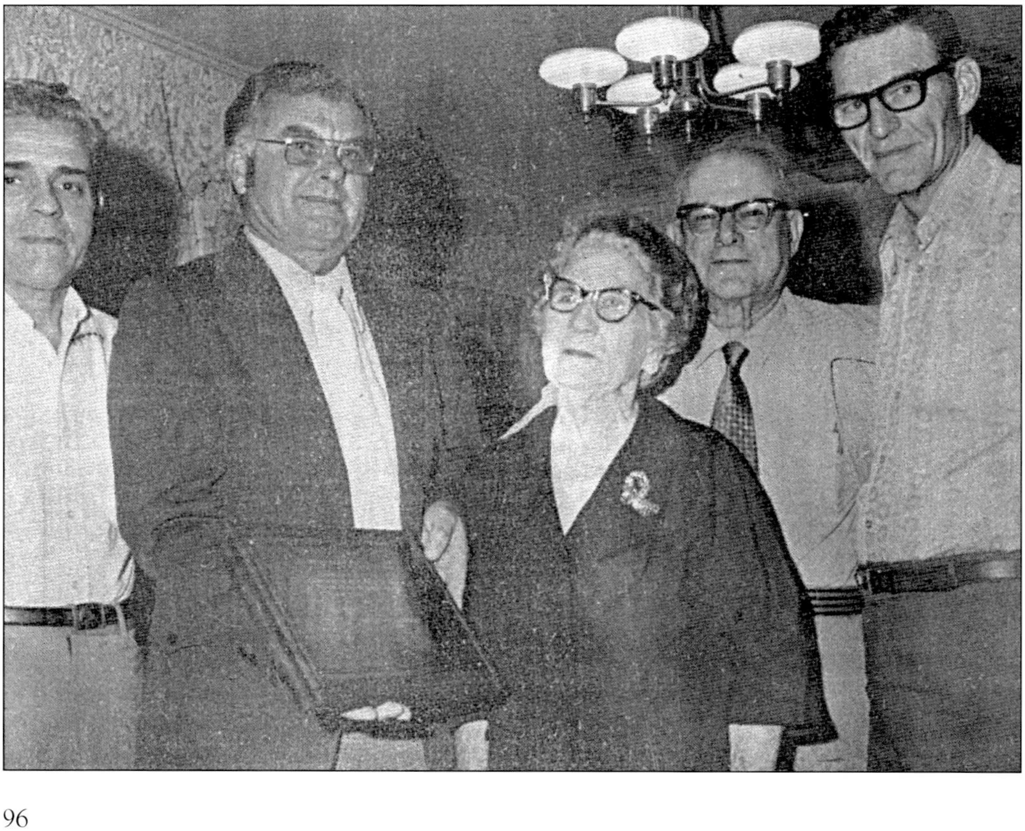

But as two-and-a-half decades of good news neared its close, tragedy struck. In July 1968, Sam Degelia Jr. (right), a Hearne grain dealer and the son of a successful Brazos River Bottoms farmer, was murdered by contract killer Charles Harrelson (seen below), father of actor Woody Harrelson. Later, Charles would go on to kill federal judge John Wood and even claim to be the second gunman in the John F. Kennedy assassination. (Courtesy of Cindy Wallace)

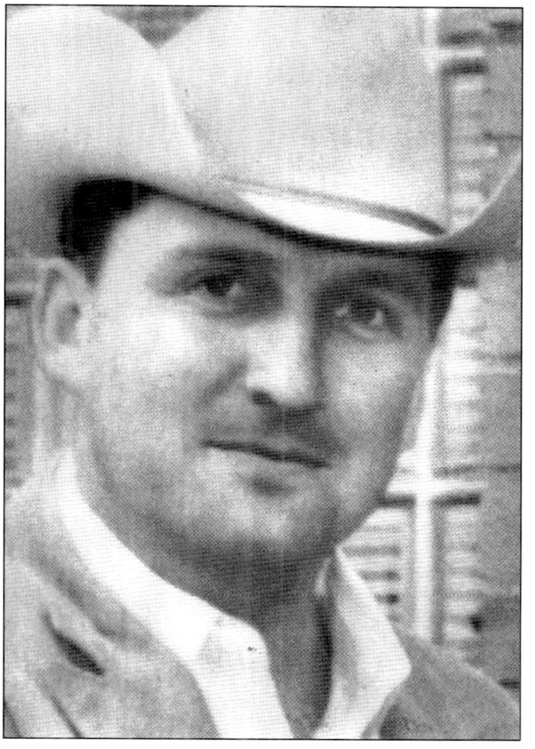

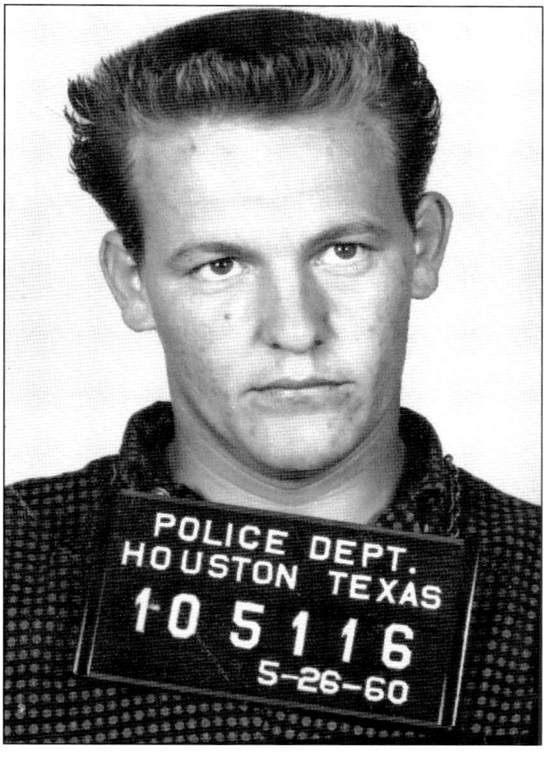

Trial testimony revealed that Pete Scamardo, Degelia's business partner, had hired Harrelson for the hit to collect on a $50,000 insurance policy. Harrelson lured Degelia to an abandoned shack near McAllen, Texas, and killed him. The first trial in which famed attorney Percy Foreman defended both Harrelson and Scamardo ended in a mistrial, but a second, called after a witness admitted to lying to cover for Harrelson, resulted in convictions. Scamardo was freed on probation; Harrelson served only five years in the Texas prison system. (Courtesy of Houston Police Department.)

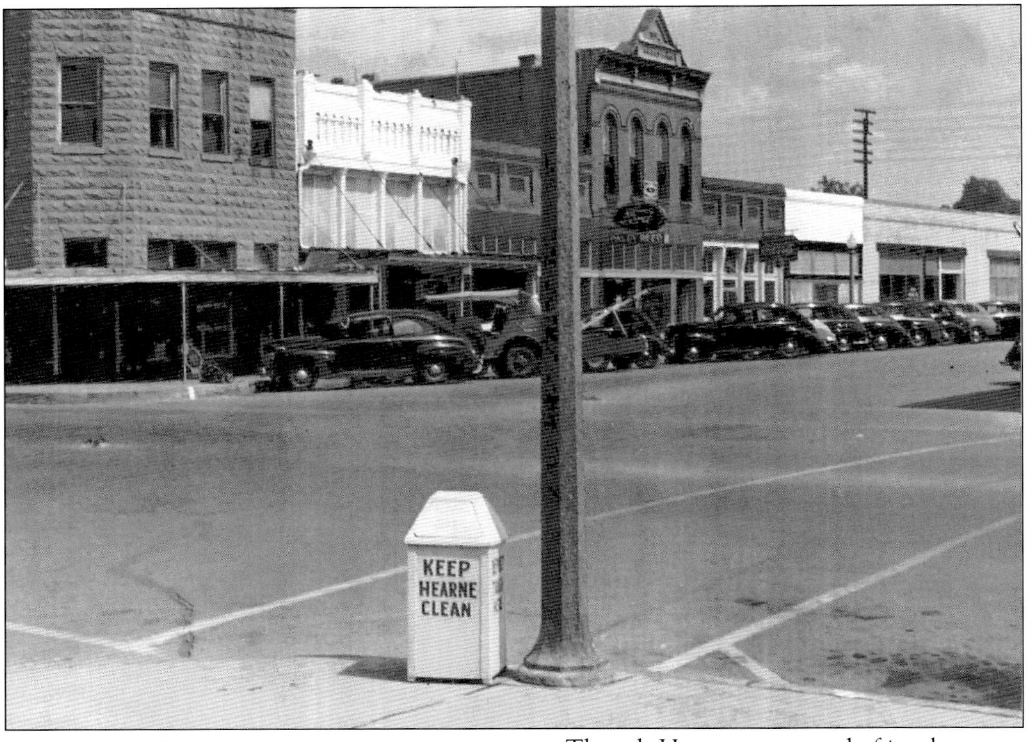

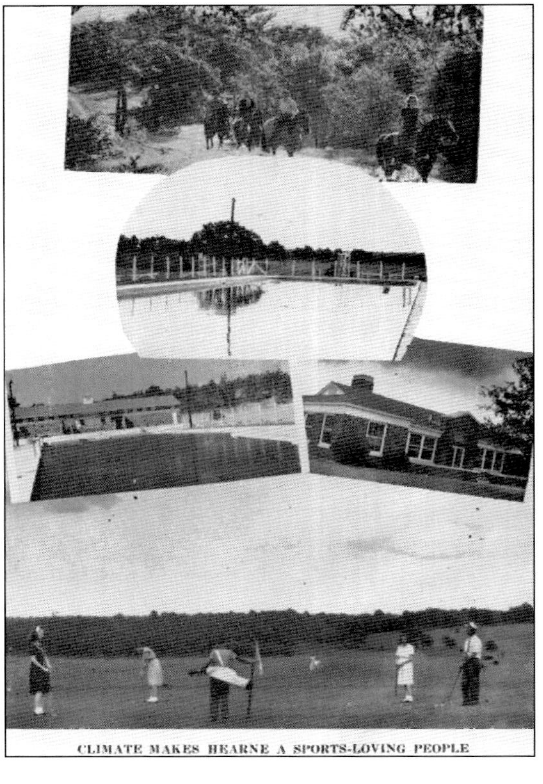

Though Hearne was proud of its clean streets, its parks, and the broad industrial base it hoped to expand, a brutal murder and rumors of corruption in city government seemed to compromise the message on its streets and in brochures touting the joys of living in Hearne. In the early 1970s, news was breaking that Hearne city officials were using their status to get additional perks—like free electricity at home. With utility costs rising, residents were not pleased. (Above, courtesy of Hearne Chamber of Commerce; left, courtesy of the City of Hearne.)

Seven

Hard Times Come to Hearne

By 1970, Hearne's population had grown to more than 5,100, its industries were booming, and the seeds of its near destruction were germinating. The next four decades would be marked by turmoil, economic decline, and courageous redefinition.

The 1970s saw federally mandated desegregation bitterly fought by Hearne's all-white school board. Bitterness in the African American community over the board's stiff resistance continues today.

Hearne was also the focus of two major legal battles: *Hearne Independent School District v. Mumford Independent School District* and *Kelly v. Paschall*, the second becoming the subject of the motion picture *American Violet*.

The slow unraveling of Hearne's economic base began as the Southern Pacific Railroad (the old H&TC) closed—one by one—its Hearne operations. So much of what had made Hearne—yard, depot, icing rack, roundhouse, and train crews—slipped away in the 1970s. Union Pacific eventually bought out both the Southern Railway and the Missouri Pacific Railroad in the late 1980s, claiming both north-south and east-west lines. It maintains an office with a few, not hundreds, of employees.

Nonetheless, Hearne's industrial base continued to be strong throughout the 1980s and 1990s with Crane Plumbing, GATX, Lifetime Doors, Stark Truss, Hearne Steel, and Wichita Metals employing hundreds. But with the decline in construction in the mid- to late 2000s, industries, beginning with Crane—Hearne's largest employer—closed, leaving workers to either relocate or look for work outside Hearne. Only GATX, Hearne Steel, and Wichita Metals remain.

On New Year's Eve 1990, the Hearne WalMart—one of a handful of WalMarts in the nation operating at a loss—closed. Unfortunately, many of Hearne's traditional downtown businesses had already closed, unable to compete with WalMart. Hearne's retail base was decimated.

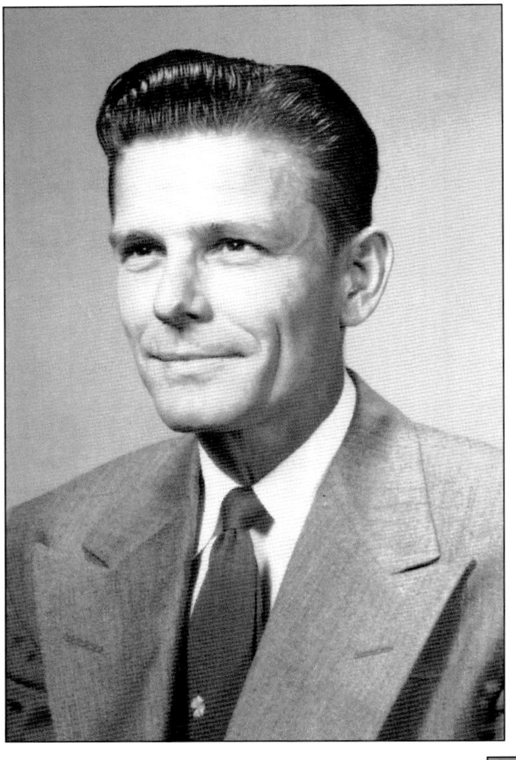

The 1970s began with shock, fear, and sorrow when in May 1972, former city councilman H.C. "Jack" Kelly (left), Hearne's banker, was brutally murdered along with his wife, Reo, and pregnant daughter Nancy Stovall. Lee Jurode, a former Hearne resident then living in Albuquerque, New Mexico, convinced John Edwardo Swift to come to Hearne with him to rob the Planters & Merchants Bank. Jurode, Swift, and Robert Duron came to Kelly's home on May 17, and when they could not convince Kelly to open the bank vault—it was set to a timer—they murdered Kelly and his family. The group fled to Oklahoma City, and after Swift murdered Duron, Swift's girlfriend Jo Ann Adams and Jurode confessed to police, fearing Swift would kill them next. District Attorney Bryan Russ (below) prosecuted the case on a change of venue in Waco. Later, Swift unsuccessfully appealed the case on the basis of racial discrimination, stating in part that no African American had ever served on a Robertson County Grand Jury. Russ admitted that to his knowledge, none had. (Both, courtesy of City of Hearne.)

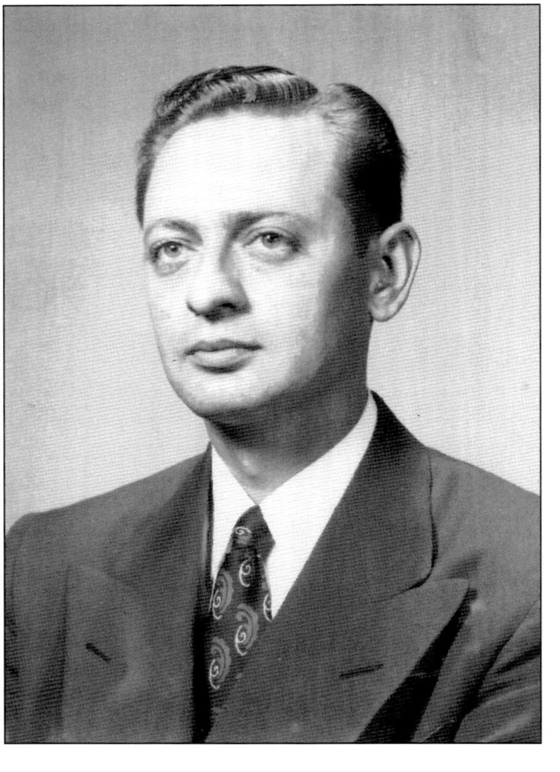

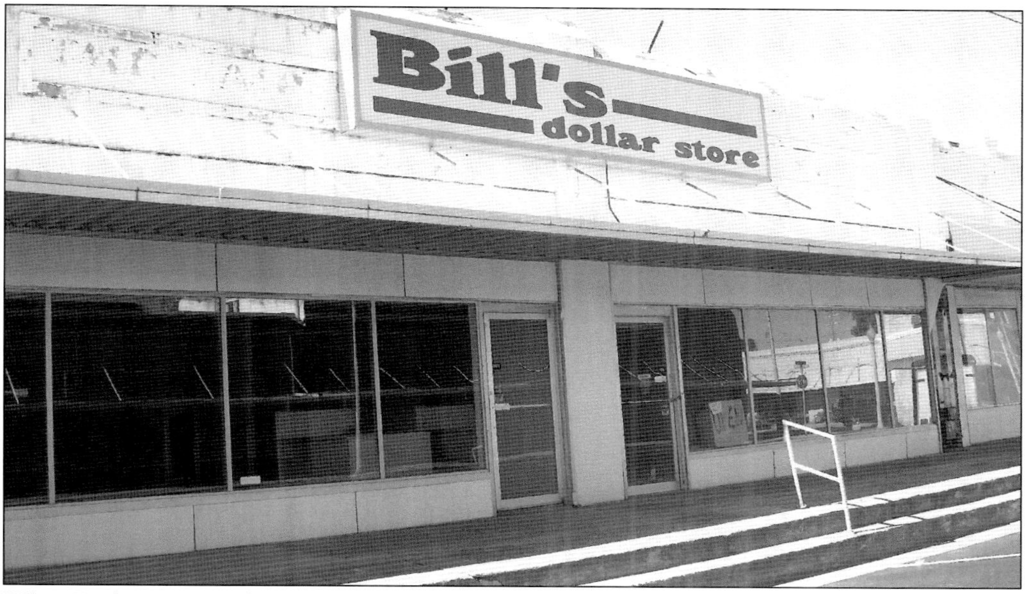

When WalMart opened a store in Hearne in 1980, residents were excited to have such a mammoth shopping venue, but within a very short period of time, Hearne's downtown stores, historically the source of its retail strength, folded. Bill's Dollar Store, K Woolens, Wilson's (clothing, not pharmacy), J.B. White's, and Perry's closed in rapid succession. And 10 years later, WalMart, one of Hearne's three largest employers, closed. It was rumored that employee theft was responsible for its failure to profit. News of the event was published in newspapers across the country, including the *New York Times*. Hearne would become the town where "you can't buy a dress or a pair of shoes." (Both, courtesy of author.)

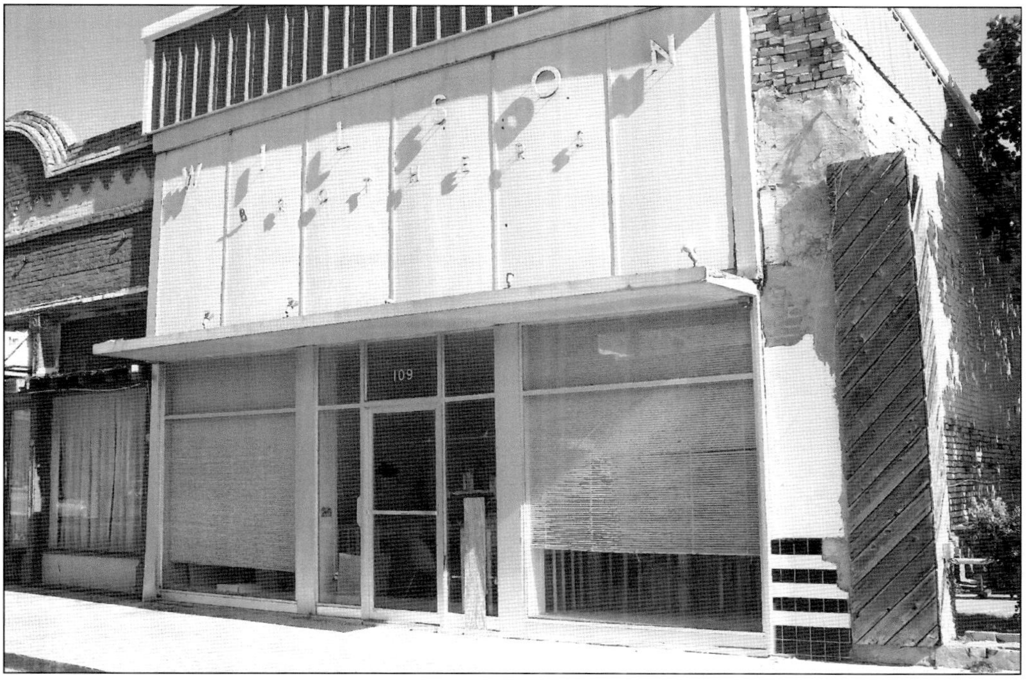

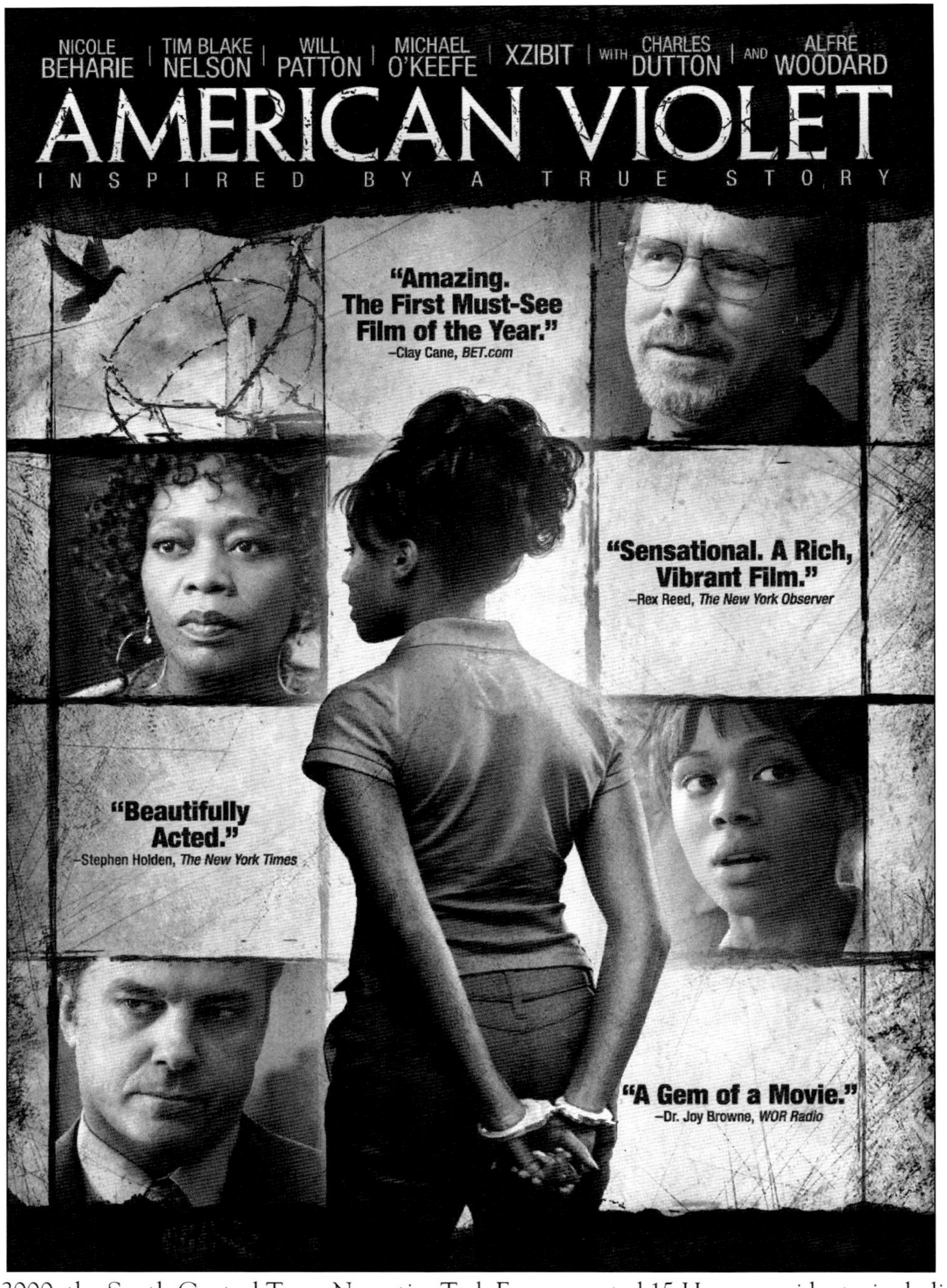

In 2000, the South Central Texas Narcotics Task Force arrested 15 Hearne residents, including Regina Kelly, on drug charges. With the aid of the American Civil Liberties Union (ACLU), Kelly fought back. Charges were promptly dropped when the testimony of the single witness was discredited. A civil suit, *Kelly v. John Paschall* (Robertson County district attorney), was settled out of court with payments to Kelly and others. The Texas Legislature disbanded the task forces as a result of this and a similar case in Tulia, Texas. The movie *American Violet* dramatized Kelly's story. (Courtesy of Uncommon Productions.)

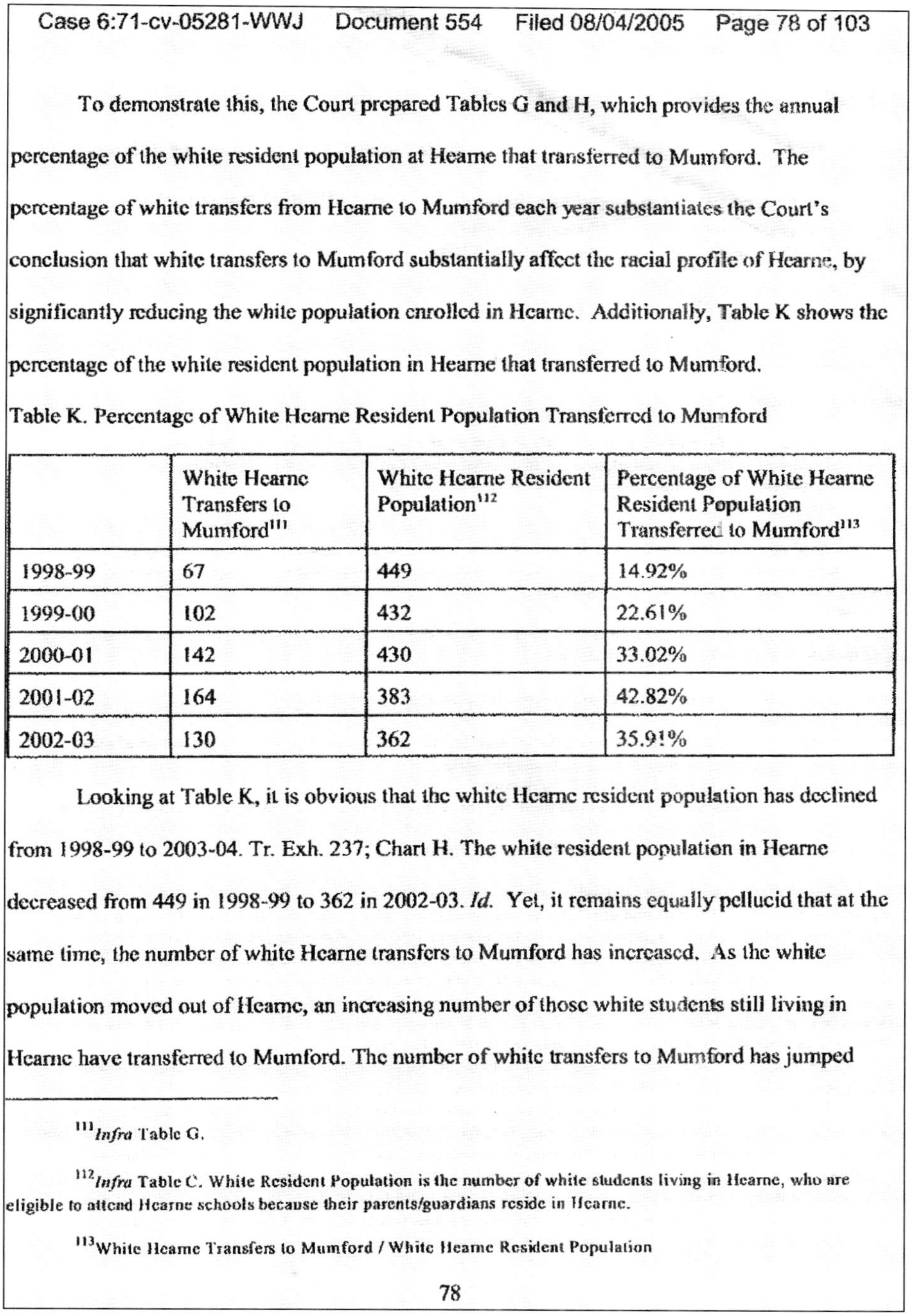
Case 6:71-cv-05281-WWJ Document 554 Filed 08/04/2005 Page 78 of 103

To demonstrate this, the Court prepared Tables G and H, which provides the annual percentage of the white resident population at Hearne that transferred to Mumford. The percentage of white transfers from Hearne to Mumford each year substantiates the Court's conclusion that white transfers to Mumford substantially affect the racial profile of Hearne, by significantly reducing the white population enrolled in Hearne. Additionally, Table K shows the percentage of the white resident population in Hearne that transferred to Mumford.

Table K. Percentage of White Hearne Resident Population Transferred to Mumford

	White Hearne Transfers to Mumford[111]	White Hearne Resident Population[112]	Percentage of White Hearne Resident Population Transferred to Mumford[113]
1998-99	67	449	14.92%
1999-00	102	432	22.61%
2000-01	142	430	33.02%
2001-02	164	383	42.82%
2002-03	130	362	35.91%

Looking at Table K, it is obvious that the white Hearne resident population has declined from 1998-99 to 2003-04. Tr. Exh. 237; Chart H. The white resident population in Hearne decreased from 449 in 1998-99 to 362 in 2002-03. *Id.* Yet, it remains equally pellucid that at the same time, the number of white Hearne transfers to Mumford has increased. As the white population moved out of Hearne, an increasing number of those white students still living in Hearne have transferred to Mumford. The number of white transfers to Mumford has jumped

[111] *Infra* Table G.

[112] *Infra* Table C. White Resident Population is the number of white students living in Hearne, who are eligible to attend Hearne schools because their parents/guardians reside in Hearne.

[113] White Hearne Transfers to Mumford / White Hearne Resident Population

78

In 2002, Hearne ISD sued Mumford ISD to regain many of its white and Hispanic students. Mumford ISD had been accepting Hearne youngsters on parents' claims that their children were "endangered." Judge William Wayne Justice, responsible for desegregating Texas schools, returned to the bench to rule in favor of Hearne with the table pictured serving as evidence. Mumford appealed to the US Court of Appeals, 5th Circuit, which overturned the ruling, contributing to the end of federal desegregation efforts in Texas. (Courtesy of author.)

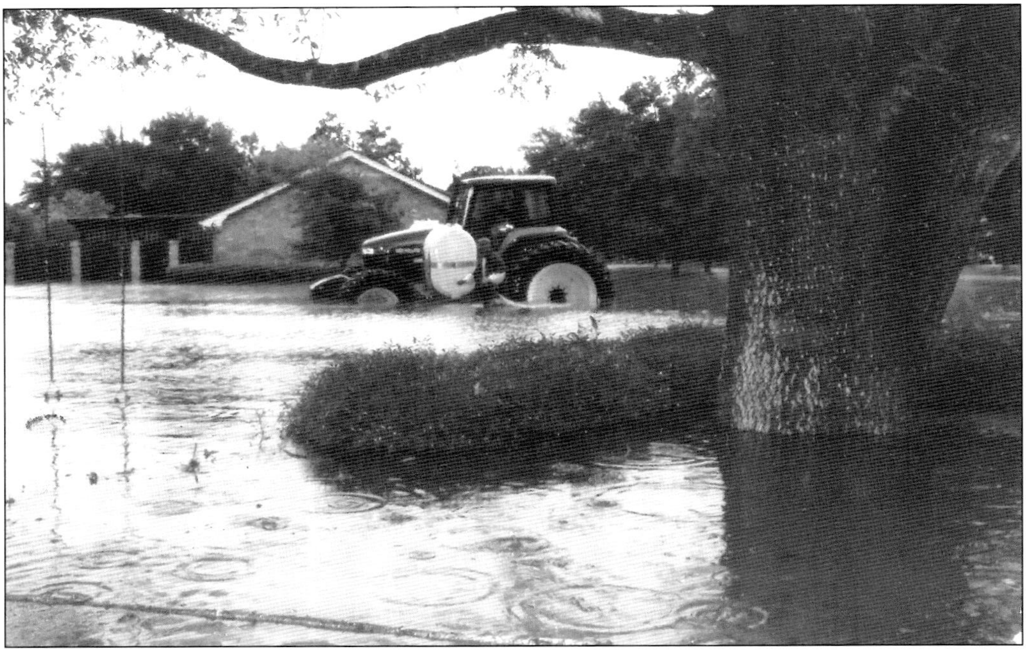

In May 2004, floodwaters not only ravaged the Brazos River Bottoms but also damaged large parts of Hearne—particularly the south side near Lost Creek. After about 18 inches of rain fell in nine hours, Lost Creek (which was filled with debris and blocked by a low-lying bridge) and the Little Brazos River overflowed their banks. (Both, courtesy of Rev. Larry Blackmon.)

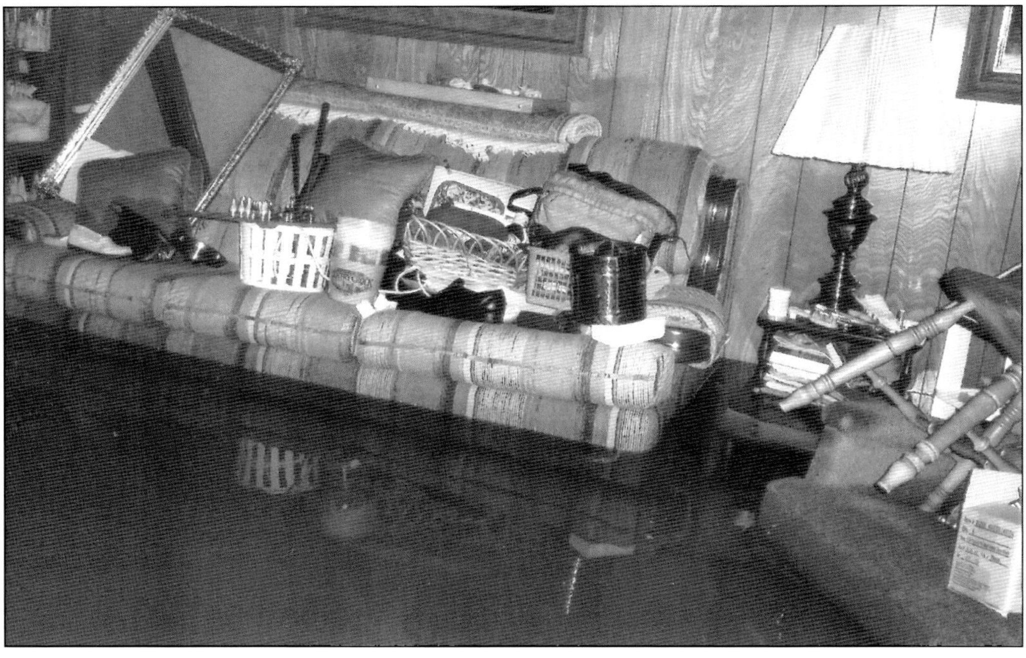

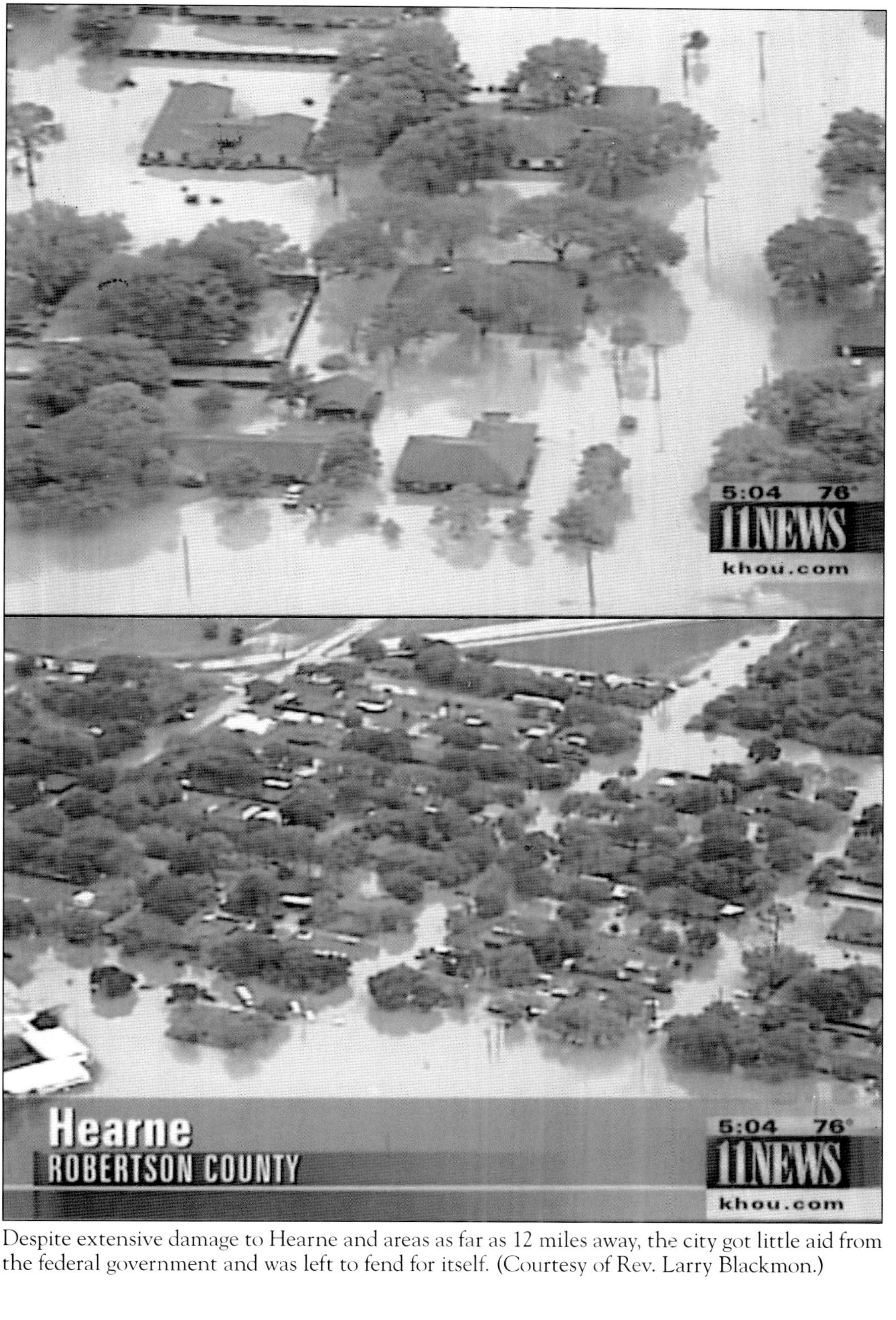

Despite extensive damage to Hearne and areas as far as 12 miles away, the city got little aid from the federal government and was left to fend for itself. (Courtesy of Rev. Larry Blackmon.)

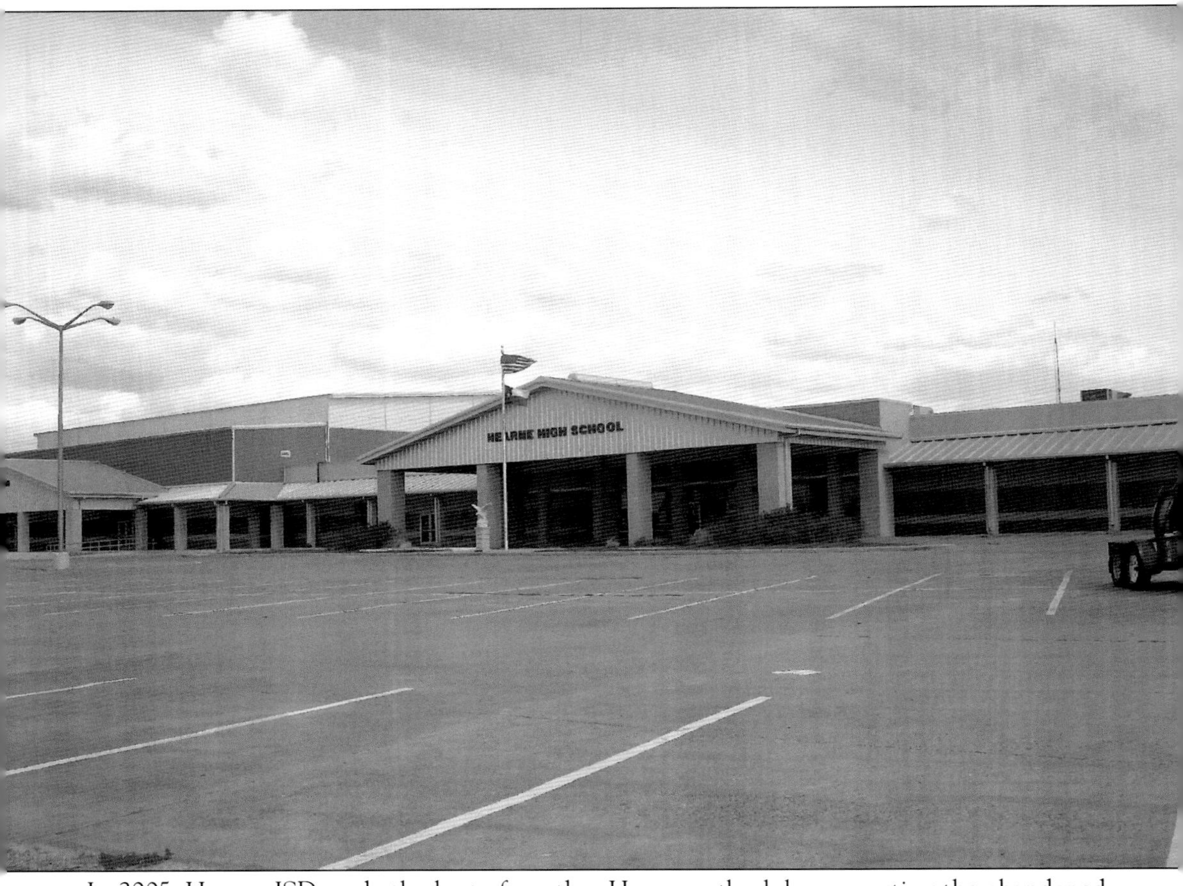

In 2005, Hearne ISD made the best of another Hearne setback by converting the abandoned WalMart into the new Hearne High School. The previous high school had been damaged by the flood. By turning one of its major sources of embarrassment into an attractive, state-of-the-art facility, Hearne demonstrated a spirit that probably accounts, more than anything else, for its survival. (Courtesy of author.)

Eight

Hearne Today

With the collapse of its industrial base and with its retail sector still in decline, Hearne is recreating itself for the fourth time. Cotton, though still grown and transported, is no longer king. Union Pacific, though still operating in Hearne, no longer hires hundreds of employees. Hearne industry has been reduced to three companies left standing: GATX, Hearne Steel, and Wichita Metals. Its retail base, though much stronger than it was in 1990 (one can buy a dress and a pair of shoes now), is still small enough that a majority of residents do most of their shopping in Bryan and College Station, 20 to 26 miles away.

Hearne, determined to survive, is finding some answers. The city sits on the busiest "small highway" in America, Texas Highway 6, which links Waco and the Bryan–College Station area with Houston. The highway and Hearne's proximity to Bryan and College Station, home of Texas A&M University, is helping to regrow the Hearne economy.

Brazos River Bottoms farmers—many with Italian last names—were hit by brutal drought conditions in 2010 and 2011, but most managed to hang on with heavy use of irrigation and better cash crops, like high-end soy beans (for baby formula) and corn (for ethanol).

Hearne is also stepping up to meet the county's medical needs. With five clinics, dental care, and a dialysis center, Hearne is becoming a medical mecca of sorts.

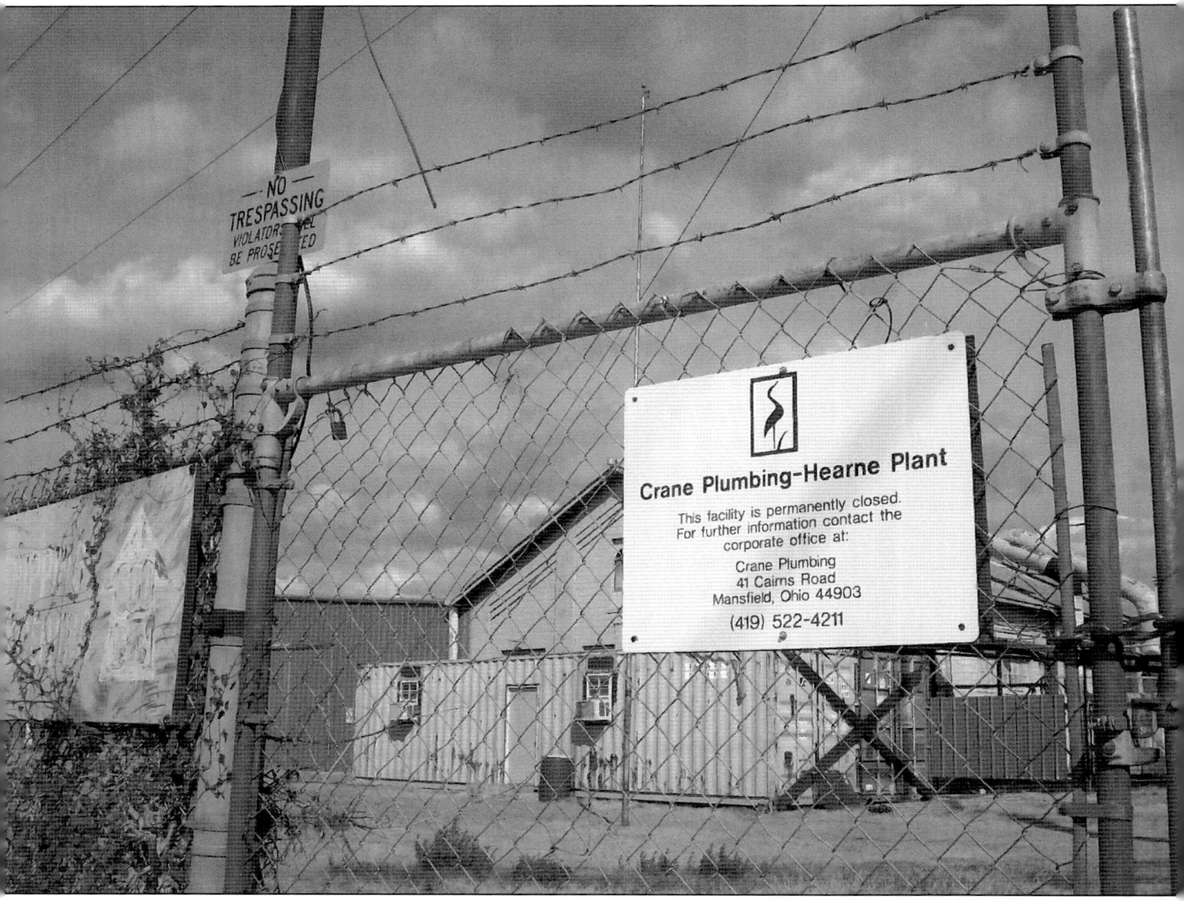

After Crane Plumbing closed its Hearne plant in December 2009, other construction-related companies followed. The Crane closing alone left about 100 workers without jobs. Abandoned industrial sites were making the Hearne landscape bleak. (Courtesy of author.)

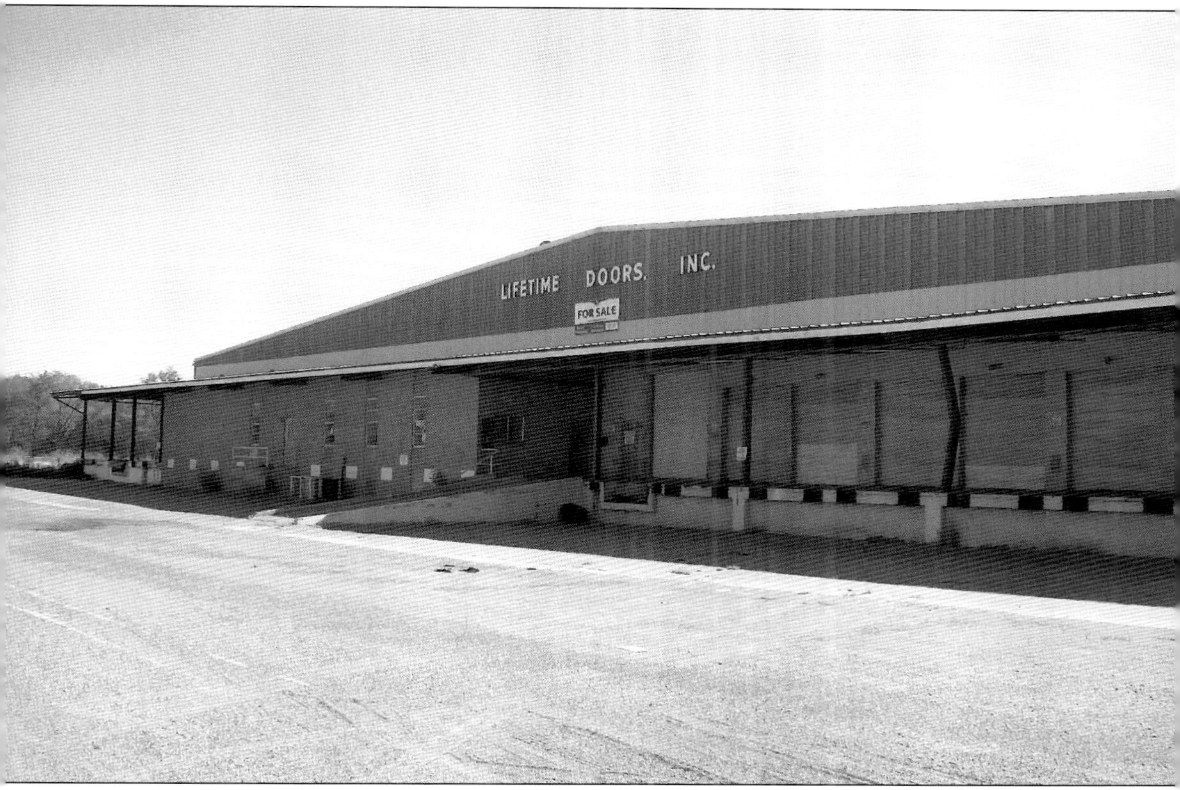

Hearne was hoping Lifetime Doors would last for the city's lifetime, but in 2010, it closed and hung the for-sale sign on the front of its construction plant. Lifetime Doors hired many people others would not, and for a generation of Hearne residents, this company and Stark Truss, which closed a few months before, represented a second chance. At one time, the two companies together had hired over 250 people. (Courtesy of author.)

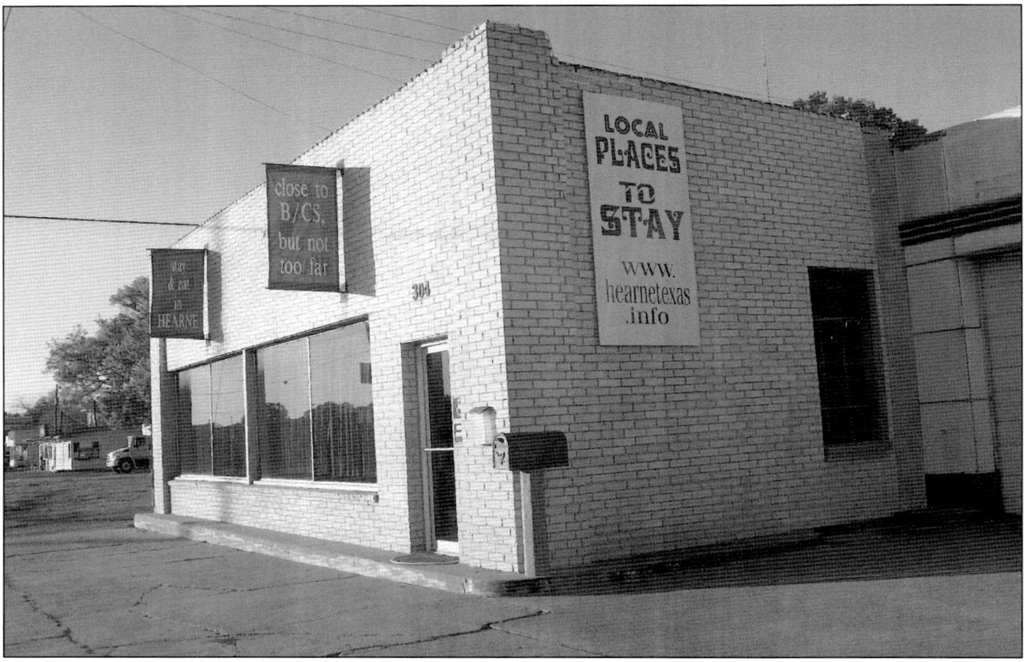

In response, the City of Hearne and its economic development office and chamber of commerce, now headed by Executive Director Kent Brunette, began focusing on two economic sectors to provide jobs and tax revenue: visitors and medicine. City Hall B is pictured above, and the Hearne Chamber of Commerce is pictured below. (Both, courtesy of author.)

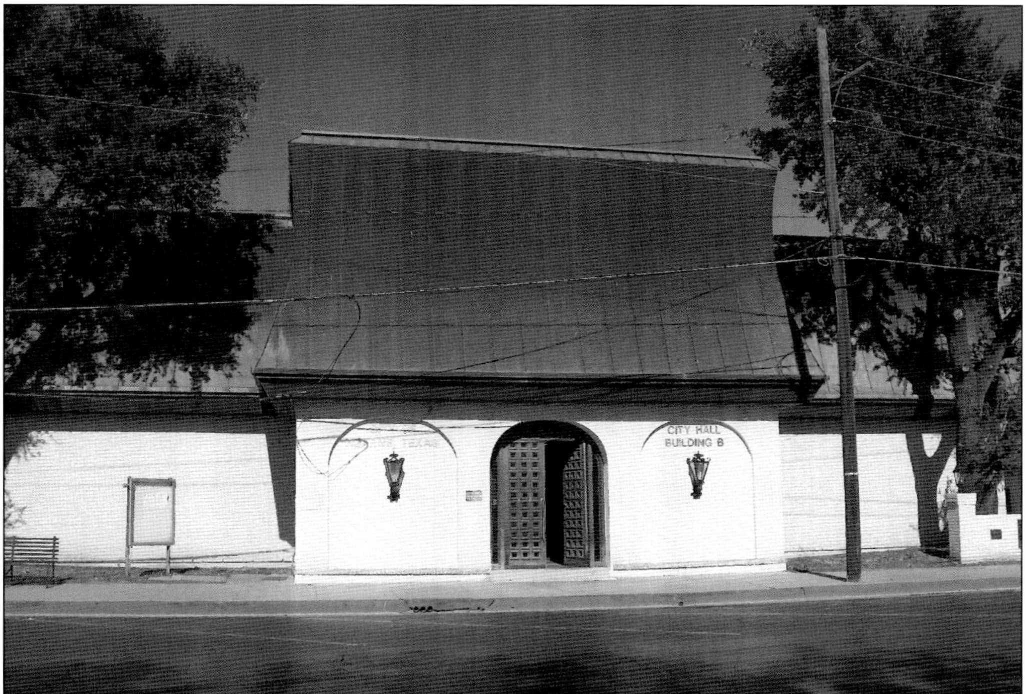

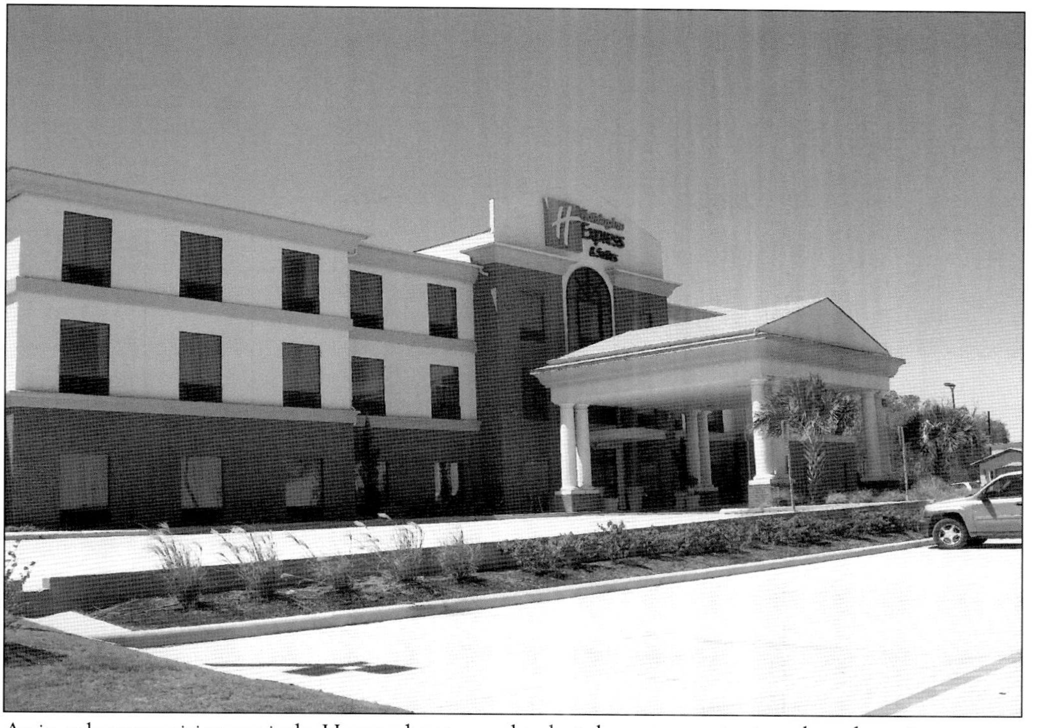

As in other transition periods, Hearne has turned to hotels, restaurants, travel, and tourism venues to bolster its economy. The Holiday Inn Express and the Budgetel Inn and Suites are examples of Hearne's new direction. The city has over 12 restaurants—most on Highway 6 or US Highway 79—to cater to diverse appetites. (Both, courtesy of author.)

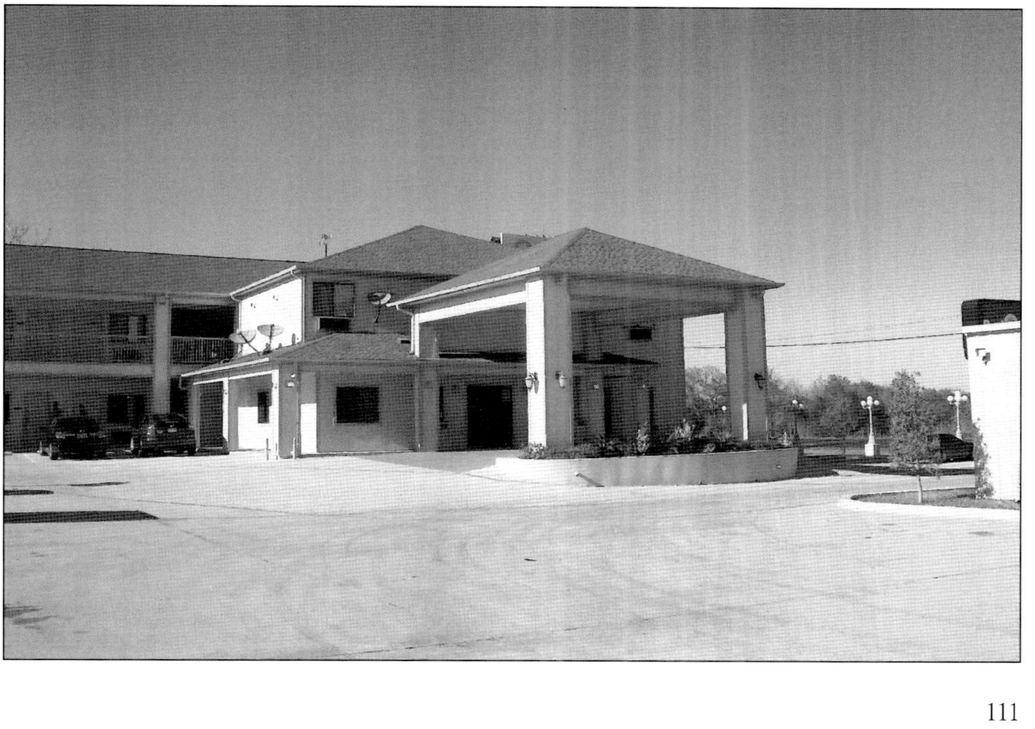

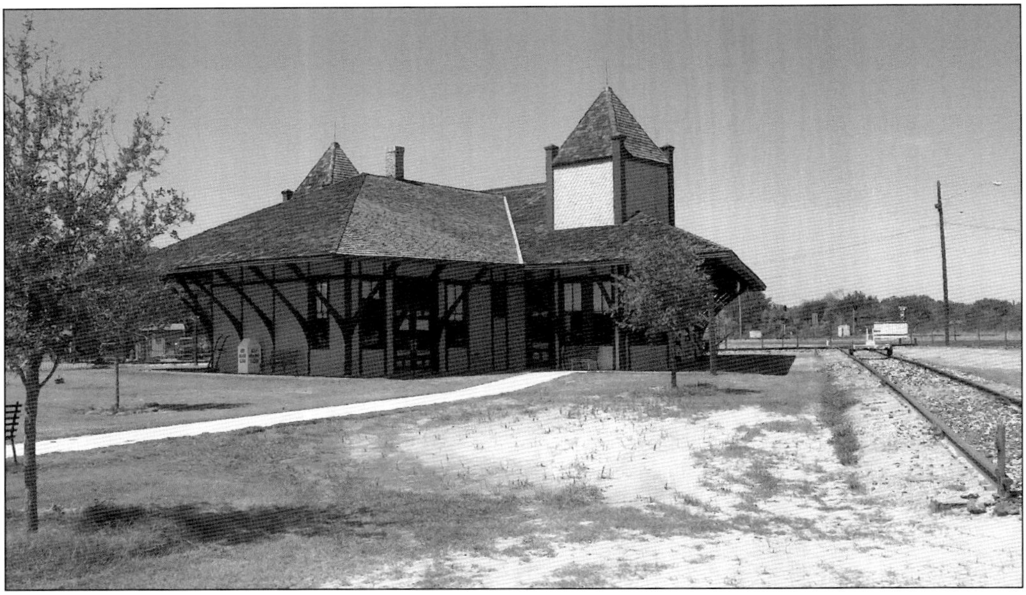

Thousands of visitors have toured the restored 1901 Hearne depot since it opened in April 2011. The depot, transformed into a train and city of Hearne historic museum, welcomed about 2,000 guests its first day and has seen about that many in the year following. Since the Hearne Heritage League originally conceived the plan to move the depot across the tracks, restore it, and transform it into a testimony to Hearne's railroading past, about 28 years passed. But when the city completed the task, the visitors came. (Both, courtesy of author.)

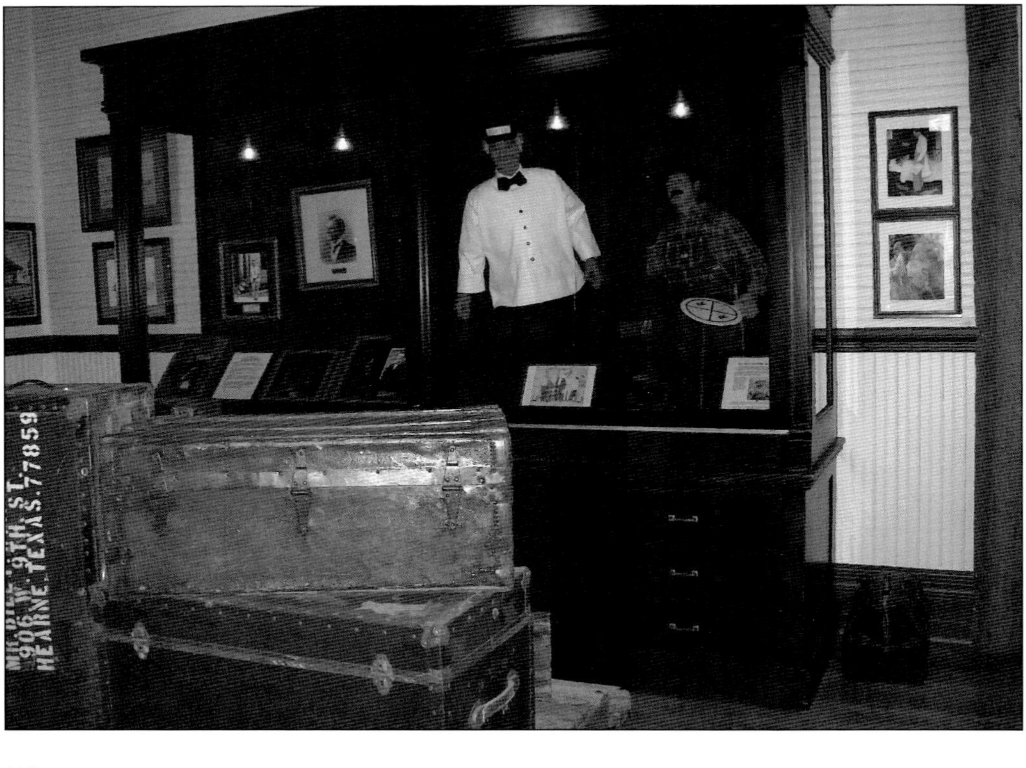

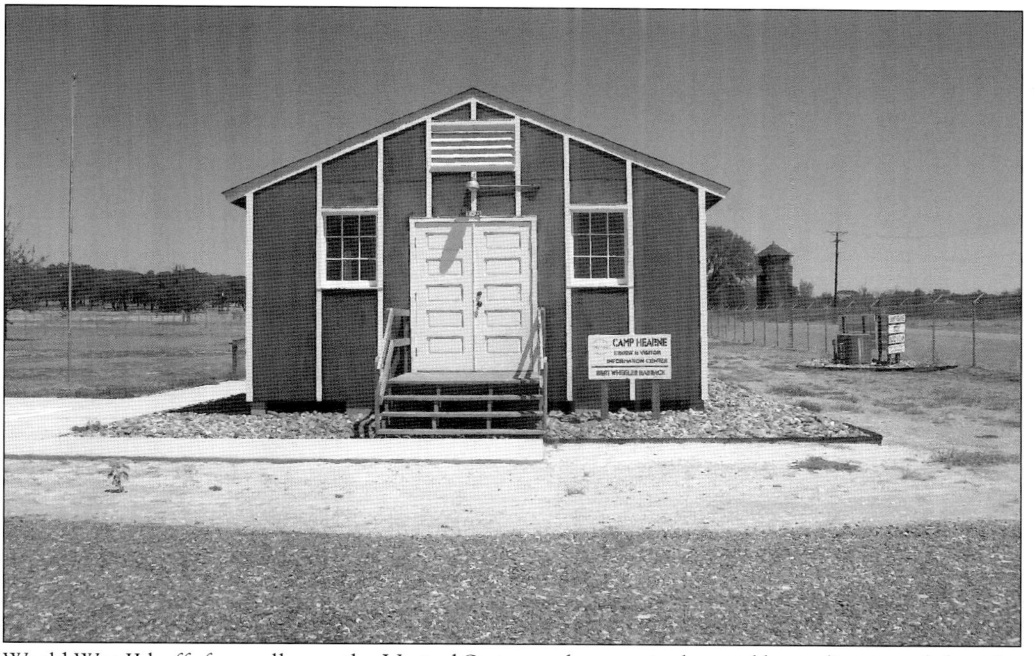

World War II buffs from all over the United States and countries beyond have discovered that the Camp Hearne Historical Site—its museum housed in a reconstructed World War II barrack—has a fascinating story to tell. The depot and Camp Hearne are within a mile-and-a-half of each other and close to Hearne's newest hotels, all on the north side of the city. (Both, courtesy of author.)

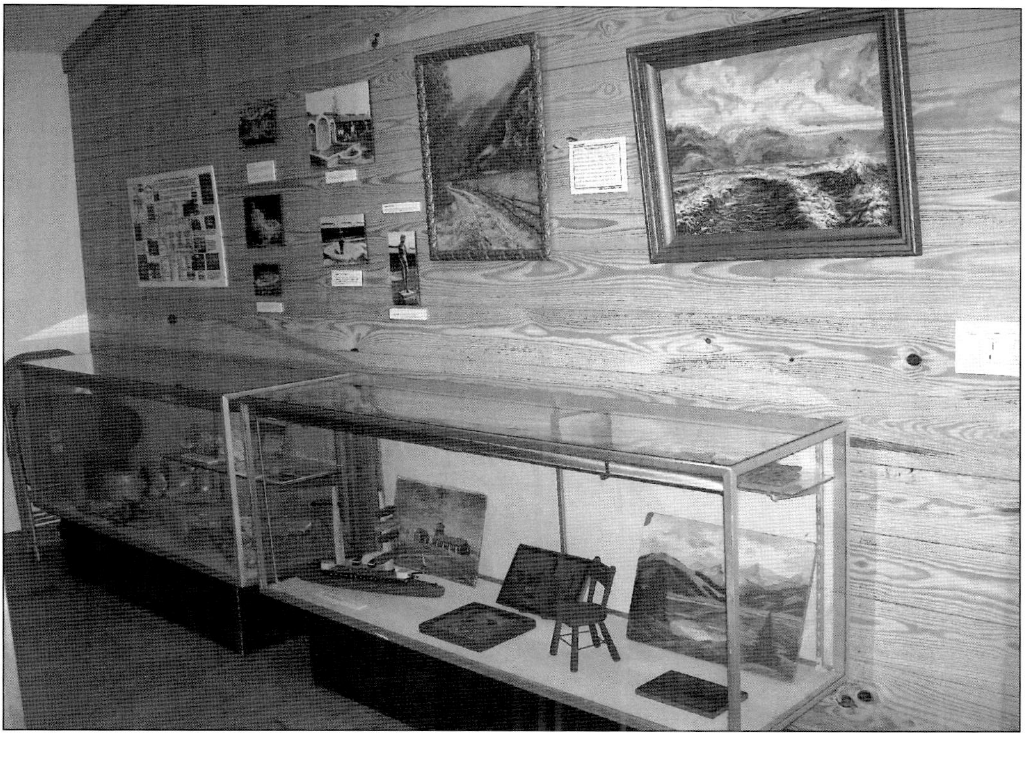

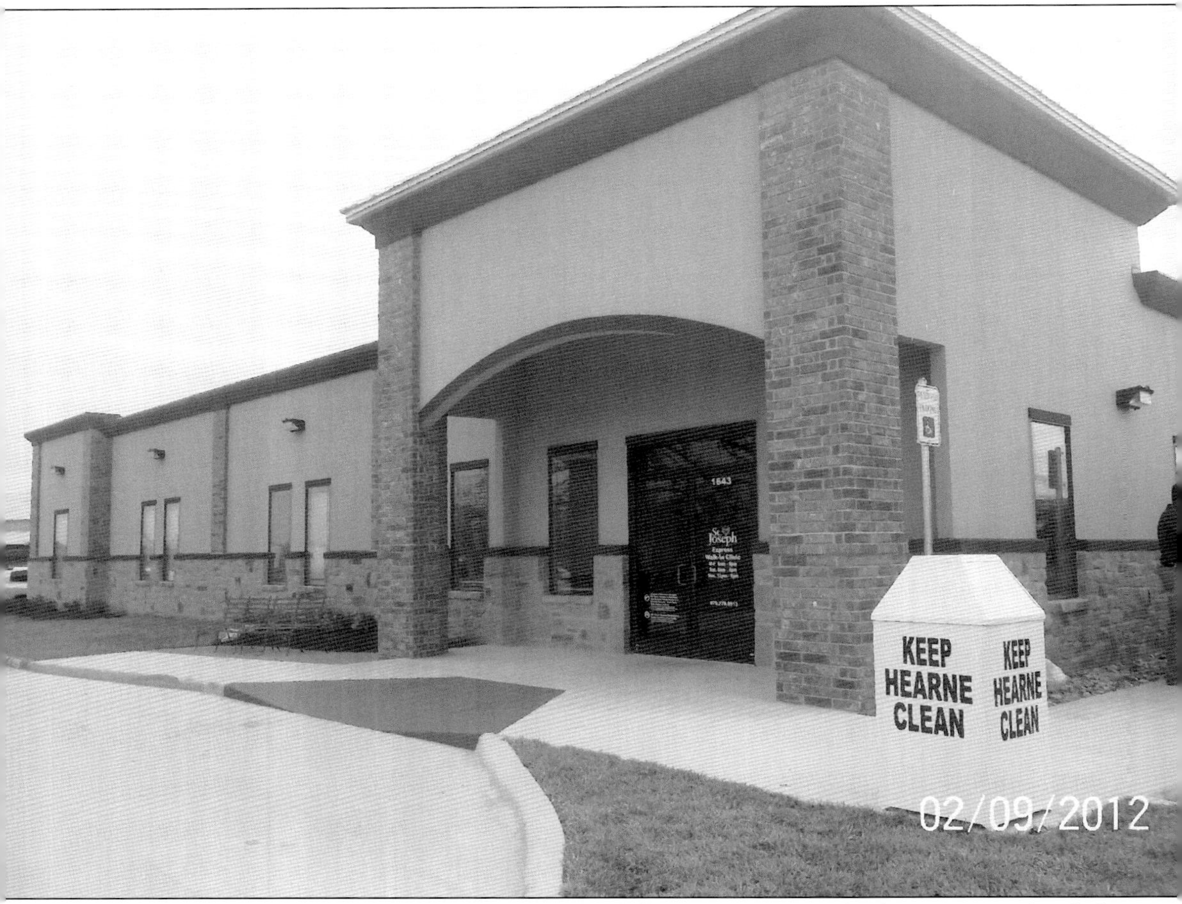

A second source of economic development and stability is Hearne's medical community, headed by the St. Joseph Regional Health Center. St. Joseph's, which has operated a clinic in Hearne for many years, opened a state-of-the-art express facility in January 2012. (Courtesy of author.)

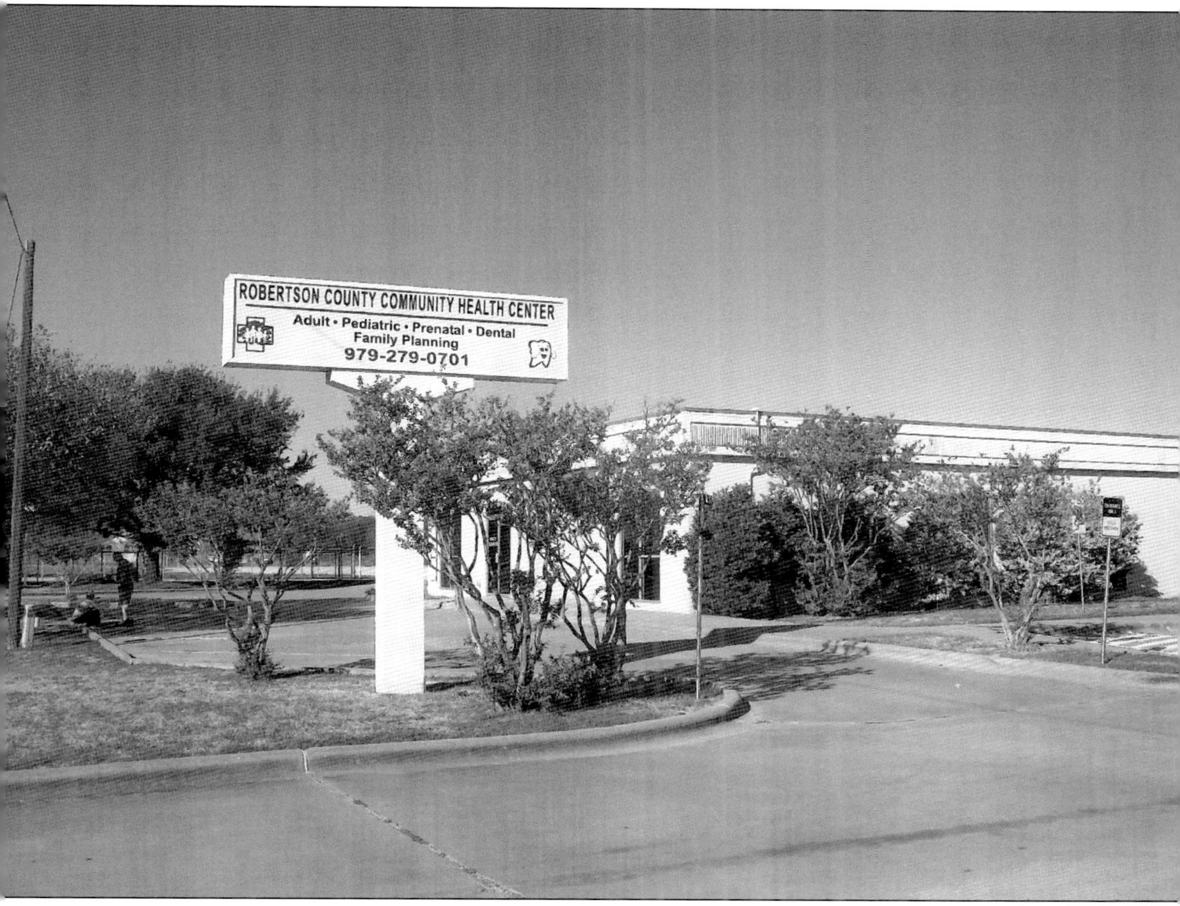

The Robertson County Community Health Center, Hearne Chiropractic, DaVita Dialysis Clinic, and the Varvel Dental Office complete Hearne's extensive health services. Though the Hearne hospital closed in the 1980s, smaller medical facilities have continued to broaden Hearne's medical services. (Courtesy of author.)

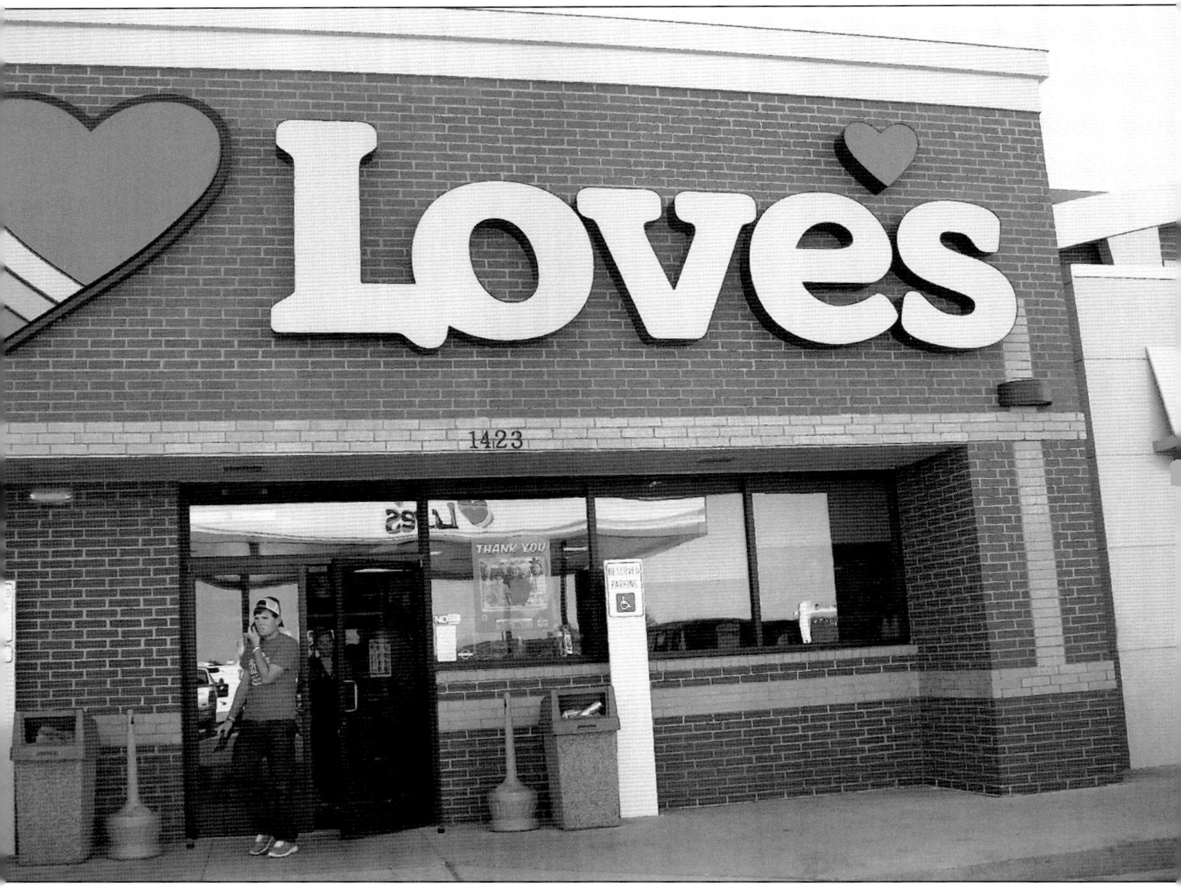

Stopping drive-by traffic to see a site, eat a meal, or rest in a modern hotel is a Hearne goal, now aided by a Love's Travel Center, which opened in 2011. For many years, Hearne has offered meals and accommodations to railroad crews; with Love's, the city is extending its hospitality to truckers and other road-weary travelers. (Courtesy of author.)

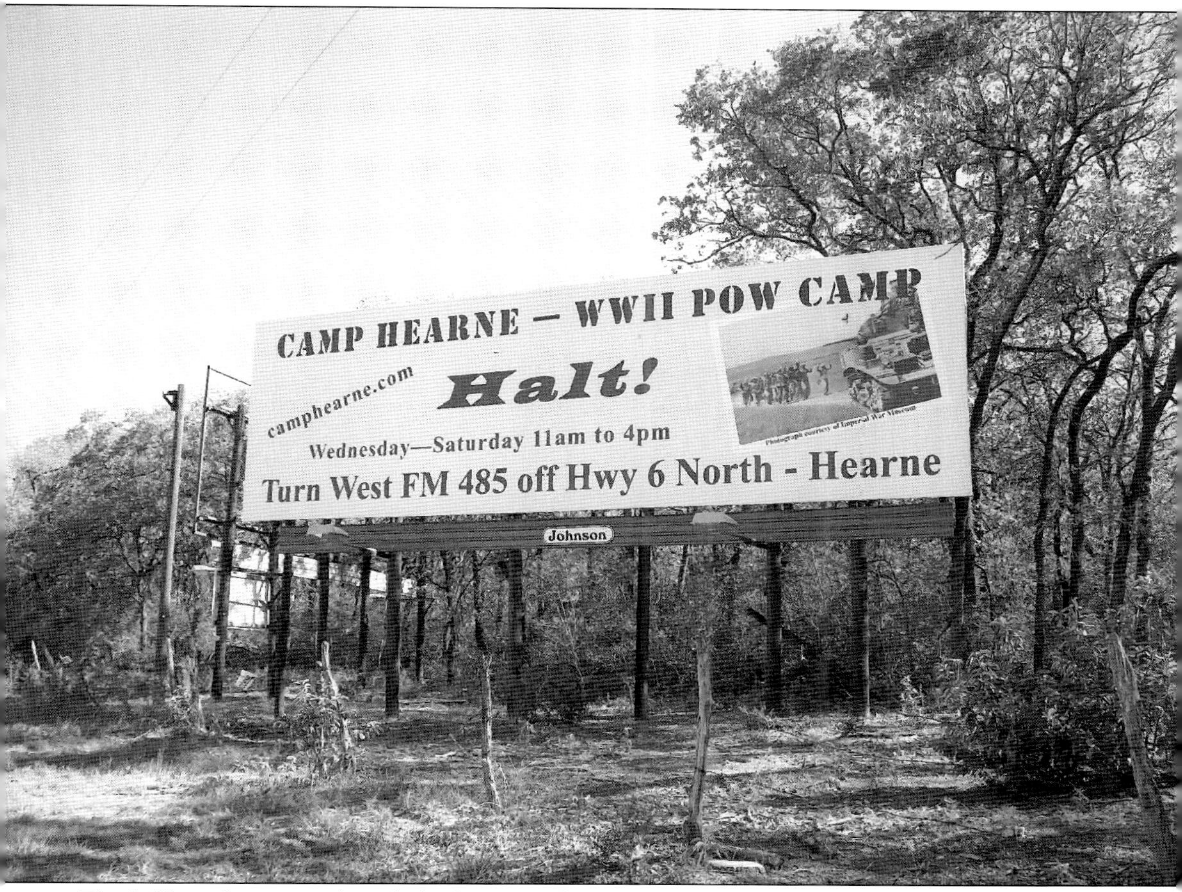

The billboard command to "halt" has actually attracted visitors on several occasions. Though primarily used to direct passing-through traffic to the Camp Hearne Museum and grounds, it also speaks to Hearne's desire to induce people to stop and stay awhile and to maybe eat lunch and visit the depot as well. (Courtesy of author.)

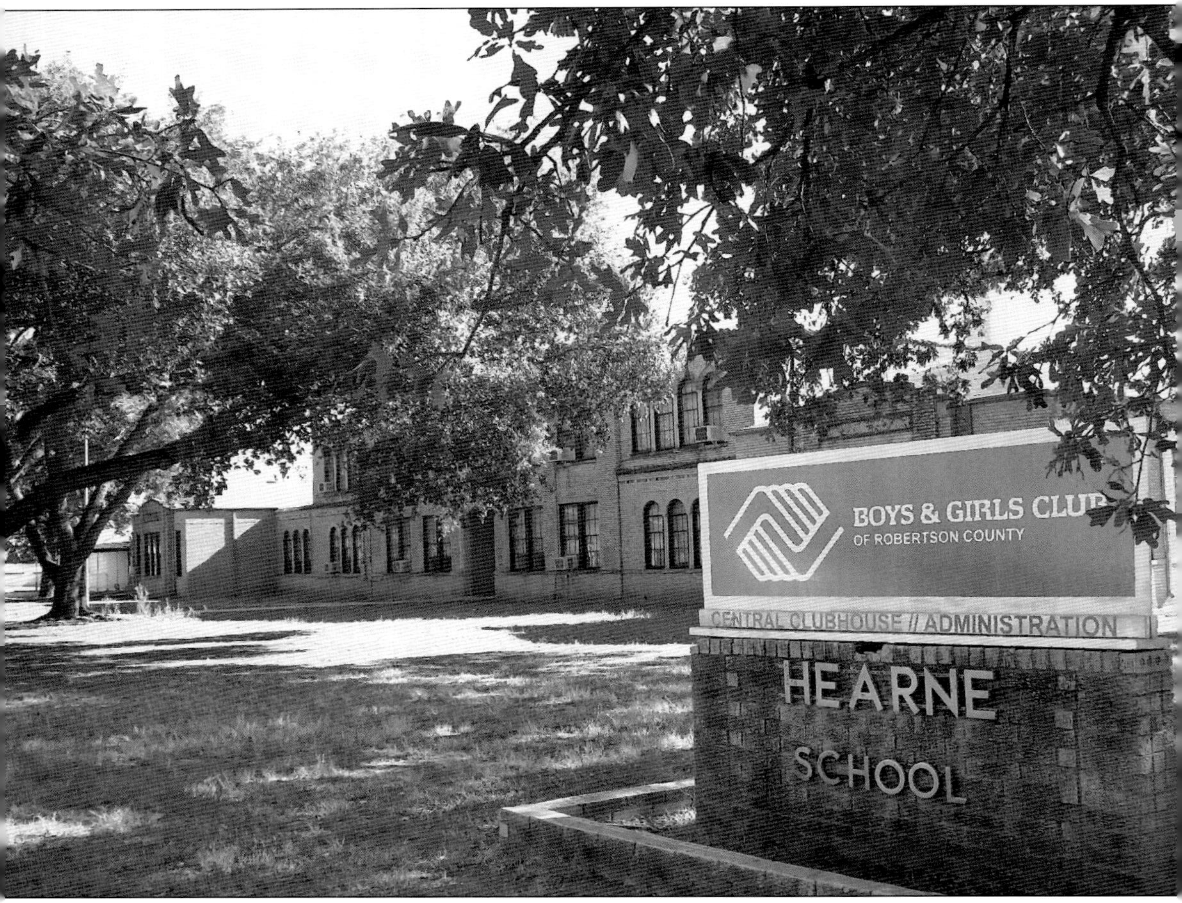

Another notable Hearne accomplishment is the opening of the Robertson County Boys & Girls Club (RCBGC). The RCBGC board worked diligently for over two years to raise more than $120,000—much of it from former and present Hearne residents—to open the club in January 2011 inside the 1930 Hearne High School building. The facility is accessible to all Robertson County children between the ages of 6 and 17. (Courtesy of author.)

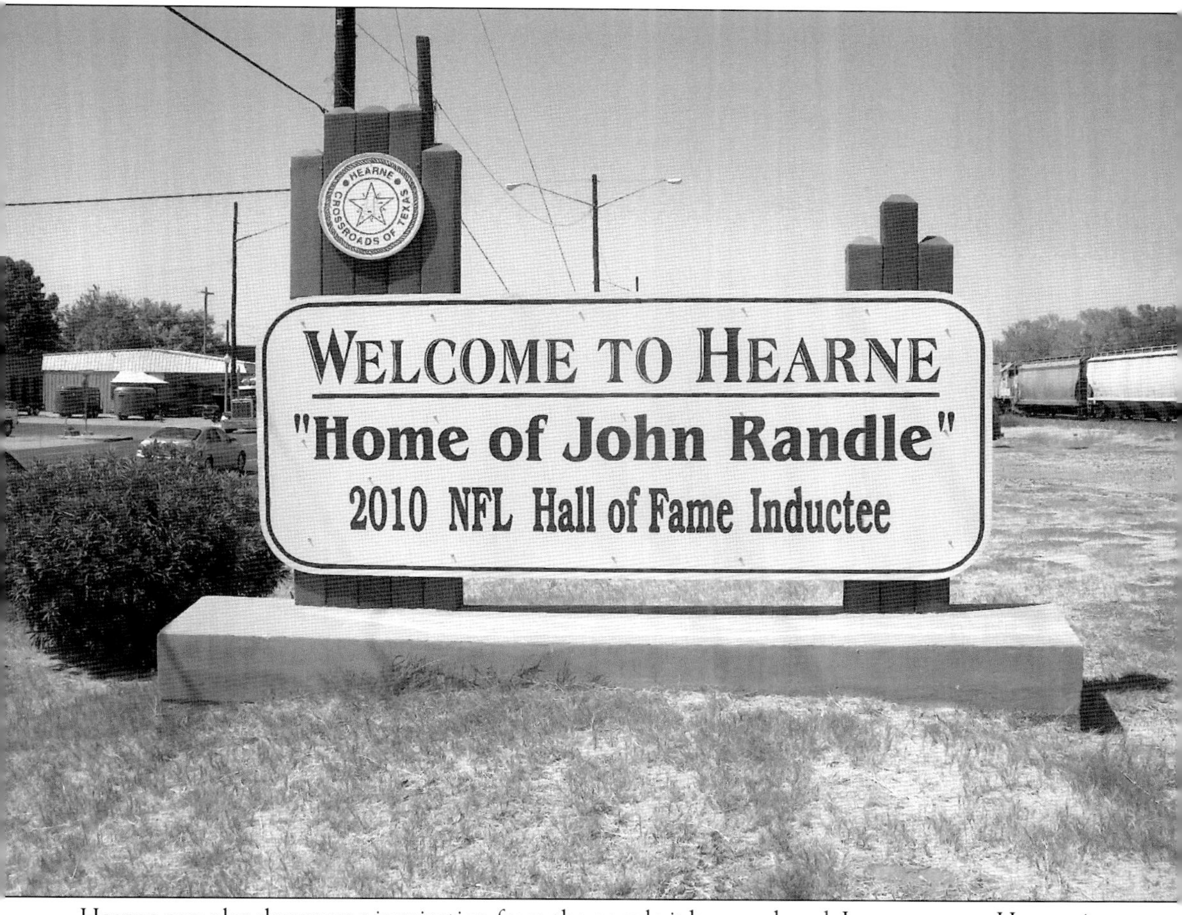

Hearne can also draw some inspiration from the people it has produced. In many ways, Hearne is a typical Texas town. It welcomes people by letting them know that 2010 Football Hall of Fame inductee John Randle graduated from Hearne High School. (Courtesy of author.)

RECORD SETTING PUNTER

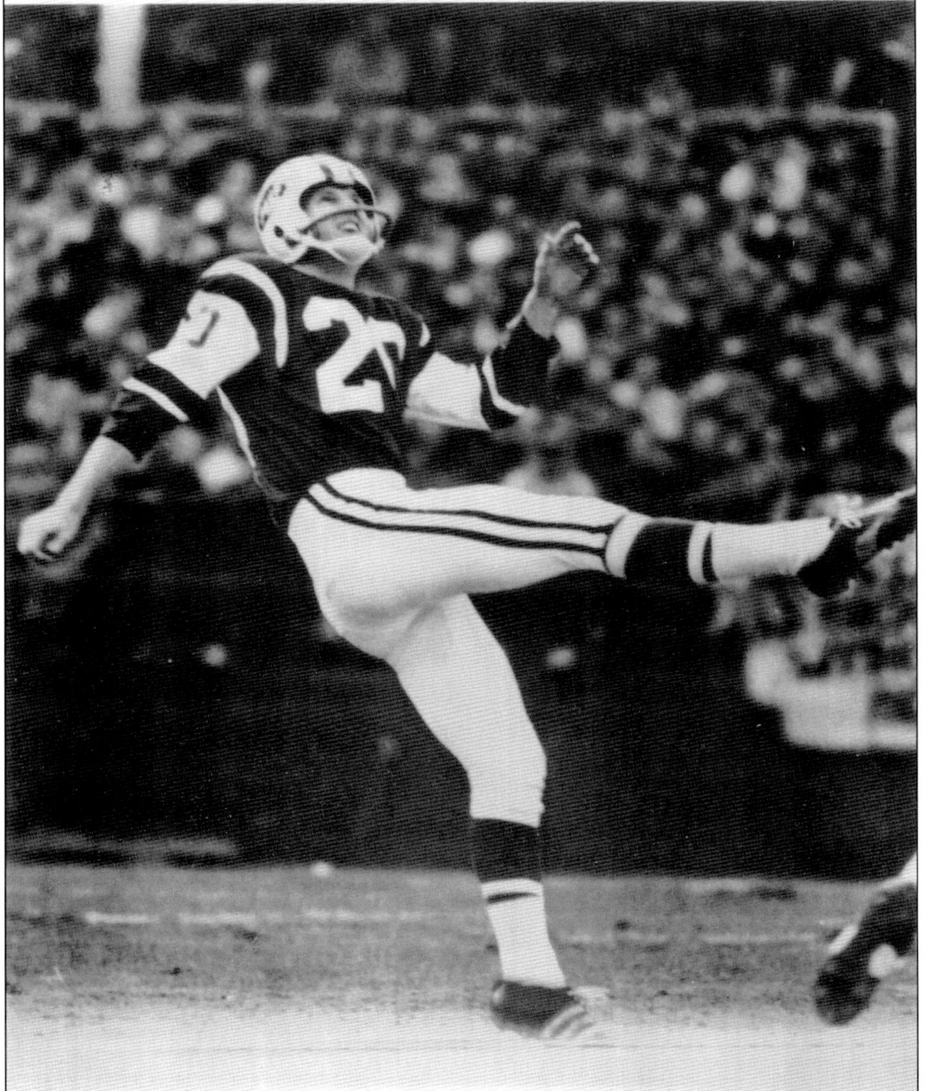

Steve O'Neal, New York Jets punter #20 (1969-1972), Set an NFL record on September 21, 1969 when he kicked a 98 yard punt in a game against Denver Broncos at Denver.

Hearne graduates who went on to the NFL also include John's brother Dennis and the man who holds the record for the longest punt in NFL history—Dr. Steve O'Neal, who punted a football that sailed for 98 yards downfield. Dr. O'Neal went on to become a dentist in Bryan, Texas. (Courtesy of *Sports Illustrated*.)

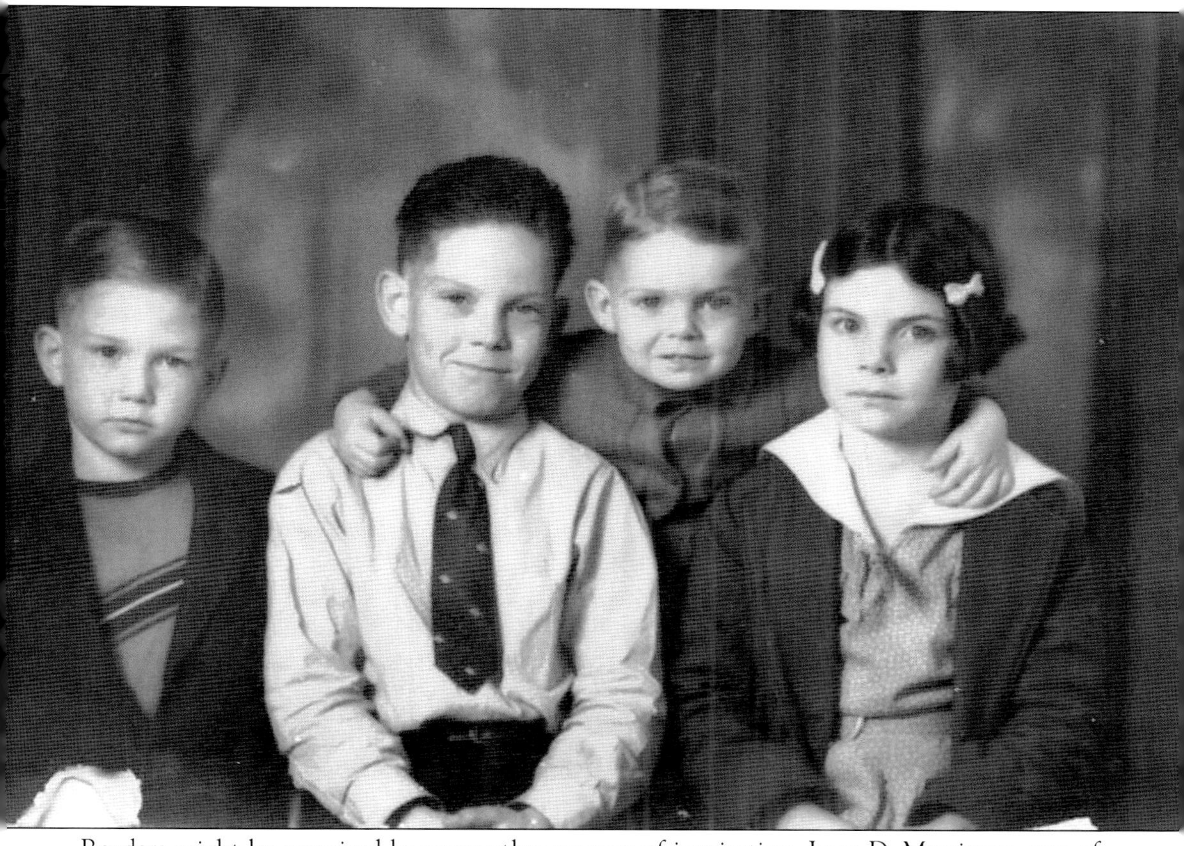

Readers might be surprised by some other sources of inspiration. Jerry D. Merriman, one of the Texas Instruments team members who invented the handheld calculator, is a Hearne High School graduate. Bobby Prado, the youngster embracing his brother and sister, invented the Prado Push, one of the most famous moves in US military aviation history. During the Vietnam War, Colonel Prado pushed a jet bomber out of North Vietnamese airspace by maneuvering his own plane underneath and lodging a hook from the wounded jet onto his windshield. (Courtesy of Carolyn Lampo.)

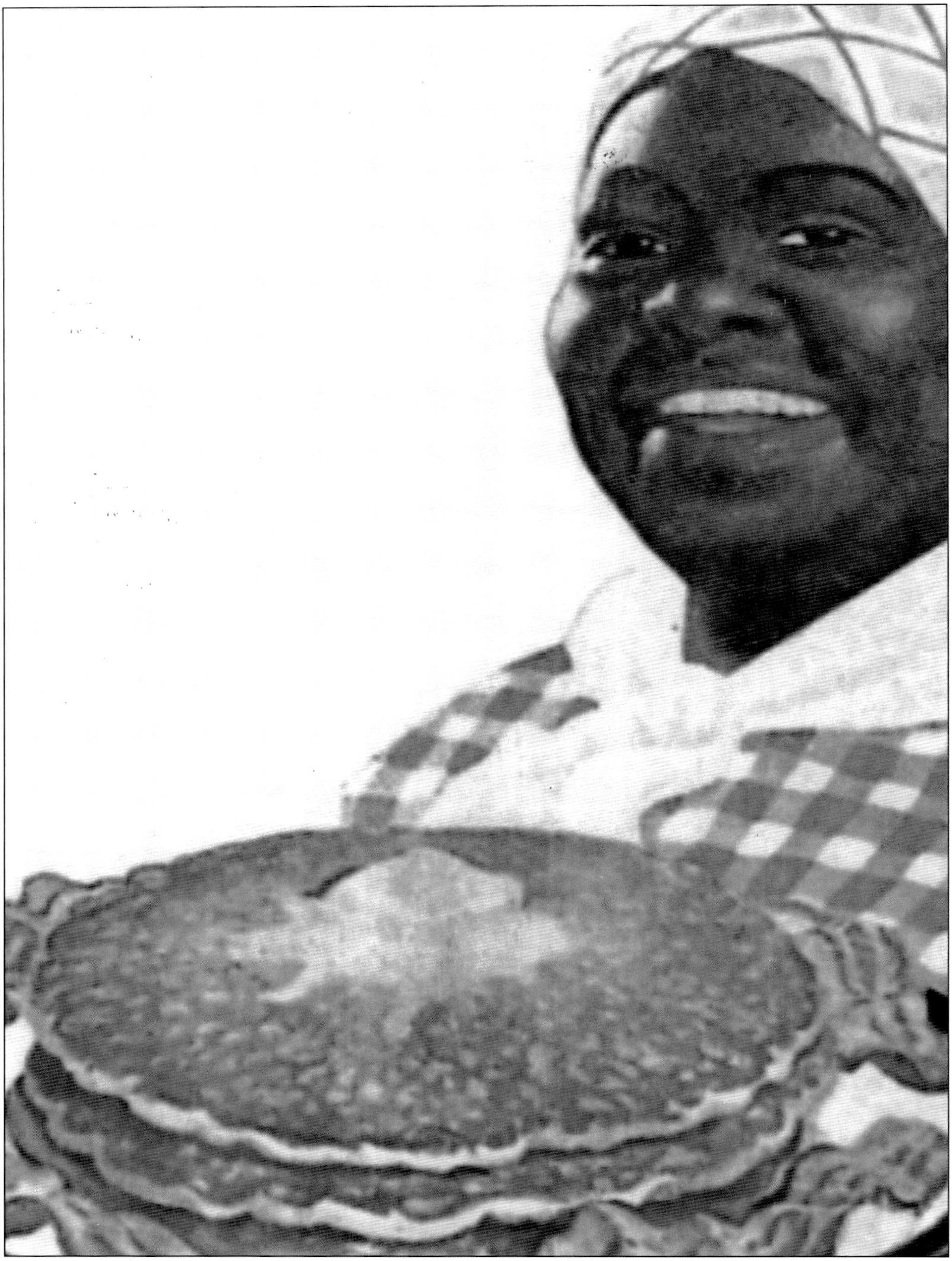

Rose Lee Moore, the model for the pancake box picture above, was also a Hearne girl from the Brazos River Bottoms. Working for Quaker Oats Company, she traveled across the country as a Quaker Oats ambassador, flipping millions of pancakes at hundreds of Quaker-hosted breakfasts. Understandably, she met a lot of people and made a lot of friends. Hearne is proud of its natives. (Courtesy of Quaker Oats.)

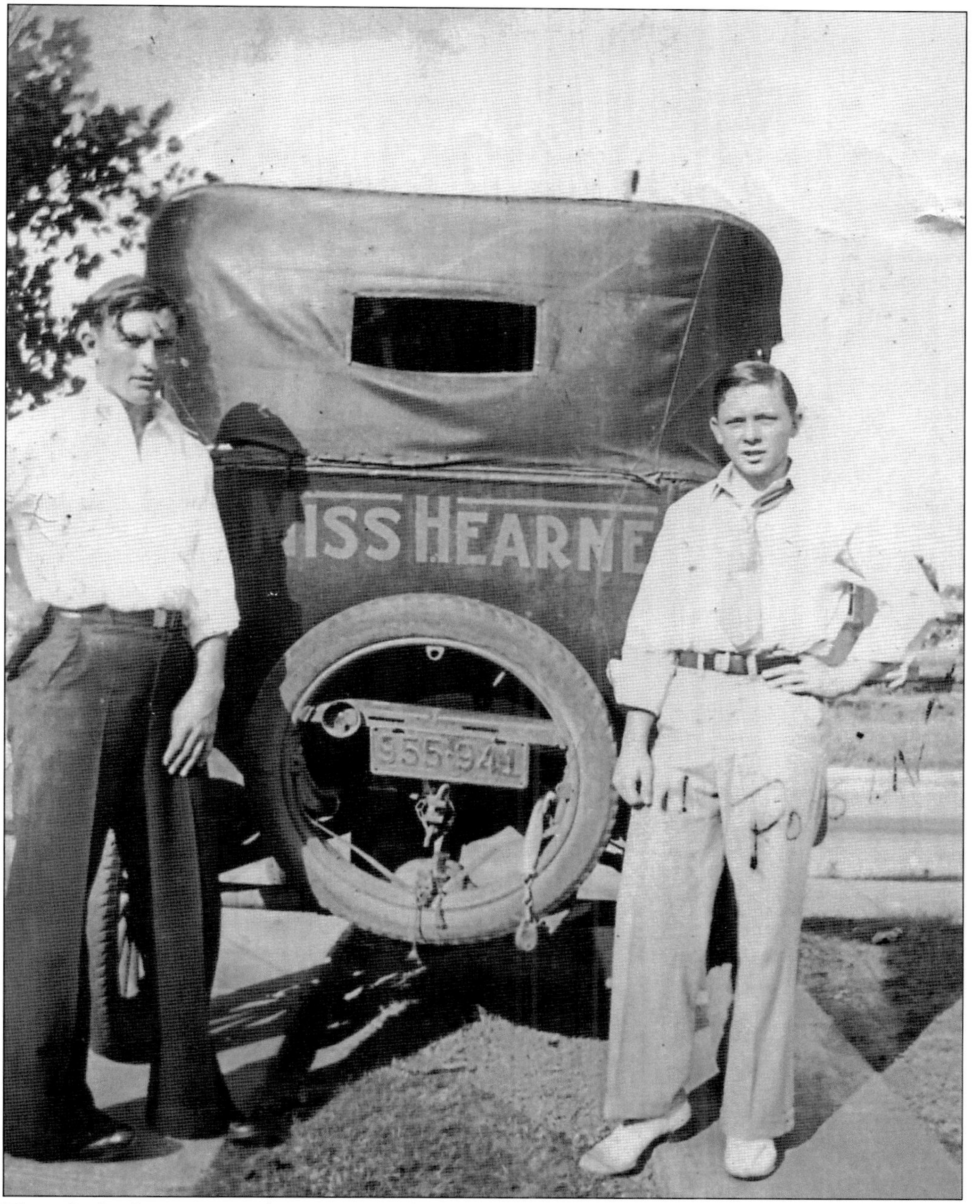

Though the last 40 years have presented one challenge after another to the people of Hearne, some of that old Hearne pride that led Demetre (the "Greek") Palmos (left) and his friend Dude Crowder (right) to name their car after Hearne remains. Miss Hearne filled up every weekend to take youngsters all over Hearne and Calvert to enjoy dances, football games, and concerts. (Courtesy of Carolyn Lampo.)

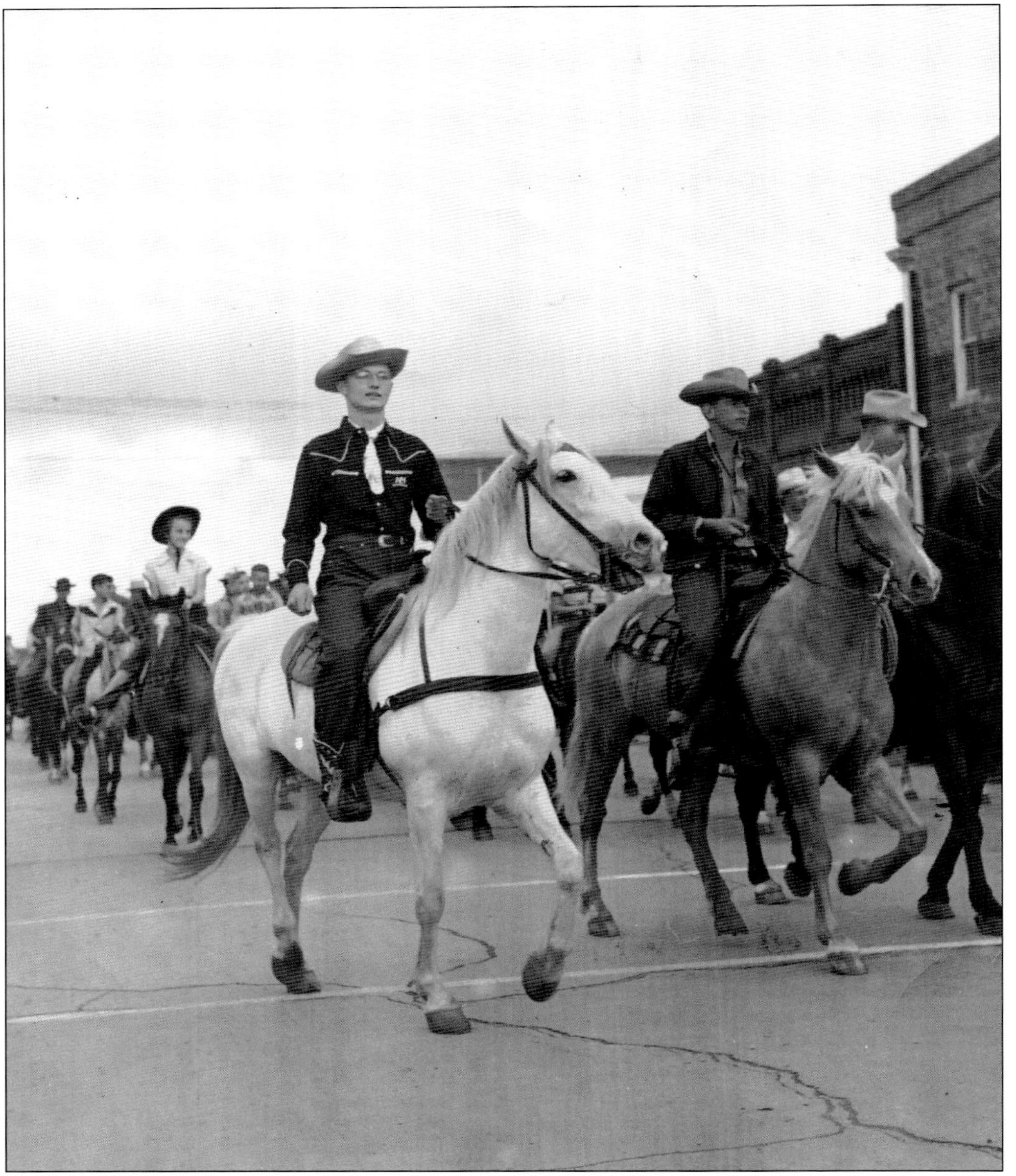

Belief in his city also inspired young Norman McCarver Jr. (front left), along with his father, Norman Sr., to write a book about Hearne. *Hearne on the Brazos* was first published in 1958 and remained in print for many years. A few copies are still available. (Courtesy of Hearne Chamber of Commerce.)

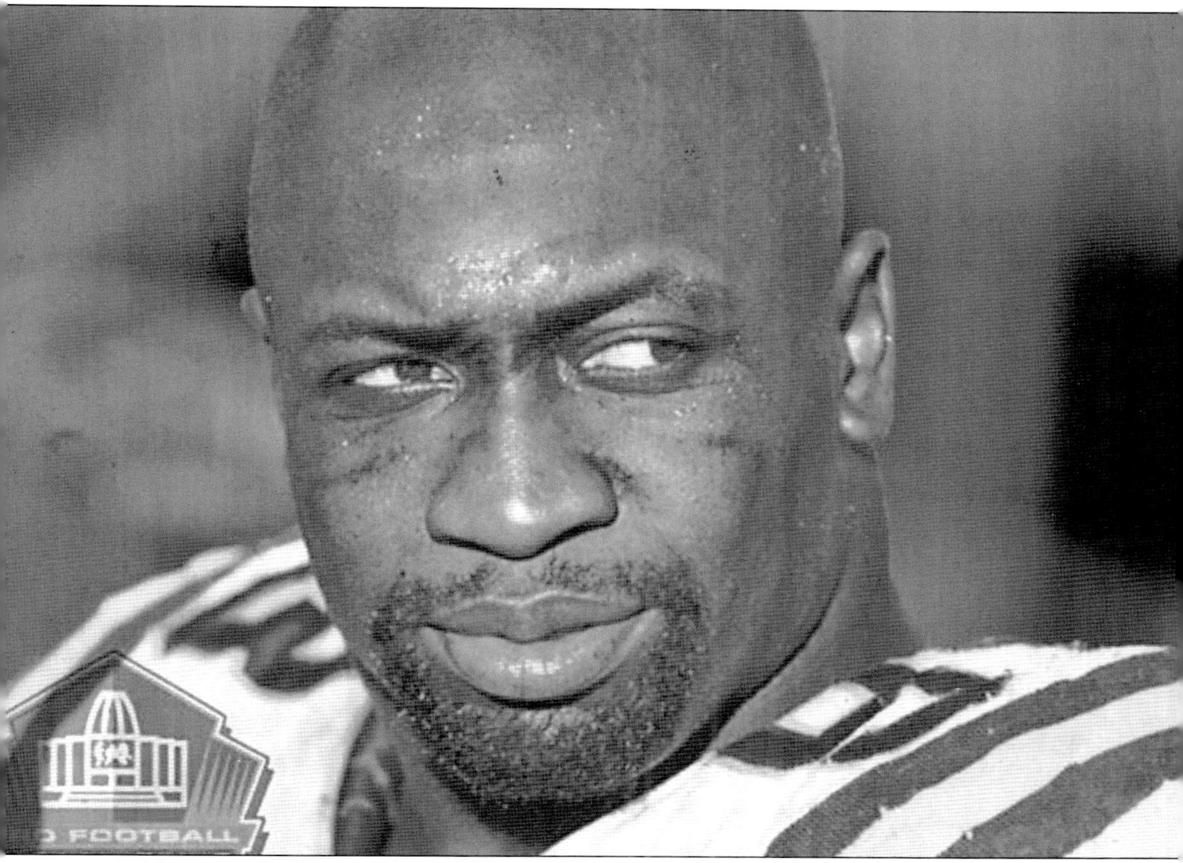

Probably something about Hearne inspired John Randle to pull a Volkswagen through the town as a football drill. That Randle creativity continued throughout his career with the Minnesota Vikings, where he became one of the most unusual on-the-line trash-talkers in the NFL. His secret was actually not talking trash. Instead, he would study opponent's biographies and ask them questions just before the ball was snapped. Then he would sack the quarterback. (Courtesy of NFL Hall of Fame.)

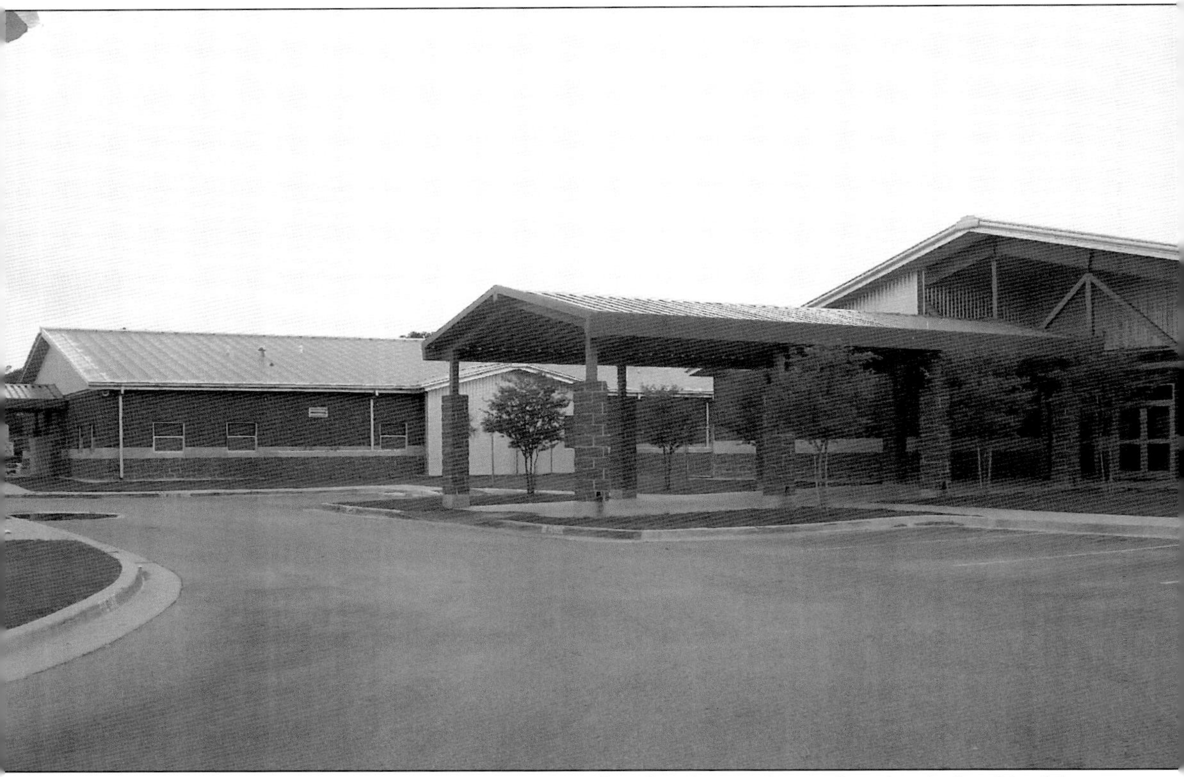

Hearne's new Hearne Elementary and Junior High Schools complete a decade of school building. All of its current classroom facilities are modern—all opening between 2004 and 2008—and Hearne ISD was one of the first districts in Texas to adopt a host of research-based curricula to maintain its "academically acceptable" rating. However, after one year of "exemplary" status, Hearne High School has struggled to regain academic acceptability. Like the city, the school district is constantly looking for ways to improve. (Courtesy of author.)

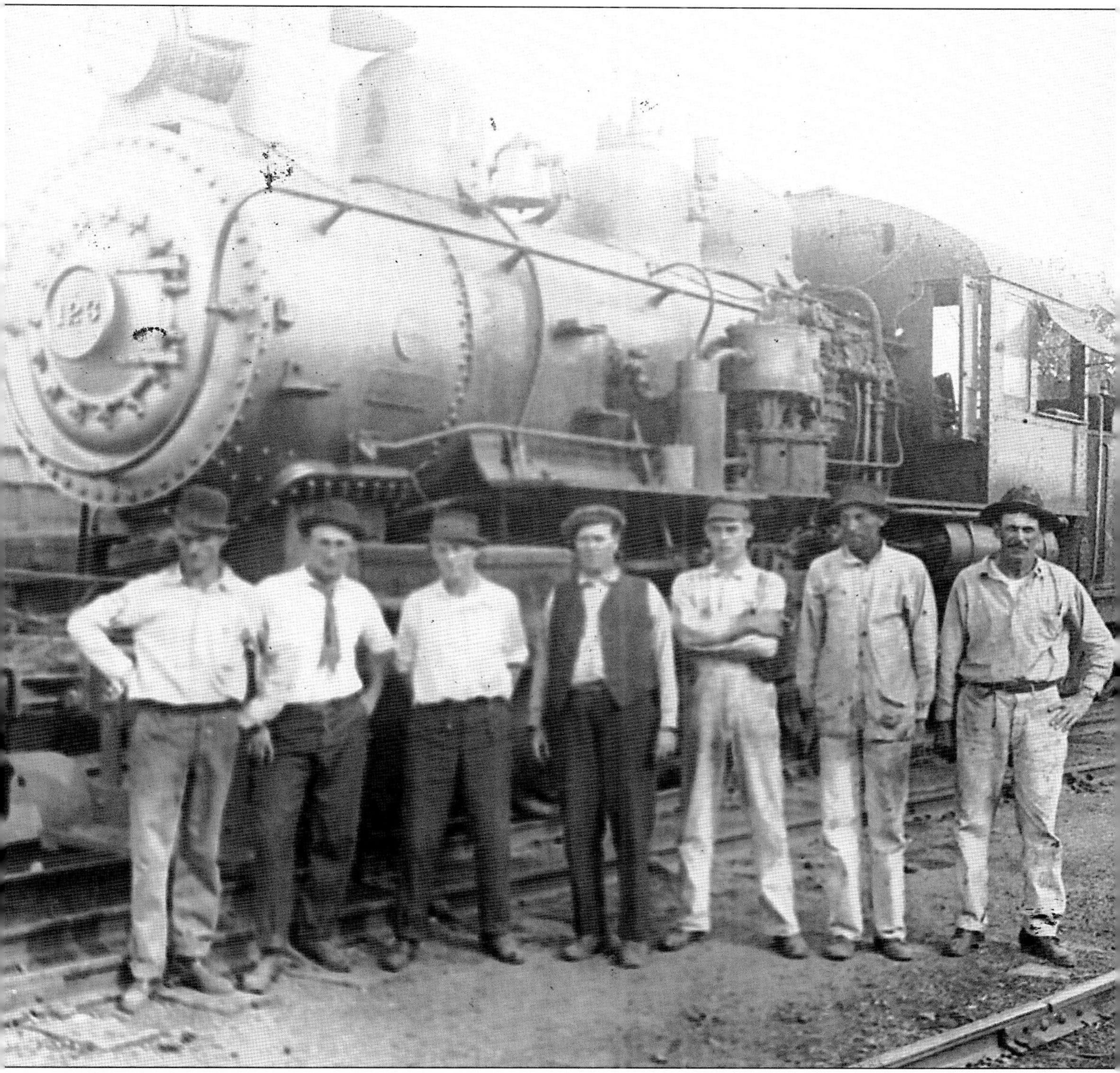

Though dreaming about the old days when sidewalks were packed with shoppers is a Hearne habit, Hearne has not given up on the future. At least as long as the trains run, Hearne will find a way to run, too. A few years before the picture of this switch engine crew, headed by engineer John Luke (far right), was taken, a Hearne switch engine crew performed a movie-worthy feat. An engine and caboose, fully engulfed in flames and missing a crew (they had jumped out to save their lives) with the brakes not fully set, barreled into the Hearne yard on January 24, 1918. A switch engine crew headed by Otho Mathews and Lynn Oliver ventured out to meet it, slowed it down, and reversed directions to push the burning wreck under the water tank, extinguishing the flames. Several crewmen were burned, but they got it done. That spirit lives on. (Courtesy of Hearne Chamber of Commerce.)